The Vampire in Nineteenth-Century English Literature

The Vampire in Nineteenth-Century English Literature

The University of Wisconsin Press

The University of Wisconsin Press
1930 Monroe Street, 3rd Floor
Madison, Wisconsin 53711-2059
uwpress.wisc.edu

3 Henrietta Street
London WC2E 8LU, England
eurospanbookstore.com

Printed in the United States of America

Library of Congress Catalogue Card No.: 87-73508

ISBN: 0-87972-424-2 Clothbound
       0-87972-425-0 Paperback

ISBN 978-0-87972-425-2 (pbk.: alk. paper)

Acknowledgements

The writer gratefully acknowledges the following journals for permission to reprint materials that were originally published in them (often in radically different form) and thanks their editors for help at varying stages in my thought process on the way to this book.

Some material on *Dracula* was first printed in *The Journal of Narrative Technique*, Volume 9, no 3 (Fall, 1979).

Other material on *Dracula* was first published in "Dracula: Stoker's Response to the New Woman," which appeared in *Victorian Studies* 26:1 (Autumn 1982), pp. 33-49.

Material on *Bleak House* originally appeared in *"Bleak House*: The Need for Social Exorcism," *Dickens Studies Newsletter*, 11 (1980), 70-73.

Other material on *Bleak House* was first published in *"Bleak House*: Dickens, Esther, and the Androgynous Mind" from the *Victorian Newsletter*, No. 64.

Some of the material on *Middlemarch* first appeared in "The Vampire in *Middlemarch* and George Eliot's Quest for Historical Reality" from Vol. 14, No. 1 of the *New Orleans Review*.

Material on *Wuthering Heights* originally appeared in "Emily Bronte's Version of Feminist History: *Wuthering Heights*." *Essays in Literature*, 12 (1985), 201-14.

Some of the material on *Jane Eyre* was first published in *"Jane Eyre* and the Evolution of Feminist History," *Victorians Institute Journal*, 13 (1985), 67-81.

Other material on *Jane Eyre* first appeared in *"Jane Eyre*: The Prison-House of Victorian Marriage," *Journal of Women's Studies in Literature*, 1 (1979), 353-59.

Some of the material on "The Vampyre" originally appeared in "Polidori's *The Vampyre*: Combining the Gothic with Realism." *North Dakota Quarterly*, Vol. 56, No 1 (Winter 1988), 197-208.

Contents

Chapter One
Blood, Eroticism and the Twentieth-Century Vampire

Sterling O'Blivion, a character in the 1984 *I, Vampire* by Jody Scott, introduces herself with a bizarre confession: "To remain young and adorable, I must drink six ounces of human arterial blood once a month. This is not an ethical choice. I was born this way. If society wants to kill or cure me, that's not up to me."[1] She adds that she has been like this for seven hundred years, but she offers no apologies, no complaints.

If Sterling O'Blivion is reconciled to her unorthodox existence, the neurotic Mr. Smith in Charles Beaumont's "Blood Brother" (1963) complains to his psychiatrist that he is less than thrilled with his present state or with the diet that prolongs it: "I always used to like my steaks rare, but *this* is ridiculous! Blood for breakfast, blood for lunch, blood for dinner. Uch—just the thought of it makes me queasy to the stomach!"[2] Even worse, however, is the violence he is compelled to commit: "Do you think I *enjoy* biting people? Do you think I don't *know* how disgusting it is? But I tell you, I *can't help it*! Every few nights I get this terrible urge.... And because of it, everybody hates me!"[3]

Smith's unhappy existence is ended by the psychiatrist, who stabs him with a wooden letter opener, but the narrator in Robert Bloch's "The Bat is My Brother" (1944) must conclude his story with an impassioned plea for the reader to bring the stake that "represents release and peace."[4]

Despite their obvious differences, these three fictional characters share a state of being, for all three are vampires, creatures from primitive folklore that are nonetheless familiar to most twentieth-century Americans. Asked to name a vampire, children today could readily name Count Chocula, the smiling figure on a box of presweetened breakfast cereal; a vampire bunny named Bunnicula that drains vegetables of their juices; the avuncular count on Sesame Street who helps them learn their numbers;[5] a variety of Hallmark trinkets for Halloween; Batman, who is described by Clive Leatherdale, as "the Count cleansed of his evil and endowed with a social conscience;"[6] or even James Warren's saucy *and* sexy Vampirella. It is *not* a monster who comes in the night to rob them of life and blood and soul. Adults might name a slightly more racy version, for the vampire has become associated with sex—generally oral sex[7]—in films with such unforgettable titles as *Count Erotica, Vampire*

1

(Tony Teresi, USA, 1971); *Does Dracula Really Suck?* (Laurence Merrick, USA, 1969); *The Horrible Sexy Vampire* (Jose Luis Madrid, Spain, 1970; Spanish title: *El Vampiro de la Autopista*); *Spermula* (Charles Maton, France, 1976); and *Lust for a Vampire* (Jimmy Sangster, England, 1970). A casual poll, however, would probably result in something more tame. In fact, asked to describe a vampire, the average man (or woman or teenager) on the street would probably mention the character in at least one of the following film versions: Bela Lugosi of Tod Browning's *Dracula* (1931), the outsider who leers at beautiful women and cowers appropriately before the movie's heroes; Christopher Lee, the feral and brutal nobleman who is destroyed in countless Hammer films only to rise again and again and again; George Hamilton in *Love at First Bite* (1979) who, horrified by a Manhattan filled with psychoanalysts by day and muggers by night, nonetheless flies off with the heroine at the conclusion; or Frank Langella in John Badham's *Dracula* (1979), the lithe and handsome midnight seducer who supplants the ineffectual hero. The poll would probably reveal that Dracula has entered the popular imagination as the vampire *par excellence*—dark, brooding, powerful, *and* generally sensual.[8] Furthermore, the more observant people polled might comment that most of the recent film versions (especially *Love at First Bite* and the Badham interpretation) as well as both books and comic books, such as Marvel's popular *Tomb of Dracula* (first issue in 1972) and *Dracula Lives* (first issue in 1973) portray Dracula as an attractive figure—far more attractive in every sense of the word than the vampire in folklore or earlier literary versions *and* far more attractive than his human adversaries.[9]

Familiar with the attractive Dracula figure in these recent films, modern readers of the novel may be surprised to discover that Stoker's original character is not always as appealing as the handsome Langella. In fact, very few films (Murnau's *Nosferatu*, 1922; Tobe Hooper's *'Salem's Lot*, 1979; and Tom Holland's *Fright Night*, 1985, are notable exceptions) do justice to the hideousness of Stoker's physical description, a characterization that adapted various folklore accounts:

The mouth, so far as I could see it under the heavy moustache, was fixed and rather cruel-looking, with peculiarly sharp white teeth; these protruded over the lips.... For the rest, his ears were pale and at the tops extremely pointed.... As the Count leaned over me and his hands touched me, I could not repress a shudder. It may have been that his breath were rank, but a horrible feeling of nausea came over me, which...I could not conceal. (Ch. II)

Resembling a bat more than a human being in this scene, Stoker's character even smells of his unsavory habits. However, despite the gruesome physical description, *Dracula* (published 1897) was a turning point for the literary vampire, for Stoker's central character is often more attractive than he is here. Indeed Stoker sometimes reveals him as no more cruel than his human opponents. Following Stoker's lead, twentieth-century writers and directors often portray the vampire as a more sympathetic character than he had been in either folklore or literature.

At the same time that vampires become more attractive (in literally every sense of the word—attractive physically, morally, and intellectually), their human counterparts become more horrifying. For example, Hans Heinz Ewers (1871-1943), who wrote "The Spider" (1921), a literal vampire story of a beautiful woman who destroys the men who love her, also wrote *Vampir* (1921), a work in which the word "vampire" is used metaphorically. In *Vampir*, Frank Braun, a young German patriot during World War I, drinks the blood of his Jewish mistress to become a better fund raiser for his country. By comparison, Clarimonde, the beautiful vampire in "The Spider," is much less horrifying for she is directly responsible for the deaths of only three men.

Like Ewers in *Vampir*, Manley Wade Wellman in "The Horror Undying" (1936) and David Drake in "Something Had To Be Done" (1976) reveal human evil that puts the vampire's bloodthirsty nature into a less horrifying perspective. "The Horror Undying" takes place in the Old West, where the violence of the vampire is unpunished for a long time, primarily because people attribute it to hostile Indians. In fact, Wellman portrays a cruel period in our nation's history when he reveals that Sergeant Stanlas has a brilliant military career before he is revealed as a vampire *and* a cannibal. Drake's story, on the other hand, presents a more recent horror, for he has his story take place in Viet Nam, during a war that apparently brought out the violence in vampires as well as men. During a three-week period, the vampire—Stefan Lunkowski— destroys five men in his outfit before his sergeant, Morezek (a man whose Old World origins apparently permit him to recognize a vampire even in a war zone), rolls a grenade into his bunk. Morezek then returns to the States, where he destroys Stefan's parents, sister, and himself with another grenade. In addition to emphasizing the human cruelty that is so often a part of war, Drake also alludes to other examples of cruelty, for he reveals that Morezek himself is dying of skin cancer, probably the direct result of exposure to Agent Orange, a chemical now linked to cancer, skin disease, and other disorders among Viet Nam veterans. At the beginning of the story, Morezek mentions, "We were out in the middle of War Zone C.... No dinks, no trees—they'd all been defoliated."[10] Drake knows that the realistic horror of Agent Orange will made the vampiric Lunkowskis appear less horrifying.

Although they are no more violent than human beings, the Lunkowskis and Sergeant Stanlas are certainly not attractive characters. Other twentieth-century writers, however, have created vampires that are considerably more appealing. Ronald Chetwynd-Hayes emphasizes the delicacy of his lovely vampire, Carola, when she is approached by her human adversary:

She made a little hissing sound; an instinctive token of defiance, and for a moment the delicate ivory fangs were bared and nipped the clergyman's hand, but that was all. There was no savage fight for existence, no calling on the dark gods; just a token resistance, the shedding of a tiny dribble of blood, then complete surrender.[11]

Weyland, in Suzy McKee Charnas's *The Vampire Tapestry*, reflects on the pain of living:

Now he knew with bitter clarity why in each long sleep he forgot the life preceding that sleep. He forgot because he could not survive the details of an enormous past heavy with those he cared for. No wonder art, or dreams, or history brought too vividly to life in human speech, were dangerous. They could tap the reservoirs of feeling buried in him under intervening sleeps.[12]

Anna, a modern young woman in Evelyn E. Smith's "Softly While You're Sleeping" (1961) finds the vampire, Mr. Varri, much more appealing than her would-be human lovers because he doesn't attempt to force his advances on her:

Her body relaxed into trembling quietness...even before she felt the prickle of the two tiny sharp teeth gently piercing the thin skin, gently drawing out her blood and, with it, her fears and anxieties and self-doubts. This *is* love, she thought wonderingly as her throat swelled to meet the vampire's kiss—a true kiss, not the clumsy suction of damp lips and the thrust of slimy tongue, not the disgusting fumble of sweating, odorous human bodies.[13]

In fact, Smith deliberately alters the fact that the vampire in both folklore and literature is a thief who coerces his victims and ultimately robs them of both blood and soul. However, she retains the fact that the vampire's love ultimately destroys the victim, for Varri attempts to persuade Anna to join him in an immortal love. Recognizing that her love for the courtly and gentle Varri will result in her death, Anna finally decides to reject her vampire lover for a more ordinary kind of love.

An equally attractive vampire is Miriam in *The Hunger* (1981) by Whitley Strieber. Beautiful, cultured, and intelligent, Miriam is the daughter of Lamia and, therefore, a member of an entirely different species. Hungering for the life of her human victims, which she absorbs by drinking their blood, she is horrifying. However, realizing that the centuries old vampire is the last of her kind, readers may be so touched by her appalling loneliness that they sympathize with her search for someone to share her immortality.

Creating even more sympathetic vampires are Jan Jennings, George R.R. Martin, and Ray Garton, who entirely remove the threat from the vampire's bloodsucking habit. In *Vampyr* (1981), Valan, an extremely attractive woman vampyr (her preferred spelling), who has never tasted human blood, leads an equally civilized group in punishing the "rogues" that prey on human beings. Joshua York, the humane vampire in Martin's *Fevre Dream* (1982), wants to save his race from their predatory habits and devotes three years of his life to discovering an acceptable substitute for human blood. Both Davey Owens and Casey Thorne in Garton's *Live Girls* (1987) are horrified at what they have become and at their thirst for blood; and Owens does everything in his power to destroy the vampires who are responsible.

Finally, Les Daniels, Kathryn Ptacek, and Chelsea Quinn Yarbro reveal that their vampire characters are appalled by human treachery and violence. Don Sebastian de Villanueva, the vampire in Daniels' *Citizen Vampire* (1981) is sickened by the violence he sees during the Reign of Terror and disgusted by the Inquisition in *The Black Castle* (1978) and the activities of the Spanish conquistidores in *The Silver Skull* (1979). August, the lamia in Ptacek's *Blood Autumn* (1985) reflects on human cruelty:

She had witnessed far worse in her long life, farther back than the time of Agamemnon, and doubtless she would see worse.... Whatever surprises mankind might hold for her, its capacity for cruelty to its own kind found her unastonished. Too often had she seen it expressed.

Far better to be what she was...for she did not kill in the name of religion, state, revenge, jealousy, greed, or any of the artificial contrivances man had invented to explain his blood lust.

She killed simply for the blood and the life that it brought her. No. more, No less.[14]

Similarly in *Hotel Transylvania* (1978), Yarbro deliberately contrasts the vampire and bloodthirsty human beings when the human Madelaine writes to her vampire lover:

In my reading of history there is war and ruin and pillage and lives snuffed out with such profligacy that my breath is stopped by the senselessness of it. One would think that all humanity had nothing better than to feed on its own carrion. I have thought as I read these books, how many much worse things there are in this world than vampires.

To know your freedom. To live in the blood that is taken with love.

Saint-Germain, Saint-Germain, I can hardly wait![15]

According to Yarbro, the vampire is no longer a cruel mirror of mankind's worst violence, but a cultured outsider who observes and comments on this cruelty. Tracing Saint-Germain's activities from ancient Egypt, to the Roman Empire, to Renaissance Italy, to Enlightenment France, and finally to twentieth-century England, she contrasts his urbane behavior to the senseless cruelty of history's numerous wars and other acts of aggression and, therefore, makes him more sympathetic by comparison.

Twentieth-century writers have used a number of strategies to make their vampire characters more attractive than their predecessors in folklore or earlier fiction. Chetwynd-Hayes, Daniels, and Yarbro, for example, reveal that vampires are less bloodthirsty than ordinary human beings; Wellman and Drake put the vampire's violence into historical perspective and reveal that the vampire is no more cruel than human beings; Scott, Strieber, S.P. Somtow (in *Vampire Junction*, 1984), and Anne Rice (in *Interview With the Vampire*, 1976, and *The Vampire Lestat*, 1985) present its unorthodox behavior sympathetically, Somtow and Rice especially showing the vampire's desire to know and experience; Richard Matheson, in *I Am Legend* (1954), reveals that vampires are the result of plague; Jennings and Martin totally eliminate the horror from its behavior; and finally writers have permitted their vampires to tell their own stories. *I, Vampire* and *The Dracula Tape* are both first-person accounts; and, like Grendel in John Gardener's retelling of *Beowulf*, the "monsters" in many of these works are extremely compelling. Jaded by the commercialism of the twentieth century, Sterling O'Blivion is attractive, both in her extreme honesty and in her desire for a less violent world:

And can the Inner Core [a C.I.A. type of group that has her under surveillance] help the poor twerp any more? Not at all!, not even as the supremely powerful Intersystem that it is, with a finger shoved up each of the world's intelligence orgs, moving their heads and arms, like the Punch and Judy dolls I hated as a child in Europe. I hated it when they whacked each other with clubs! The other children all howled in delight. The *normal* children—which may tell you something.[16]

Like Yarbro, Scott reveals that ordinary human behavior is both frightening and cruel. The vampire, an oppressed outsider who is frightened by this ordinary behavior, thus becomes less horrifying by comparison. Equally compelling is Dracula in Fred Saberhagen's series. *The Dracula Tape*, the first novel in the series, retells Stoker's novel from Dracula's point of view and directs the reader's attention to certain inconsistencies in Stoker's novel.[17] In the following passage, Dracula explains that he was not responsible for Lucy Westenra's death:

Lucy I did not kill. It was not *I* who hammered the great stake through her heart. *My* hands did not cut off her lovely head, or stuff her breathless mouth—*that mouth*—with garlic, as if she were a dead pig.... Only reluctantly had I made her a vampire, nor would she ever have become a vampire were it not for the imbecile Van Helsing and his work.[18]

The astute reader of the two novels will remember that Dracula is correct in his assessment of the situation; and the rest of *The Dracula Tape* continues to vindicate the vampire. As a result Saberhagen's Dracula is an appealing figure while his human opponents appear to be both stupid and brutal.

Somewhat less appealing are the first-person accounts in "Conversion" (1976) and "The Bat is My Brother," in which narrators reveal their horror when they discover that they have died and been reborn as vampires. However, even here, seeing the events from the vampires' point of view makes these twentieth-century vampires considerably more attractive than their merely bestial predecessors in folklore, who were victims of their uncontrollable hunger for human blood.

More attractive than their predecessors, twentieth-century vampires do remain bloodsuckers even though Saberhagen, Yarbro, Jennings, Martin, and Charnas manage to eliminate most of the horror from this trait. In addition, some twentieth-century works alter the original superstition and make blood sucking a metaphor. For example, the unnamed subject of Fritz Leiber's "The Girl with the Hungry Eyes" (1968) is neither literally dead nor literally a bloodsucker although Leiber is obviously aware that the traditional vampire is a corpse that destroys the souls of its victims by drinking their blood. Thus he makes his human subject (who finally comes to symbolize the false promises of modern advertising) more deadly than the supernatural vampire:

There are vampires and vampires, and the ones that suck blood aren't the worst.... She's the smile that tricks you into throwing away your money and your life. She's the eyes that lead you on and on, and then show you death. She's the being that takes everything you've got and gives nothing in return. [19]

In Leiber's story, although the word "vampire" is a metaphor rather than a literal belief, it is no less deadly.

In addition to sucking blood, a number of vampires rebel against authority. The unnamed woman vampire in Everil Worrell's "The Canal" (1927) refuses to acquiesce to any kind of authority, and she sneers at the narrator's offer of assistance:

'Do you think you would be helping me, to tie me to a desk, to shut me behind doors, away from freedom, away from the delight of doing my own will, of seeking my own way? Rather this old boat, rather a deserted grave under the stars for my home!' [20]

Accustomed to admiring this kind of romantic independence, many readers are likely to find this refusal to conform to arbitrary social standards initially attractive, but the narrator reveals that his lovely vampire has purchased her freedom for an awful price, for she is a child murderer.

More attractive, though equally deadly, is Erich in "Night Life" (1976) by Steven Utley, a rebel against a corrupt twentieth-century society who preys on other less attractive rebels. Coming to America from Europe, he chooses to prey on the "muggers, hookers, pimps, pushers, rip-off artists, two-bit con men, low-priced killers-for-hire. In the nights to come, he would come to know them all better."[21]

Finally, a rebel against authority in a more recent work is Juliette (based on Sade's novel of the same name) in *Citizen Vampire*. She and Sade, who makes a brief appearance in the novel, are both libertines, defined as "Society's criminals, and nature's heroes."[22] Eager for ever new sensations, she revives Don Sebastian, a centuries old vampire, who ultimately becomes her lover and who turns her into a vampire to help her escape the guillotine. However, Juliette, who has rebelled against the authority of her husband, the monarchy, and the revolution, is incapable of following the restrictions required of vampires either. Thus her grave is discovered by the young woman who had been her personal servant before the revolution, and she is destroyed.

Many vampires in twentieth-century literature are portrayed as bloodsuckers or rebels, but the single trait that distinguishes almost all of them is their overt eroticism, a characteristic that is generally presented as a positive trait. For example, Mr. Varri, the vampire in Smith's "Softly While You're Sleeping" is a tender, solicitous lover even though his courtship would ultimately result in Anna's death. Miriam in *The Hunger*, Valan in *Vampyr*, Weyland in *The Vampire Tapestry*, and Anya in *Live Girls* (a work that locates much of the action in a peep show and a club, where clients can pay for additional services) are described as sensuous and physically ardent; and, like Sterling of *I, Vampire*, all four have taken numerous lovers of both sexes over the centuries. Moreover, while Miriam and Sterling do require human blood to sustain their existence, neither they nor Valan are dangerous because of their eroticism; and Anya is dangerous only because her eroticism is combined with the vampires' plan to take over the world.

Other twentieth-century vampires seem to take definite delight in their sexuality, some even being characterized as polymorph perverse. For example, Dracula and the other vampires in Fred Saberhagen's novels (*The Dracula Tape*, 1975; *The Holmes-Dracula File*, 1978; *An Old Friend of the Family*, 1979; and *Thorn*, 1980) clearly take erotic pleasure in their relationships with "breathing human beings." The same pleasure applies to Saint-Germain and his followers in the novels of Chelsea Quinn Yarbro (*Hotel Transylvania*; *The Palace*, 1978; *Blood Games*, 1979; *Path of the Eclipse*, 1981; and *The Saint-Germain Chronicles*, 1983).

While the preceding pages indicate that the vampire in the twentieth century is certainly not a consistent character, there are some definite family resemblances among most of these vampires. The one trait that links them all is their need to drink blood although many twentieth-century writers eliminate the horror from this characteristic by letting the vampire substitute animal blood for human blood or by reducing the amount that is required. (In addition, many writers have eliminated another horrifying aspect by making the vampire a member of a different race instead of a reanimated corpse.) For example, Sterling's need for six ounces of human blood a month hardly seems excessive; and the fact that neither she, St. Germaine, Saberhagen's Dracula, nor Valan need to kill for this blood makes them even less monstrous. In addition, the twentieth-century vampire is often rebellious—sometimes violent in the rebellion against the society that has rejected him or her. A generally attractive figure, Sterling nonetheless preys on the hopes and dreams of ordinary human beings in the Max Arkoff studio where she works because she rejects the trivial nature of their desires. Saint-Germain also rebels against the societies in which he lives and continues his scholarly quest for a better world. Less attractive vampires, on the other hand, simply reject the human world with which they are forced to coexist. Finally, the twentieth-century vampire—especially in film, but also in books—is almost always an erotic creature. In fact, eroticism is so much a part of the vampire's character in the twentieth century that it is easier to mention the few exceptions to this rule: The timid Smith in "Blood Brother;" the brutal Sergeant Stanlas in "The Horror Undying;" Stefan Lunkowski in "Something Had to Be Done;" and the dogs in *Hounds of Dracula* (1977) are the only examples of vampires in twentieth-century popular culture for whom brute strength is more important than seduction.

In addition to these three characteristics—bloodsucking, rebellious behavior, and overt eroticism—vampires in twentieth-century literature sometimes have other distinct characteristics. Among these are the ability to change shape, the aversion to certain culturally important symbols (such as the cross, holy water, or the Host), the necessity of sleeping in their native soil, and other purely physical characteristics such as sharp teeth, hypnotic eyes, and extreme pallor. However, almost all these characteristics reinforce the three main characteristics. The aversion to culturally important symbols reaffirms the vampire's rebellion against authority and, therefore, against the symbols of that authority. The sharp teeth usually reinforce the vampire's need to drink blood although certain modern writers, including Yarbro and Saberhagen, use it only to point to the vampire's "otherness." The hypnotic eyes are important to a creature who "captures" its prey by seduction rather than by physical strength while the pallor is fairly typical of dead bodies—reanimated or not. Finally, the necessity of sleeping in native soil is a carryover from folklore, a requirement that the neurotic vampire in "Blood Brother" reveals is a major inconvenience to the vampire in the twentieth century. Stripped of his roots *and* his family crypt, he must purchase a family plot so he can sleep in that native soil: "Then you bring home a couple pounds of dirt and spread it around the coffin. Wake up at night and you're covered with it."[23] Thus a serious folklore belief about the importance of tradition becomes trivialized in the twentieth century.

Looking back over these examples of twentieth-century literary vampires reveals one striking fact about the vampire today. Although the sheer number of vampires in the twentieth century reveals that the vampire remains an important mythic figure (and therefore a figure worthy of serious study), it is undoubtedly a character of popular culture rather than of serious literature and drama—a creature that stalks the films, television programs, paperback books, and comics of the modern world. (It would be possible to cite numerous other examples; Raymond T. McNally's bibliography in *Dracula Was a Woman* cites more than a hundred and fifty individual entries—novels in vampire series, individual vampire novels, and short stories—although McNally is not overly scrupulous about distinguishing vampires from their near relatives—werewolves, zombies, and human beings who resemble the vampire). [24] There are exceptions, such as Anne Rice's *Interview With The Vampire*, a book that was taken seriously by literary critics as well as enjoyed by members of The Literary Guild, and its sequel, *The Vampire Lestat*, but these exceptions merely prove the rule.

Moreover, the vampire in the twentieth century—more often than not—is an attractive figure. (Here too are exceptions, of course, such as the appropriately named Faustine in Cornell Woolrich's "Vampire's Honeymoon" (1939), Barlow in Stephen King's immensely popular *'Salem's Lot* (1976), [25] Janos Stromberg in Mark Ronson's *Blood Thirst* (1979), Prince Conrad Vulkan in Robert R. McCammon's *They Thirst* (1981), Dolores in *Last Rites* (1985) by Jorge Saralegui, Jerry Dandrige in *Fright Night* (1985) by John Skipp and Craig Spector, and Dracula in *Sherlock Holmes vs. Dracula* (1978) by Loren Estleman, in *Bloodright* (1977) by Peter Tremayne, or *Dracula in Love* (1979) by Peter Shirley. However, most of these unattractive vampires are little more than clones of Stoker's Dracula with a little folklore thrown in for good measure.) The vampire today is now Frank Langella, the handsome and sensitive (far more sensitive than his human counterparts) vampire in John Badham's *Dracula*, the pensive Miriam in *The Hunger*, the inquisitive Lestat and St. Germain, or the saucy and sexy Vampirella.

However, if the vampire in twentieth-century popular culture is largely an appealing figure, such was not always the case. Originating in folklore, an earlier equivalent of popular culture, the vampire generally inspired fear, horror and revulsion. Moreover, that same horrifying figure from primitive folklore became an important literary motif in England during the nineteenth century, where it inspired some of that century's most capable writers and thinkers and became a character in serious fiction (*Wuthering Heights, Jane Eyre, Bleak House*, and *Middlemarch*) and non-fiction (*Capital* and *The Condition of the Working Class in*

England) as well as in works, such as the penny dreadful *Varney the Vampire*, that were clearly directed to an unsophisticated mass audience.

Not only did the vampire appear in serious literature during the nineteenth century, but it was treated seriously by the writers who chose to use it. Often a kind of camp figure today, nauseated by his "nasty" habits and rejected by the human beings around him, the vampire in the nineteenth century often inspired genuine fear, horror, and more than a little awe as the following chapters on the vampire in nineteenth-century literature will reveal.

That change is one of the primary reasons for this study. Familiar with the bestial character from folklore, the powerful vampire in nineteenth-century literature, and the vampire in the twentieth century, a figure that James B. Twitchell describes, with some justification, as "rude, boring, and hopelessly adolescent,"[26] I saw a figure that has definitely evolved over time. Thus I wanted to look at the relationship between this particular literary character and the social history that influenced its creation. While psychological studies of the vampire tend to see only similarities in vampires from different historical periods (Ernest Jones's classic study, for example, argues that the superstitious fear of the vampire is "derived from early incest conflicts)."[27] and other studies of the vampire tend to see only individual cases without drawing any conclusions about the character in general, this study sees characteristic differences in the portrayal of the vampire at different historical periods. Moreover, since I am especially interested in the relationship between Victorian literature and the culture that influenced its production, this study looks closely at the nineteenth-century works that feature the vampire and at the historical reasons that so many major nineteenth-century writers chose to treat the vampire seriously. Seeing reasons for the change from the powerful figure in the nineteenth century to its less powerful but more attractive twentieth-century offspring reveals a number of profound differences between our predecessors in the nineteenth century and ourselves. Of particular interest to me as a woman and a feminist are the ways that so many of these writers use the vampire motif to explore sexual roles and human identity.

Although I originally planned to include various kinds of vampiric characters (a strategy that would have enabled me to include discussions of *Christabel*, "Lamia," and *The Sacred Fount* because I was reasonably sure that Coleridge, Keats, and James were familiar with the vampire and were using it deliberately),[28] I ultimately decided to try to avoid the problems of my predecessors. Included in these problems are the approach that simply lists different types of vampires or vampiric characters without paying attention to the traits and tendencies that make these characters similar and the approach that fails to differentiate the vampire on the one hand from other types of preternatural characters and the vampiric character from other types of exploiters. Therefore, I decided to limit this study to a smaller body of works, specifically to literary works where there is some internal evidence, such as a character's actually being described as a vampire, that the writer is familiar with the belief in vampires and is, therefore, using it deliberately to create certain expectations in the reader's mind. As a result, my study includes *Jane Eyre* but not *Christabel*. Even though Geraldine's supernatural origins more nearly resemble those of the vampire from folklore, Coleridge never uses the word vampire to describe her. Bronte, on the other hand, has Jane describe Bertha as a vampire. She also has Jane soon learn the truth when Rochester takes her to the third floor of Thornfield to introduce her to her predecessor: Instead of being a horrifying supernatural figure, Bertha is another suffering human being. That Bronte chose the word "vampire" means that she was consciously using a belief with which she expected her readers to be familiar. Furthermore, because she tells Rochester that the creature *reminded* her of "the foul German spectre—the Vampyre" (Ch. XXV), readers can be reasonably sure that she was deliberately manipulating a familiar literary figure and that she had a particular reason or reasons for drawing an analogy between that supernatural figure and the all-too-human Bertha.

Finally, because so many other studies include vampires, vampire-like creatures from folklore, and real human beings (including Gilles de Rais and Vlad Tepes, the Renaissance Wallachian ruler on whom Stoker modeled Dracula) and literary characters and, therefore, overlook the obvious differences between life and literature, I chose to restrict my study to the literary character, primarily to works of imaginative literature and to works in which the writer does *not* believe in real vampires but uses the belief consciously as a literary motif. Moreover, because of the differences between the vampire in the nineteenth and twentieth centuries, I decided to limit my study to the vampire in nineteenth-century English literature. Beginning with the nineteenth century also has a certain justification because the motif seemingly sprang full grown like Aphrodite onto the English literary scene right at the turn of the century. In fact, a reviewer in *The Monthly Review* (July 1796) observes the sudden popularity of the motif:

It will appear extraordinary that a poem [Burger's *Lenore*], written a considerable time since, and known in this country at least some years, should on a sudden have excited so much attention as to employ the pens of various translators.... Unless this has been a matter of mere accident, it must be considered as a proof of the increased relish among us for the modern German school of literature—a school, of which the marvellous, the horrid, and the extravagant, constitute some of the most prominent features.[29]

Prior to these translations the vampire had never appeared in English literature.

Finally, because so many earlier studies of the vampire lack coherence and consistency, I chose to limit my study only to vampires that met a certain definition. Although numerous definitions of this preternatural creature exist, other writers on the subject have simply thrown up their hands in despair. Twitchell, for example, admits that he isn't interested in definition; and *The Living Dead* is an interesting discussion of Romantic literature, but not a particularly informative discussion of the vampire. Summers, on the other hand, begs the question entirely by saying that an "exhaustive study is well-nigh impossible...owing to the very vague definition and indeterminate interpretation one is able to give to vampirism from a purely literary point of view" because it is difficult to "differentiate the malignant and death-dealing spectre or it may be even corpse who returns to wreak his foul revenge from the Vampire."[30]

Despite the difficulties in definition, it is important to begin with some coherent sense of how our ancestors saw the vampire. Therefore, I chose to begin with Margaret L. Carter's definition because it is both succinct and comprehensive and because it defines almost all vampires in nineteenth-century literature although *not* all vampires in the twentieth century. Moreover, Carter's definition of the vampire as "a reanimated corpse that sustains its immortality by feeding on blood, and, in doing so, drains the victim's life force and transforms the victim into a likeness of itself"[31] also has the virtue of agreeing with most nineteenth-century definitions.[32]

Carter, therefore, in defining the vampire focuses on four important characteristics:

1. The vampire is a reanimated corpse, a *dead body*, rather than a different species.
2. The vampire sustains its immortality by drinking blood.
3. The vampire's need for blood destroys the victim.
4. The vampire turns its victims into vampires.

The vampires included in this study (indeed almost all vampires in nineteenth-century English literature) all meet the first three characteristics except that these characteristics are used metaphorically in *Jane Eyre*, *Middlemarch*, and *Bleak House* as well as in the works of social criticism. However, Lord Ruthven and Carmilla—perhaps even Dracula himself—do not meet Carter's fourth characteristic. There is absolutely no evidence that Lord Ruthven's victims do anything but die; Baron Vordenburg, the vampire expert in "Carmilla," explains that victims of vampire attack "almost invariably, in the grave, develop into vampires" (Ch. XVI), but this curious explanation suggests that not all do. Certainly, Dracula does not turn the sailers on the *Demeter* into vampires, for their bodies—drained of blood—are apparently thrown into the ocean.

Because no study of the vampire in nineteenth-century literature would be complete without Lord Ruthven, the first vampire in English fiction; Carmilla; or Dracula, perhaps the most famous vampire in all literature, I chose to modify Carter's otherwise excellent and comprehensive definition. Therefore, this study centers on literary vampires that meet the following definition:

The vampire is a reanimated corpse that perpetuates its unnatural existence by feeding on blood, an act of parasitism that drains the victim's life force and can transform the victim into a vampire; it is also an ordinary human being who is characterized as a vampire and who is clearly modeled on vampires with whom writer and reader are familiar.

Thus, because my study treats the vampire as an aberrant *human* character, it does not discuss in any detail the odd variants of the vampire motif in the nineteenth century that Christopher Frayling mentions:

...assorted vampire plants (such as H.G. Wells's *Strange Orchid*, 1895), psychic sponges (such as Conan Doyle's *The Parasite*, 1891), vampire houses and portraits (such as in *The Desires of Men* by L.T. Meade, 1899), evil scientists posing as vampires to keep the peasants away (such as in *Carpathian Castle* by Jules Verne, 1892) and even a 'winged kangaroo with a python's neck' (the Robinsons' *Last of the Vampires*, 1890).[33]

Frayling adds, however, that "most of these bizarre variants date from the 1890s, when the genre had either to diversify or repeat itself."[33] Furthermore, as the earlier part of this chapter suggests, twentieth-century writers have continued this process of diversification—so much so that the vampire in twentieth-century popular culture is no longer a reanimated corpse; it no longer destroys its victims; and it no longer turns its victims into vampires. Although vampires in the twentieth century often retain remnants of their formerly horrifying propensities, little besides a vague family resemblance links vampires so different as Count Chocula and King's Barlow.

There is much greater coherence in the vampire in nineteenth-century literature, so much that—despite the different degrees of sophistication with which the motif is handled—treatments of the vampire in imaginative literature fall into three divisions. These divisions then became three of the major sections for this study of the literary vampire:

1. The first section focuses on fictional works in which living-dead characters actually drink the blood of their human victims and in which the human characters all agree (or come to see) that "real" vampires exist within their fictional world. Works treated in this section include Polidori's *The Vampyre*, *Varney the Vampyre*, "Carmilla," and *Dracula*.

2. The second section covers fictional works in which one of the characters suspects another of being a vampire; however, because that suspicion is never proved conclusively, the reader is led to focus on ordinary human evil rather than on supernatural evil. This chapter

focuses on *Wuthering Heights* and Stoker's *The Lady of the Shroud* as the only major literary examples of this type.

3. The third section includes fictional works in which one of the characters deliberately uses the term "vampire" as a significant metaphor for destructive human behavior and shows, therefore, that he or she is aware of the literary tradition and of the social/historical significance of the vampire motif. Works discussed in this chapter include *Jane Eyre*, *Bleak House*, and *Middlemarch*. Because the vampire is connected to so many concerns—especially an interest with the past and its relationship to the present, an awareness that certain individuals and groups exploit others, and a concern with sexual identity—and because this chapter explores these writers' conscious manipulation of an existing motif, the chapter may seem disproportionately long. However, the significance of the vampire motif lies in precisely its connection to other areas.

In addition, each chapter looks at the correlation between the three kinds of works that feature vampires and the development of realistic fiction during the nineteenth century. While definitely not a straight line (the obviously Gothic "Carmilla" was published in 1872 and the equally unrealistic *Dracula* in 1897), the general tendency in nineteenth-century fiction is away from Gothic—even the kind of explained Gothic written by Ann Radcliffe—and toward a realistic depiction of ordinary life and manners. Moreover, this trend toward realism would seem to lead away from such an obviously supernatural figure as the vampire. However, quite the contrary is true, for the vampire (and the reader is advised to think of other Gothic characters, such as those discussed in Nina Auerbach's *Woman and the Demon*,[35] continues to be adapted—although as a metaphor instead of as an actual belief—in realistic fiction.

Besides the three chapters that focus on imaginative literature, the study includes a chapter that discusses folklore and other source materials that led to the unique character of the vampire in nineteenth-century literature as well as a final speculative chapter that attempts to answer some of the questions about the relationship between literature and social history that are raised in the rest of the study. The reason for the chapter on folklore is obvious, for understanding what makes the vampire in nineteenth-century literature unique necessitates our understanding the tradition that the individual writers discovered and adapted to their own use.

The reasons for the final chapter may be less immediately clear. Students of significant literature are likely to agree with Twitchell that the vampire in the twentieth century is trivial and derivative—the end of a genre. Nonetheless, the vampire remains one of the twentieth century's most powerful myths—as powerful in our popular culture as the belief embodied by the tale of Cinderella, by the Horatio Alger paradigm, or by the myth of the innocent green world that George Lucas revives in

Return of the Jedi; and the sheer quantity of recent works that feature the vampire attests to our continued fascination with this powerful erotic being, the outsider and rebel. No less important to nineteenth-century literature, the vampire was nonetheless a very different creature as the earlier part of this study has suggested and as the three chapters on nineteenth-century literature will prove. Understanding that difference as well as the cultural reasons for the evolution of an attractive figure from the bloated and inhuman nightmare figure from folklore will reveal something important about the vampire and—much more important— about human culture as well.

According to tradition, vampires have no mirror reflection. Thus they are incapable of seeing themselves, and we are equally incapable of seeing them clearly. Nonetheless, their hidden countenance is always there—a reflection of our deepest fears and desires. Therefore, as we hold the mirror up to our unnatural counterparts, we see that the nature of those fears and desires has changed dramatically over the past three centuries. Seventeenth-century peasant, nineteenth-century poet, or twentieth-century teenager—we see in the vampire something different— something that we often fear, sometimes desire.

Chapter Two
The Origins of Modern Myth

In the last chapter we saw that the vampire is such a familiar character today that adolescent readers of comic books, devotees of serious literature, and watchers of late-night "Creature Features" can all recognize the family resemblances in vampires as diversified as Dracula (played as an urbane eighteenth-century gentleman by George Hamilton) in *Love At First Bite*, the hauntingly beautiful Miriam (Catherine Deneuve) in *The Hunger*, or the misunderstood punster Sterling O'Blivion of *I, Vampire*.

Returning to the nineteenth-century, readers discover that the ancestors of these familiar figures, though no less common to people, were somewhat different. Sir Frances Varney in the penny dreadful *Varney the Vampire* (originally printed in parts in the early 1840s), for example, is much less urbane than Hamilton's version. His face—not to mention his courtship—is dreadful:

It is perfectly white—perfectly bloodless. The eyes look like polished tin; the lips are drawn back, and the principal feature next to those dreadful eyes is the teeth— the fearful looking teeth—projecting like those of some wild animal, hideously, glaringly white, and fang-like. It approaches the bed with a strange, gliding movement. It clashes together the long nails that literally appear to hang from the finger ends....He drags her head to the bed's edge. He forces it back by the long hair still entwined in his grasp. With a plunge he seizes her neck in his fang-like teeth— a gush of blood, and a hideous sucking noise follows. *The girl has swooned, and the vampyre is at his hideous repast!* (Vol. I, Ch. 1, Rymer's italics)

Here is none of the playful sensuality of Hamilton or Langella or even Lee's raw eroticism. Indeed, the reader's first glimpse of Varney reveals something more bestial than human, a creature with fangs and claws who comes in the night to drink the blood of his unwilling victim.

The following excerpt from "Carmilla" (first published in the magazine *The Dark Blue* in 1871) reveals a being slightly more recognizable to twentieth-century readers:

The grave of the Countess Mircalla was opened: and the General and my father recognized each his perfidious and beautiful guest.... Her eyes were open; no cadaverous smell exhaled from the coffin. The two medical men, one officially present, the other on the part of the promoter of the inquiry, attested the marvelous fact, that there was a faint but appreciable respiration, and a corresponding action of the heart. The limbs were perfectly flexible, the flesh elastic; and the leaden coffin floated with blood, in which to a depth of seven inches, the body lay immersed. Here then, were all the admitted signs and proofs of vampirism. (Ch. XV)

Earlier sections of LeFanu's "Carmilla" reveal a being who, like the beautiful Miriam, is cultivated—even genteel. However, when LeFanu reveals that Carmilla's natural habitat is the crypt, not the drawing room, he also gives her characteristics that distinguish her from most twentieth-century vampires.

Ranging from the Count on Sesame Street to Chelsea Quinn Yarbro's St. Germain, the twentieth-century vampires that were introduced in Chapter One are often more human than their predecessors. No one describes this phenomenon better than Anne Rice whose vampire Lestat announces: "Try to see the evil that I am. I stalk the world in mortal dress—the worst of fiends, the monster who looks exactly like everyone else."[1] Rice continues to take the vampire seriously although she does not really present it as an evil force. However, many of her contemporaries create vampires so benign that they are often camp figures—mere parodies of the vampire's horrifying former self.

What the reader sees in the vampire in nineteenth-century literature is the result of writers combining at least three broad strands: folkloric treatments of posthumous magic, earlier literary characters—such as the rake and the villains and temptresses of the Gothic novel, and (later in the century—as Chapters Three, Four, and Five will demonstrate) responses to genuine changes in social roles for men and women.

The beginnings are, of course, in folklore; and writers who have studied the phenomenon (two of the best-known are Montague Summers in *The Vampire in Europe* and *The Vampire: His Kith and Kin* and Anthony Masters in *The Natural History of the Vampire*)[2] observe that almost no culture is free of the superstition of blood-sucking ghosts. Specifics, however, differ from culture to culture. The Rumanian Stigoi is a reanimated corpse, made live again by the return of the soul. Both Polish and Russian vampires emerge from their coffins only between midday and midnight; in addition, their coffins are filled with blood, and they have such enormous hunger that they eat their winding sheets as a matter of course. The Malaysian Langsuir is a flying female demon who sucks the blood of children while the Portuguese Bruxsa seduces travelers and drinks the blood of children. The Scottish baobham sith takes the form of groups of beautiful girls to drain victims of blood while the Danish Mara takes human form during the day and destroys those who fall in love with her.[3] No single vampire is as horrifying as the following ghastly composite by Summers that combines traits from many European versions:

A Vampire is generally described as being exceedingly gaunt and lean with a hideous countenance.... When, however, he has satiated his lust for warm human blood his body becomes horribly puffed and bloated, as though he were some great leech gorged and replete to bursting...the nails are always curved and crooked, often well-nigh the length of a great bird's claw, the quicks dirty and foul with clots and gouts of black blood. His breath is unbearably fetid and rank with corruption, the stench of the charnel.[4]

Summers' portrait of the folkloric vampire makes even Varney appear charming, for the vampire from folklore is a prisoner of physical urges, a creature animated only by his thirst for blood. It is the vampire's gross corporality that most disturbs the writer in *Colburn's New Monthly Magazine*, for he points to the vampire's lack of human feeling and to his desire to "banquet a monstrous thirst acquired in the tomb, and which, though he walks in human lineaments, has swallowed up every human motive in its brutal ferocity" (p. 141).

While the belief in vampires is almost universal, England seems to have been singularly free from this superstition. Both Kittredge in *Witchcraft in Old and New England* and Summers in *The Vampire in Europe* refer to the twelfth-century accounts of William of Newburgh and William of Malmesbury as the only historical accounts of this belief in England; an article in an 1855 issue of *Household Words* refers to a third example, an Anglo-Saxon poem on the Vampyre of the Fens; and Nicholas K. Kiessling uses linguistic evidence to argue that Grendel's mother is an English lamia:

His mother, the *merewif*, sea woman (line 1519), is conceptually similar to the Old English *meremenin*, sea sprite, the gloss to Latin *Sirena*, and to the Old High German words for sea sprite, forest hag and witch (for example, *mermine minie*, *waltminne*, *holzvrowe*, and *strigae*). These Old High German words in turn are glosses to Latin *lamia*.[5]

Even accepting these historical accounts, one can hardly make a case for a vampire tradition in England. Moreover, since there is a hiatus of almost seven centuries, such references are too remote to influence nineteenth-century writers. (One should not ignore the fact—noted in the November 14, 1896 issue of *Chamber's Journal*—that "the burial of suicides at cross-roads with a stake thrust through them, usual in England till well into this century, closely resembles the precaution used in Slavonic lands for inducing vampires to cease from troubling" [pp. 730-31].) Although the English have a long tradition of ghostly visitors, no evidence suggests that these ghosts returned to suck the blood of the living or to destroy human beings through sexual exploitation. Generally—like the ghost of Hamlet's father or the Bodach Glas that appears to Fergus in *Waverley*—they return because of human motives: revenge, unfinished business, jealousy.[6]

England had no native tradition of vampires, but reports of vampire epidemics on the continent could have provided writers with the necessary information. During the eighteenth century, the subject of vampirism was an obsession in Europe. Pamphlets, newspapers and conversations centered on the vampire; and despite the ridicule of philosophers, sovereigns sent officials to report on the vampire epidemics, which centered "in Istria (1642), East Prussia (1710 and 1721), Hungary (1725-30), Austrian Serbia (1731-2), East Prussia (1750), Silesia (1755), Wallachia (1756), and Russia (1772)."[7] Gabriel Ronay cites Dom Augustin Calmet, author of the first anthology of vampire material, who offered one possible cause of these epidemics: Fear of vampires began in Hungary, Moravia, and Silesia during the late seventeenth century, a period when the conflict between the Roman Catholic Church and the Greek Orthodox Church had reached a crisis.[8] Ronay explains that reports of vampires came from border areas where Catholic Hungarians and Orthodox Serbs and Walachs intermingled. That the names of the alleged vampires were Slavonic suggests that they were probably followers of the Greek faith who came from villages that had lost their Hungarian population during the Turkish occupation. After the Turks were ousted from this area, these newly colonized villages were subject to considerable pressures from the Hungarian government and the Catholic Hapsburg military regiments who administered the villages.[9] Racial and cultural differences in this area led people to suspect and distrust their neighbors, and the proximity in which these different people lived intensified suspicions. These suspicions—combined with a well-established belief in vampires in this part of the world—may have led to the vampire epidemics in the eighteenth century.

Ronay adds that there were other reasons to distrust one's neighbors since this area was cursed with epidemic disease during this period: the Black Plague between 1692 and 1694, smallpox in 1708 and again in 1719. Before scientists discovered the causes of disease, people often attributed epidemics to supernatural intervention.

The Continental vampire epidemics apparently had a direct impact on both English literature and English law. According to folklore in many East European countries, one sure way to become a vampire was suicide; and Summers, Masters, and Twitchell all cite the laws regarding the treatment of suicides in England in the early nineteenth century. Such laws made it illegal to dig up the body of an alleged vampire to drive a stake through it.

The impact of the vampire epidemics on English literature were somewhat less direct. In fact, it took over a century for writers and thinkers to capitalize on the social aspects of the vampire motif, to translate disease into moral contagion,[10] and to study the characteristics that made the vampire an alien. (Just as primitive people often regard outsiders as potential vampires, many Victorian writers emphasize that the vampire is an outsider: Bertha Mason is a Creole; Heathcliff's origins are unknown although he is sometimes described as looking like a gypsy; and Dracula, who describes himself as a descendant of Attila, comes to England from exotic Transylvania.) The English interest in the vampire comes directly from Germany. During the eighteenth century, German universities were the center of debate about the vampire epidemics and the ensuing mass hysteria; and these debates led to the publication of monographs and philosophical treatises on vampires. Frayling suggests how the discussion of vampires moved from folklore to scientific speculation within a fairly short period:

> If the fashionable journals made much of the Arnold Paole story [one of the best documented cases of vampirism] for a season or two, the interest aroused in intellectual circles by this prototypical example of 'peasant superstition' lasted much longer. The report of 1732 directly stimulated at least fourteen treatises and four dissertations; at one time or another the debate involved such leading figures of the Enlightenment as the Marquis d'Agens, Voltaire, Rousseau, Van Swieten (Empress Maria Theresa's personal physician and adviser) and the Chevalier De Jaucourt (a prolific contributor to the great Encyclopedia).[11]

These philosophical works in turn inspired various literary treatments of the vampire, especially in Germany. Encouraged by Herder's romantic nationalism and by the romantic quest for mystery, many German writers turned to folklore and to classical Greek and Latin mythology for subject matter. The vampire was simply one more example of a mysterious subject that appealed to the German Romantics. Ossenfelder wrote *Der Vampir* in 1748; Burger wrote *Lenore* in 1773; and Goethe wrote *The Bride of Corinth* in 1797. These works were soon translated into English. In addition, because of the German influence, the English came to associate the vampire with Germany as when Jane Eyre tells Rochester about the strange woman who had appeared in her room and states that it reminded her of the "foul German spectre— the Vampyre" (Ch. XXV).

Already enamoured with the ghastly figures from the Gothic novel— the Manfreds, Antonios, and Old English Barons—English writers and readers were prepared to experience that odd love-hate relationship with the vampire that lasted almost the entire nineteenth century. (Oddly enough, there are no vampires in the novels of Ann Radcliffe, William Godwin, Clara Reeve or the other writers that can be accurately described as the first generation of Gothic writers. While their works are peopled with numerous vicious characters, none is literally a supernatural bloodsucker.[12] Because the writers of these novels could not have been unaware of the vampire epidemics in Eastern Europe, one must assume that the vampire did not serve the needs of their imaginations and that something—or combination of things—occurred later to make it a suitable literary subject.)

The evolution of the vampire motif from folklore to serious literature is not quite so simple as the previous paragraph suggests, of course. According to the *Oxford English Dictionary*, the first reference to the vampire in English occurs in 1734, almost a century before the vampire enters literature: "These Vampyres are supposed to be the Bodies of deceased Persons, animated by evil Spirits, which come out of the Graves, in the Night-time, suck the Blood of many of the Living, and thereby destroy them." The O.E.D. plainly defines a peasant superstition—and nothing more. There is at least one earlier reference, however—in the May 1732 issue of the *London Gentleman's Magazine*—and that extremely early reference already suggests the writer's awareness of metaphoric possibilities in the vampire superstition:

This Account, of Vampyres, you'll observe, comes from the Eastern Part of the World, always remarkable for its Allegorical Style. The States of Hungary are in subjection to the Turks and Germans, and govern'd by a pretty hard Hand; which obliges them to couch all Complaints under Figures. This Relation seems to be of the same kind.[13]

This reference focuses on the vampire as a kind of social metaphor, a way of illustrating political oppression.

Despite the early interest in the metaphoric richness of the vampire, there is always the possibility that part of the interest stemmed from genuine belief.[14] Jeffrey B. Russell's discussion of witchcraft, for example, illustrates that the uneducated nineteenth-century Englishman was very superstitious. Although the laws against witchcraft (a superstition that has a number of interesting parallels to vampirism) were repealed in 1736, beliefs lingered in rural areas where occasional violence against suspected witches continued well into the twentieth century.[15]

Most discussions of vampirism during the nineteenth century, however, focus on rational explanations of the phenomenon. For example, the vampire epidemics led to a number of attempts during the eighteenth and nineteenth centuries to expose superstition to the cold scrutiny of science. These rational explanations, according to Twitchell, focused on two areas: studies of people whose abberrant behavior resembled that of the vampire and studies of the similarities between the symptoms of certain diseases and the supposed results of vampire attack. In addition, Twitchell points to the discovery of an actual creature that resembled the vampire of folklore, the "Desmodus rotundus," more commonly known as the vampire bat.[16] Unknown in the Old World, this little bloodsucker might have come straight from nightmare. All these philosophical and scientific treatises kept the vampire before the eyes of the reading public in the eighteenth and nineteenth centuries and thereby reinforced the various literary treatments of the vampire. In addition, it is probable that these rational explanations were the view of the majority of literate Englishmen. For example, an 1841 work by Charles Mackay, *Extraordinary Popular Delusions and the Madness of Crowds*, summarizes an attitude toward superstitious beliefs that was probably common among educated Victorians:

We all know the strange pranks which imagination can play in certain disease; that the hypochondriac can see visions and spectres.... Science has lifted up the veil, and rolled away all the fantastic horrors in which our forefathers shrouded these and similar cases. The man who now imagines himself a wolf is sent to the hospital instead of the stake, as in the days of the witch mania; and earth, air, and sea are unpeopled of the grotesque spirits that were once believed to haunt them.[17]

Science attacked two characteristics of the vampire: the fact that the body did not decompose like other dead bodies and the fact that the vampire left its grave to prey on the living. *Blackwoods* printed an article in 1847 that attributed vampirism to premature burial. The article refers to the epidemics in Eastern Europe and argues that the alleged vampires were people who, because of a cataleptic trance or some other physical condition that made them appear dead, had been buried alive. The author refers to recorded cases of people who had been buried alive or who had narrowly escaped being buried alive and adds that similar cases would have been more common in areas where bodies were not embalmed and during epidemics, when bodies were buried more quickly than at other times. Premature burial would also explain the existence of corpses that had rolled over in their graves and of those that had bloodied themselves in their futile attempts to escape. That these natural phenomena led to vampire epidemics in some areas, the writer attributes to hysteria, arguing that fright can bring on fits and that "certainly no ghastlier terror can there be than the accredited apprehension of Vampirism."[18] The 1855 article in *Household Words* agrees with the *Blackwoods* article while the 1896 article in *Chamber's Journal* explains that the belief in vampires is nothing but the workings of a diseased imagination.[19] None of these rational interpretations adequately explains why the subject of vampires attracted such widespread attention in nineteenth-century England (My speculations on reasons for the vampire's popularity are included in Chapter Six), but the numerous treatments of the motif in both fiction and popular journalism indicate that people were aware of the belief in vampires and that this interest did not stem from a genuine belief in supernatural manifestations.

The preceeding pages suggest that nineteenth-century English writers learned about the vampire from at least three distinct sources: folklore, eighteenth-century German literature, and scientific discussions of primitive beliefs. However, many specifics of the vampire's character, including the emphasis on its social relations and destructive traits are reminders of one more subtle influence—popular literature, most particularly the Gothic novel.

The earliest examples of vampires (in some cases vampire-like characters instead of actual vampires) in both German and English literature occur in poems that look back to the Middle Ages or to classical Greece. Thus, *Lenore, Christabel,* and "La Belle Dame Sans Merci" derive much of their mystery from their medieval settings while *The Bride of Corinth* and *Lamia* rely on the exoticism associated with the ancient world. Similarly the earliest Gothic novels are set either in a timeless world or are, like Walpole's *Castle of Otranto,* set in a deliberately medieval one, where the reader could believe that supernatural events might easily occur.

However, while early Gothic works are set in the remote past or in a timeless never-never land, quite different from the England inhabited by both writers and readers, the second generation of Gothic writers (Mary Shelley and Polidori, for example) move their mysterious tales to their own era and to more ordinary settings. Interested in exploring the psychology—often the abnormal psychology—of characters who appear perfectly ordinary, in probing the more mysterious occurrences of life, and in avoiding the stultifying rationalism that they associated with their predecessors in the Enlightenment and with many of their contemporaries, the second generation of Gothic writers discovered that they could create realistic characters and settings and still relate the profound sense of mystery achieved by the early Gothic writers.

In fact, by 1816, when Polidori wrote "The Vampyre" as part of the same story-telling contest that inspired Mary Shelley to write *Frankenstein,* the emphasis is on realistic detail. Both works use contemporary settings instead of shadowy backgrounds, remote in time and place, and both works rely on characters with whom the reader can identify. Victor Frankenstein is a young student—perhaps more ambitious than most, but equally callow and unthinking; and Shelley demonstrates that the horrors of *Frankenstein* occur not because of the title character's bizarre scientific experiments but because of the absence of a very human quality: love.

The characters in *The Vampyre* are equally recognizable. The two central characters are young men who set off on the continental Grand Tour together. One is the naive but honorable narrator while the other, Lord Ruthven, might have been modeled on Mr. B, Lovelace, or any of the other rakes in eighteenth-century literature. (That he is also modeled on Lord Byron can be explained by the current popularity of the Byronic hero and by Polidori's personal relationship with Lord Byron. As Byron's personal physician he apparently felt that he was in the shadow of his famous benefactor just as young Aubrey feels inferior to the more experienced Ruthven. At any rate, the similarities between Byron and his literary offspring were apparently obvious to many readers.) Lord Ruthven seduces women, gambles, and duels even before the narrator discovers that he is also a vampire, and the reader would be equally uncertain were it not for a long preface that discusses source materials. However, Polidori establishes the destructive elements of Lord Ruthven's character long before revealing his vampire's supernatural abilities.

Nonetheless, Lord Ruthven, the first *literal* vampire in English fiction is a model for the vampire in English fiction. A new kind of literary figure, Ruthven's distinctive character comes from at least three sources: folklore, scientific discussions of primitive belief, and popular literature.

Tracing the development of the vampire as a literary motif from its origins in folklore, one sees it evolving from reports of "posthumous magic." Frayling's discussion of the Arnold Paole story is a model of this evolution:

Predictably enough, this unusually detailed report caused a sensation: at the annual Leipzig fair, in 1732, a cheap version of the Arnold Paole story became an instant best-seller; on March 3rd, the *Dutch Gleaner* (which was very popular in Versailles court circles) ran a detailed and suitably embellished account.... Some English periodicals, including the *London Journal* and the *Gentleman's Magazine*, immediately cobbled together translations or adaptations, which appeared from March to May 1732.... Augustin Calmet anthologized all these articles in his full-length *Treatise*.[20]

By the end of the nineteenth century, however, peasants such as Arnold Paole have evolved into characters as rich and diversified as Eliot's Rosamond Vincy and Stoker's Dracula.

The preceding lengthy discussion confirms what M.M. Carlson argues in *Folklore Forum*. Explaining that the vampire is actually a literary character rather than a "figure from folklore," Carlson shows that, though the vampire originated in folklore, "literature has greatly reworked and remolded the vampire into a recognizable literary type to suit its own needs and purposes"[21] and cites several obvious differences between the two. For example, the literary vampire generally chooses victims outside his own ethnic group and of the opposite sex while the vampire in folklore "does not distinguish his victims by sex. He also begins by appearing to his own family first, then to other relatives and friends in the village."[22] In addition, as Leatherdale observes, the literary vampire is much more powerful:

In literature, the social background of the undead is commonly transformed from the peasantry to the nobility, and they are able to travel beyond their native community to plague great cities where they can hide in total anonymity.[23]

There are other differences, of course, but these examples suggest that nineteenth-century fiction writers saw in the vampire something vastly different from what was seen by superstitious Eastern European peasants.

In addition, the vampire also evolves over the course of the century. Varney and Carmilla retain characteristics that seem to come straight from folklore: the fangs and claws attributed to Varney and his otherwise bestial behavior and Carmilla's need to reside in her blood-filled coffin. However, by the end of the century, most literary vampires have lost the gross physical characteristics *and* the mysterious behavior of their predecesessors in folklore.

Equally important is the fact that many of the changes in the vampire during the nineteenth century are connected to the development of fiction during the nineteenth century. Originating in Gothic works, such as *The Vampyre*, "Carmilla," and *Dracula*, the vampire also appears in realistic fiction such as *Middlemarch*, in works that combine realistic elements with romance (*Wuthering Heights*), and even in non-fiction such as *Capital* and *The Condition of the Working Class in England*. The Gothic, which had originated in the eighteenth century as a distinct genre, becomes in the nineteenth century the heart of many realistic novels, what Northrop Frye describes in *The Secular Scripture* as the hidden romance center.[24]

Realistic fiction is not a nineteenth-century development, and the movement from romance to realism is not a strictly chronological one. Nonetheless, it is possible to see a heightened interest in realistic fiction as the century progressed; and this movement from sensationalism to realism is often revealed most transparently in some of the minor novelists, as Edith Birkhead demonstrates in the following discussion of an almost forgotten Gothic novelist:

It is noteworthy that by 1820 even Miss Wilkinson had learnt to despise the spectres in whom she had gloried during her amazing career. In *The Spectre of Lanmere Abbey* (1820) the ghost is ignominiously exposed, and proved to be "a tall figure dressed in white, and a long, transparent veil flowing over her whole figure," while the heroine Amelia speaks almost in the accents of Catherine Morland.[25]

That some of the first generation of Gothic novelists—Godwin and Radcliffe being the best known—had provided such rational explanations for the supernatural within their works is a reminder that Gothic literature had an oddly dual existence from the moment it appeared within English literature, one component accepting supernatural occurrences as literal within its fictional world, the other insisting that the mystery originally attributed to the supernatural can be explained logically.

Birkhead's reference to *Northanger Abbey*, however, is a reminder that realistic writers often adapt certain Gothic elements. (Austen, of course, parodies the more extreme elements of her Gothic predecessors, but she also reveals how much she learned from their exploration of matters that are hidden beneath the social surface.) Similarly Charlotte Bronte adopts the convention of the mysterious nun in *Villette* only to expose it as a sham. In *Jane Eyre*, she adopts the supernatural belief in vampires to focus on a more plausible horror (one that Elizabeth Gaskell claimed that Bronte actually knew about)—attempted bigamy and an incarcerated mad wife.

Austen and Bronte are not the only writers to incorporate aspects of the Gothic into their otherwise realistic works. In *Ghosts of the Gothic*, Judith Wilt focuses on Austen, Eliot, and Lawrence, saying that she does not intend to enclose them "within the defined Gothic...but rather to suggest that these great novelists' imaginations function not to break out of or abandon that core but to embrace it."[26] Whether one agrees with Wilt's assertion or with Frye's argument that all realistic social novels encompass buried romance, one has to agree that almost all nineteenth-century novels—even the most realistic—include Gothic elements. Therefore, this study of one literary motif, the vampire, has significant ramifications for other works of nineteenth-century fiction, especially those that adapt motifs from earlier forms of literature as well as those that explore predatory images.

Realistic nineteenth-century novels do not adopt all aspects of the Gothic (missing, for example, from most realistic novels is the Gothic interest in architecture as well as the interest in foreign lands), but the evolution of the vampire within nineteenth-century literature is linked to those that are most often adopted—the sense that human life is mysterious and the belief that certain human beings exist outside the community.

The Gothic emphasis on mystery and awe is incorporated into realistic nineteenth-century fiction. Varma, in *The Gothic Flame*, mentions that the "interesting plots in Victorian novels bear impress of the widespread and long enduring vogue of Gothic romance, and reveal that notable writers were conscious of the power of the weird and eerie."[27] Looking at novels by Scott, the Brontes, or Dickens, one quickly sees how their plots are influenced by the Gothic emphasis on mystery and suspense. However, one also sees that this emphasis on mystery extends beyond plot. Wilt, for example, argues that efforts to explore mystery unite Scott, Dickens, and the Brontes, but she is especially interested in Austen, Eliot, and Lawrence because these three writers understand how much that Gothic sense of "overwhelmingness" matters "to the individual, the race, even the species of man.... They are united too in their perception of the *uses* of anxiety and dread as a way of recognizing and admitting the fact of overwhelmingness."[28] Wilt does not mention the extent to which the fear and horror featured in the Gothic novel (and in the sensation novels of the 1860s, which transfer this overwhelmingness to the mundane social world) eventually become a part of mainstream realistic fiction, but most readers recognize that the ability to see shocking details as a part of ordinary life is one characteristic of nineteenth-century realism. Thus, while the Romantic poets focus on the awe and mystery inspired by the natural world and the Gothic novelists on the awe and dread in mysterious people and places, the nineteenth-century realistic novelists encourage their readers to see that awe and dread—in many cases, even horror—are present in the most mundane social situations.

George Eliot, for example, encourages readers to see the utter destructiveness of ordinary egoism by comparing four of the characters in *Middlemarch* to the vampire in folklore. Likewise, Thackeray, who chooses to adapt the siren from Greek mythology instead of the vampire into his portrait of everyday life and manners, also encourages the reader to see that horror often lies just beneath the pleasant social surface:

They look pretty enough when they sit upon a rock, twanging their harps and combing their hair, and sing, and beckon to you to come and hold the looking-glass; but when they sink into their native element, depend on it those mermaids are about no good, and we had best not examine the fiendish marine cannibals, revelling and feasting on their wretched pickled victims.[29]

By comparing his human character to a mythic figure, Thackeray creates a metaphor that enables the reader to see the horror and destructiveness within the mundane reality. At the same time, his metaphor encourages the reader to see that awe and dread are a part of everyday life, not something to be consigned to Ancient Greece or the Middle Ages or even to the Eastern Europe of the recent past.

Another Gothic characteristic that is incorporated into the realistic novel is the conflict between the individual and the community. Referring to Raymond Williams's study, *The English Novel From Dickens to Lawrence*, Wilt explains that the "search for community is the subject of the nineteenth-century English novel."[30] Certainly that notion of community unites novels as otherwise different as *Vanity Fair, The Mill on the Floss, Middlemarch, Barchester Towers*, and *Little Dorritt*. However, as the idea of a genuine community becomes more and more of an impossibility—even a sham—the Gothic sense of alienation becomes more apparent. This alienation is described by G.R. Thompson when he argues that characters in Gothic literature reside in an ambiguous world instead of "the clearcut world of the Middle Ages," a world that they have "no hope of comprehending" and in which they cannot make the proper moral choices even though some occult power seems to hold them responsible for their choices.[31] Realistic novelists, especially those who wrote during the second half of the nineteenth century, often replace the power of God with the power of the community, a community that may be false, nonexistent, or merely perverse. Nonetheless, this community continues to retain its importance in fiction, and writers persistently see it as a source of values. In fact, to be rejected by the community—even by a corrupt community—is to be an outcast. Jane Eyre regrets not being accepted into the communities at Gateshead and Thornfield Hall even though she is highly critical of both; Maggie Tulliver tries to appease the community that looks disdainfully at her; and the little band of vampire hunters in *Dracula* despairs of being able to tell the story of their conquest of the vampire to the community they have just saved from certain destruction.

If realistic fiction in the nineteenth century incorporates Gothic elements, including the sense that human life is mysterious and occasionally awe-inspiring, and focuses on the individual who is ostracized by the community, it is also unique in itself. Unlike the Gothic, a form that emphasizes the tormented inner world of the isolated individual, the realistic novel examines human beings as social creatures within a community setting. Therefore, realistic novels such as *Adam Bede, Villette, North and South, Hard Times* or *Middlemarch* analyze the relationship between the individual and society and emphasize the social forces that shape the individual's consciousness. Although anything that concerned human beings could become a suitable subject for realistic fiction, the following are especially significant to Victorian novelists: industry and the relationship between labor and capital; marriage as an institution and the social and economic forces that shape people's concepts of romantic love; the family, especially the way that changing social patterns alter the traditional family; and the community, another social institution that changed radically during this period, primarily because of the rise of industrialization and the growth both of cities and of new forms of transportation. Thus writers of realistic fiction shape and adapt the world around them as subjects for literature instead of creating a fantasy world peopled by gods, heroes, and supernatural creatures.

A literary movement that originated during a period when the world was changing rapidly, realism focuses on man and society. In addition, because it also came to fruition during an age that was scientific and positivist, it emphasizes the external objective world and ordinary human beings—the kind that would have been familiar to both writer and reader. George Eliot describes the typical character of realistic fiction in the following excerpt from *Adam Bede*:

These fellow-mortals must be accepted as they are: you can neither straighten their noses, nor brighten their wit, nor rectify their dispositions; and it is these people amongst whom your life is passed—that it is needful you should tolerate, pity, and love.... So I am content to tell my simple story, without trying to make things seem better than they were;

dreading nothing, indeed but falsity, which, in spite of one's best efforts, there is reason to dread. Falsehood is so easy, truth so difficult.[32]

As a result of her striving to create realistic human characters and situations, the people in Eliot's fiction are identifiable human beings, who are shaped by their society and who behave plausibly, people who might have lived next door to her readers.

The realistic nineteenth-century novel shares elements with realistic works from other periods, such as its emphasis on external, objective details and its reliance on characters who are interesting precisely because they are ordinary, but it also has several unique characteristics. One is the intensity with which it probed the social problems associated with ordinary life and manners—the kinds of social details that mattered to contemporary readers. Another is the degree to which it incorporated Gothic elements and focused the reader's attention on the mysteries that lay just beneath the social surface.

Furthermore, if the combination of Gothic elements with realistic makes nineteenth-century English fiction unique, it also makes the nineteenth-century vampire very different from both its ancestors in folklore and its twentieth-century offspring. Originating in the exotic past and in primitive cultures, the vampire enters English literature through Romantic poetry, where it remains an exotic supernatural creature. Within two decades, however, the vampire enters the second-generation of Gothic fiction in works such as Polidori's *The Vampyre* or the penny dreadful *Varney the Vampire*, works that accept the vampire's supernatural abilities as givens. Later in the century, however, the vampire becomes a character in realistic fiction, not always a central character assuredly but one that can be used to shed new light on this form of literature and on the social and intellectual forces that made it such a popular form during the Victorian Era. These matters will be covered in the following three chapters.

Chapter Three
The Vampire as Gothic Villain

Dracula. As Chapter One suggests, the name has practically become a synonym for vampire in the twentieth century. However, Bram Stoker's original character is a transitional figure that has links to both the hideous creature from folklore and the more appealing modern version in *Love At First Bite*, John Badham's *Dracula*, and the novels of Fred Saberhagen and Chelsea Quinn Yarbro. Similarly the novel in which he is the title character is a transitional work that looks back to its predecessors in Gothic literature and forward to twentieth-century popular culture.

Stoker is careful to reveal the truth about Dracula slowly. To create this suspense, he narrates the first sections of the novel through Jonathan Harker, a young English lawyer who has gone to Transylvania to handle some real estate transactions for Count Dracula, who has purchased property in London. It takes Harker, who—like most of the other characters in the novel—is a rationalist and a sceptic, some time to realize the truth about Dracula. However, even before he realizes that Dracula is a supernatural being, Harker recognizes that the Count wields considerable economic and physical power. Count Dracula is, first of all, a nobleman who is accustomed to having power over others; and he announces proudly: "Here I am noble; I am *boyar*; the common people know me, and I am master...I have been so long master that I would be master still—or at least that none other should be master of me" (Ch. II).

In addition to social and political power, Harker learns that his host also has a great deal of erotic power over women. Not only does he live in a castle with three women (These are women with whom he had evidently had sexual relationships at one time though the centuries have altered that relationship to something from which all passion has disappeared), but he easily seduces both Lucy Westenra and Mina Harker. Lucy, for example, positively blooms after her first encounter with the vampire; and even the newlywed Mina confesses that she did not want to prevent his advances. Furthermore, he announces enigmatically that Lucy and Mina may not be his only English conquests: "Your girls that you all love are mine already; and through them you and others shall yet be mine—my creatures to do my bidding and to be my jackals when I want to feed" (Ch. XXIII). Thus, even without the vampire's supernatural ability to conquer death or to change shape at will, Dracula is a character of considerable power.

Stoker, however, is careful to mention Dracula's supernatural characteristics as well. For example, Harker first realizes that Dracula is a being unlike himself when he discovers that Dracula has no mirror reflection. In addition, Stoker creates Van Helsing—a doctor, lawyer, and scholar—who relates the traditions and superstitions associated with the vampire. Describing Dracula as a being who can not be destroyed "by mere passing of the time" and who flourishes by drinking the blood of his living victims, he cites other supernatural abilities:

Even more, we have seen amongst us that he can even grow younger; that his vital faculties grow strenuous, and seem as though they refresh themselves when his special pabulum is plenty.... He throws no shadow; he make in the mirror no reflect.... He can transform himself to wolf.... He can come in mist which he create. (Ch. XVIII)

Moreover Van Helsing also informs his young companions that they must destroy Dracula or risk becoming vampires like him: "But to fail here, is not mere life or death. It is that we become as him; that we henceforward become foul things of the night like him—without heart or conscience, preying on the bodies and the souls of those we love best" (Ch. XVIII). Thus Van Helsing both reinforces Dracula's supernatural abilities and links those abilities with evil.

Very different from his twentieth-century offspring, Stoker's character is clearly a creature of supernatural evil and immense power, a Gothic figure in a work where all the characters (even the scientists and skeptics for whom acceptance of the irrational and mysterious is initially difficult) come to accept him as an actual and threatening presence.

However, if Dracula's power is modeled on that of the vampire from folklore and from earlier literature, other characteristics anticipate the more appealing modern vampire, for Stoker presents his title figure as a lonely and isolated figure who is hunted and finally destroyed by opponents who use both the ancient power of religion and the modern power of technology against him. Stoker suggests that the odds are against Dracula from the beginning and also takes considerable pains to reveal his monster's human side. For example, he has Dracula serve as both coachman and chef for Harker, the latter activity all the more difficult for someone who hasn't tasted ordinary food in at least three centuries. He also has Dracula reveal his vulnerability to Harker by confessing his eagerness to learn English to avoid being recognized as a stranger: "But alas! as yet I only know your tongue through books. To you, my friend, I look that I know it to speak" (Ch. II). Once in England Dracula apparently acquires some of the English bourgeois respect for cleanliness even though he is a somewhat erratic housekeeper as his opponents learn when they break into his Piccadilly house and discover "notepaper, envelopes, and pens and ink...covered up in thin wrapping paper to keep them from the dust" as well as a clothes brush, a brush and comb, and a jug and basin—the latter containing dirty water which was reddened as if with blood" (Ch. XXII). However, having acquired English housekeeping traits, he has nonetheless not learned all there is to learn about the English way of life. For example, the reader sees him as a stranger when Mina describes him fleeing England. Even though he does not wear the opera cape associated with his film offspring, the date is October; and Dracula is inappropriately dressed "all in black, except that he have a hat of straw which suit not him or the time" (Ch. XXIV). In Transylvania, on the other hand, he wears Harker's clothes when he goes out prowling for food. Despite Dracula's professed desire to be remain inconspicuous, clothing—one of the ways by which realistic writers identify characters—always reveals him as strange and Other.

In addition to including such realistic details as Dracula's toilet articles and inappropriate dress, Stoker has much of the novel take place in nineteenth-century England. (That he begins in Transylvania, where he locates Dracula's castle, also reveals his familiarity with the folklore, of course.) Carter observes that Stoker's use of "a prosaic, modern setting" is responsible for the novel's "peculiar excellence":

In the wilds of Greece or the remote mountains of Styria, the vampire is a natural part of the scenery. In the...England of railway and telegraph, he is a blasphemous abnormality. Count Dracula's advent on the tranquil shore of Whitby represents the icy touch of the Unknown upon our well-ordered, materialistic lives.[1]

Not only is the setting realistic, but Stoker also uses the journals and personal letters of ordinary human beings and newspaper clippings— the very written record of everyday life—to tell his story. The result is the most famous example of one kind of vampire work, the type in which living-dead characters actually suck the blood of their victims and in which the human characters identify "real" vampires in their fictional world.

While *Dracula* is a work that anticipates twentieth-century popular culture, it also looks back to its predecessors. One of the first in English literature (and the first example in fiction) is *The Vampyre*, an elegant little work that was written by Byron's personal physician and travelling companion, John Polidori. A work that earned a certain notoriety in the nineteenth century because of its association with the Byron-Shelley circle in Geneva (when it was first published in *The New Monthly Magazine* in 1819, it was erroneously attributed to Byron) and in the twentieth because it originated in the same ghost-story contest at the Villa Diodati that produced *Frankenstein*. It deserves to be better known in its own right.

Polidori's vampire, Lord Ruthven, is definitely modeled on the vampire from folklore, a fact made obvious by a lengthy introduction that explains that the belief in vampires is "very general in the East,"[2] where it has resulted in many wonderful stories "of the dead rising from their graves, and feeding upon the blood of the young and beautiful" (xix). The introduction also provides a brief synopsis of the Arnold Paul story and alludes to various studies of vampirism:

> The veracious Tournefort gives a long account in his travels of several astonishing cases of vampyrism, to which he pretends to have been an eye witness; and Calmet, in his great work upon this subject, besides a variety of anecdotes, and traditionary narratives...has put forth some learned dissertations, tending to prove it to be a classical, as well as barbarian error. (xxiv)

The introduction shows that Polidori is familiar with the folklore that identified the vampire as a dead body; and the work itself introduces a character whose "dead grey eye" (p. 27) and "the deadly hue of his face, which never gained a warmer tint, either from the blush of modesty, or from the strong emotion of passion" (p. 28) are clearly modeled on the vampire from folklore. Moreover, Ruthven is demonstrably a dead body that requires blood to sustain his unnatural existence, for he is shown to drink the blood of at least two young women, Ianthe and the narrator's sister; and he also comes back to life after being "killed" by bandits.

However, if Polidori is faithful to his sources in folklore, he also adds some touches of his own. For example, Twitchell observes that Polidori is the first to suggest that moonlight can rejuvenate a vampire,[3] a talent that the author of *Varney the Vampire* will use to excess. Polidori is also the first to present the vampire as an aristocrat; and nineteenth-century writers will continue to present the vampire as an aristocratic threat. In addition to Lord Ruthven, there is Sir Frances Varney, Countess Mircalla, and the most famous vampire of all, Count Dracula. Finally, Polidori also provides an erotic twist—one of the first of many additions to the superstition—when he has one of his characters explain that the vampire is "forced every year, by feeding upon the life of a lovely female to prolong his existence for the ensuing months " (p. 42). While the vampire in most folklore versions had been simply a hungry corpse with no special preferences about the choice of victim, Polidori suggests an erotic attachment—often perversely so—between vampire and victim, an attachment that will become much more than a suggestion in both "Carmilla" and *Dracula*, not to mention many of the twentieth-century versions.

The brutality of the attack on Ianthe might have come directly from folklore, for it is apparently a crime of simple hunger. However, the circumstances involving Ruthven's second victim are more complex and interesting because the vampire takes time to seduce Aubrey's sister and even to make her his wife. Only after the wedding do Miss Aubrey's guardians discover that "Lord Ruthven had disappeared, and Aubrey's sister had glutted the thirst of a VAMPYRE!" (p. 72).

Despite these changes, Polidori leaves the reader with very little doubt that Ruthven is modeled on the Eastern European vampire, for he is shown to destroy at least two people by drinking their blood. A young Greek woman with whom Aubrey has fallen in love, Ianthe—the first victim—is attacked by a vampire when she attempts to warn Aubrey from an area known to be frequented by vampires, and the unwitting Aubrey even grapples with the vampire though without seeing his opponent's face. (However, Lord Ruthven drops his dagger during this scuffle; and Aubrey, who had already "wondered at the many coincidences which had all tended to excite a belief in the supernatural power of Lord Ruthven" [pp. 42-43], now knows the truth: his former traveling companion is a vampire.)

While adapting material from folklore, Polidori also creates a character that is more unique and interesting than the vampire in folklore. In addition to making Lord Ruthven a vampire who destroys certain victims by drinking their blood, Polidori also makes his vampirie a moral parasite, "a man entirely absorbed in himself," (p. 31). To reinforce his character's moral flaws, Polidori chooses to emphasize a minor detail from some of the folklore versions:

In many parts of Greece it is considered as a sort of punishment after death, for some heinous crime committed whilst in existence, that the deceased is not only doomed to vampyrise, but compelled to confine his infernal visitations solely to those beings he loved most while upon earth—those to whom he was bound by ties of kindred and affection. (xxii)

According to most versions, people—like Arnold Paul—became vampires simply because they were unfortunate enough to be attacked by another vampire, because they were stillborn, or because of certain hereditary causes, not because they were punished for evil deeds. Nor were they *compelled* to attack their loved ones although the vampire in folklore often began his "career" with family members.

In addition, Polidori emphasizes that Lord Ruthven is a cruel man who ruins some of his unsuspecting victims financially and socially. In this respect he resembles various characters from popular literature: Lovelace, Squire B, and other eighteenth-century rakes as well as the mysterious and unpredictable villains of Gothic novels—the Schedonis, the Ambrosios, the Manfreds. He also, as should be mentioned here, resembles the Byronic hero. Not only was Polidori personally familiar with Byron, but he was obviously thinking of him when he created his vampire, for he named the character Lord Ruthven, the name used in

Glenarvon, Lady Caroline Lamb's notorious roman a clef, to satirize the poet.

Seeing Ruthven as both a vampire and a derivative of the eighteenth-century rake, Polidori often chooses to emphasize his character's moral failure rather than his supernatural ability. Even before the reader learns that Ruthven is a vampire (a revelation that doesn't occur until the work is half over), Polidori reveals him as a destroyer of others, one whose touch leads to the "death" of the victim's reputation and will. For example, although Aubrey believes that Lord Ruthven is attracted only to virtuous women, he later discovers: "...all those females whom he had sought, apparently on account of their virtue, had...thrown even the mask aside, and had not scrupled to expose the whole deformity of their vices to the public gaze" (p. 37). Finally, Aubrey observes that even Ruthven's money is tainted with death:

> ...when the profligate came to ask something, not to relieve his wants, but to allow him to wallow in his lust, or to sink him still deeper in his iniquity, he was sent away...with rich charity.... All those upon whom it was bestowed, inevitably found that there was a curse upon it, for they were all either led to the scaffold, or sunk to the lowest and most abject misery." (p. 33-34)

His condition is thus contagious, a characteristic that Carrol L. Fry observes is common to both the vampire and the "rake of the popular novel" who "pass on their conditions (moral depravity in the former and vampirism in the latter) to their victims."[4]

Clearly influenced by both folklore and by a popular literary tradition in his portrait of the vampiric Lord Ruthven, Polidori also contributes greatly to the modern concept of the vampire. Among his contributions is the recognition that the vampire exists in civilized settings as well as in primitive ones. Like *Dracula*, much of *The Vampyre* occurs in areas that would have been familiar to Polidori's contemporaries—nineteenth-century English drawing rooms and Continental resorts, for example; and M.L. Carter observes that Polidori was partially responsible "for the greater emphasis on contemporary settings in horror tales, rather than shadowy backgrounds remote in time and space."[5] Carter is right, for certainly much of the horror of Polidori's tale occurs when the reader realizes that unspeakable things can happen in the most ordinary places and to the most ordinary human beings.

Another critic, James Rieger, emphasizes a slightly different aspect of Polidori's technique when he observes that both *Frankenstein* and *The Vampyre* achieve their unique quality by rejecting characteristics of the "outdated 'shudder-novel' ":

The doctor candidly admitted in his "Introduction" to *Ernestus Berchtold* that, "A tale that rests upon improbabilities, must generally disgust a rational mind; I am therefore afraid that, though I have thrown the superior agency into the back ground as much as was in my power, still, that many readers will think the same moral, and the same colouring, might have been given to characters acting under the ordinary agencies of life; I believe it, but had agreed to write a supernatural tale, and that does not allow of a completely every-day narrative."[6]

Despite the disclaimer, Polidori is obviously interested in the Gothic emphasis on the mysterious and the horrifying. The end result of this combined interest in Gothic fiction and the recognition of the excesses of the genre is that he manages (as Stoker and LeFanu will do later in the century) to have it both ways—to have his vampire as well as "characters acting under the ordinary agencies of life."

The most important of these ordinary characters—indeed the only one Polidori presents in any detail—is Aubrey, a young man who is fascinated and eventually destroyed by the vampire. Polidori introduces Aubrey by commenting on his naivete; at the same time, he reveals the perfectly ordinary human weakness that will prove fatal to himself and to those he loves:

...he cultivated more his imagination than his judgment. He had, hence, that high romantic feeling of honour and candour, which daily ruins so many milliners' apprentices. He believed all to sympathise with virtue, and thought that vice was thrown in by Providence merely for the picturesque effect of the scene, as we see in romances. (p. 30)

Aubrey is thus a young man who cannot distinguish fact from the most unrealistic kinds of fiction; and Polidori is obviously amused by his innocent character, a young man who resembles himself when he went off to Europe with Lord Byron. (There are other ways that Polidori incorporates aspects of his own life, including his use of the name Lord Ruthven for his patently Byronic character. For example, Polidori and Aubrey share several important characteristics, including innocence and a strong sense of honor. In fact, Polidori's life could be described as a case of life's imitating art, for William Michael Rossetti claims in his introduction to Polidori's diary that in "August 1821 he committed suicide with poison—having, through losses in gambling, incurred a debt of honour which he had no present means of clearing off."[7] Despite these points of similarity, however, it is important not to overemphasize the autobiographical details in *The Vampyre* because there are very specific differences in Polidori's life and in that of his characters. For example, Aubrey is an orphan; and Polidori came from a large and close-knit family. Moreover, it was Byron who suggested that the two part company,[8] not Polidori.)

Polidori is also careful to point out the limitations of Aubrey's naivete, for he describes a dreamy character who believes "that the dreams of poets were the realities of life" (p. 30). He then goes on to satirize a young man who could take Gothic literature seriously by observing that Aubrey was

...startled at finding, that, except in the tallow and wax candles that flickered, not from the presence of a ghost, but from want of snuffing, there was no foundation in real life for any of that congeries of pleasing pictures and descriptions contained in those volumes, from which he had formed his study. (p. 31)

A masculine version of Catherine Morland, Aubrey is fascinated by the mysterious Lord Ruthven and agrees to become his traveling companion for the continental grand tour. He later becomes disenchanted, however, when Lord Ruthven's plans to seduce a young woman acquaintance force him to realize that his companion is not an honorable man. The two are effectively contrasted in the following brief scene:

Lord Ruthven answered, that his intentions were such as he supposed all would have upon such an occasion; and upon being pressed whether he intended to marry her, merely laughed. Aubrey retired.... He ordered his servant to seek other apartments, and calling upon the mother of the lady, informed her of all he knew, not only with regard to her daughter, but also concerning the character of his Lordship. The assignation was prevented. (p. 38-39)

It appears that virtue triumphs here, as it does in both popular romances and Gothic novels. However, Polidori is clearly moving toward a more realistic depiction of life, for he has Aubrey discover later that life is much more cruel than fiction:

...his first inquiries were concerning the lady he had attempted to snatch from Lord Ruthven's seductive arts. Her parents were in distress, their fortune ruined, and she had not been heard of since the departure of his lordship. (pp. 52-53)

Although Aubrey suspects his former companion, the reader never learns whether Lord Ruthven actually drinks the blood of this young woman. What is important is that this scene provides yet one more opportunity for Aubrey to see that vice is not simply picturesque as well as another opportunity to see his human limitations.

Aubrey discovers these limitations again, when he returns to England, where he is expected to safeguard his sister, her entry into society having been delayed until the time that "he might be her protector" (p. 53). Having promised Lord Ruthven, however, that he will not reveal the vampire's true identity for a year and a day, he is powerless to tell the truth even when Ruthven also returns to England and starts courting his sister. Enraged by his inability to reveal the truth, Aubrey has a fatal stroke before his sister becomes Lord Ruthven's victim. Thus his high ideals and poor judgment are at least indirectly responsible for his own death and for the death of his only sister.

Looking closely at *The Vampyre* reveals how quickly writers transformed the merely brutish character from folklore into a complex and interesting literary character. For example, Polidori, although he adapts material from folklore in his portrait of Lord Ruthven, makes his human characters responsible for much of the death and destruction that occur and therefore focuses his readers' attention on the horrors of everyday life. As a vampire, Lord Ruthven is shown to be *directly* responsible for the deaths of only two people—Ianthe and Miss Aubrey (and Miss Aubrey, despite her apparent innocence and interest in matters beyond the material world, is at least a willing participant, for she accepts his proposal of marriage). The others—those he ruins at the gambling tables as well as the women whose reputations he destroys—may be corrupt even before meeting Lord Ruthven.

Although other writers—notably Stoker and Dickens—will explore the part the victim plays in its relationship with the vampire, Polidori does not develop this aspect of his story. He does provide, however, the merest suggestion of the ways that writers, such as the Brontes and George Eliot, will use the vampire as a social metaphor when he gives the reader brief glimpses of a corrupt society where the wealthy, plagued by ennui, seek to alleviate their boredom by flirting with vice. The vampire, a creature that preys on human beings, is a logical member of such a society.

The first English example of a fictional work that features the vampire, Polidori's work—despite its relative sophistication—remains close to folklore in a number of ways. The most important of these is that it includes a vampire that actually sucks the blood of his human victims. Moreover, it is a work in which the characters come to identify "real" vampires within their fictional world. On the other hand, Polidori's work anticipates some of the ways that other writers will use the vampire as a social metaphor in realistic fiction.

In the decades following its publication, numerous works were based on *The Vampyre*. In fact, Frayling and Mario Praz assert that the immense popularity of Polidori's work and the "close identification of *The Vampyre* with accepted mythologies about Lord Byron seriously limited the possibilities of character development within the genre."[9] Whether the influence of Byron proved as important as Frayling and Praz suggest is perhaps debatable. (In Chapter VI, I propose that various cultural changes are responsible for the significant changes in the literary vampire.) Beyond question is the fact that dramatic versions of Polidori's story proliferated over the next decades. Twitchell, for example, mentions "numerous French and English melodramas and two operas,"[10] and

Summers observes that the French were especially interested in the vampire:

> Immediately upon the furore created by Nodier's *Le Vampire* [a work closely based on Polidori's tale] at the Porte-Saint-Martin in 1819 vampire plays of every kind from the most luridly sensational to the most farcically ridiculous pressed on to the boards. A contemporary critic cries: "There is not a theatre in Paris without its Vampire![11]

Although the French seem to have acquired a reputation for their fascination with the vampire in the first quarter of the nineteenth century, the vampire was also important in English melodrama. Besides the various adaptations of Polidori's story, a dramatic version of *Thalaba the Destroyer* opened at the Royal Coburg Theatre on Monday, August 18, 1823. In addition, the vampire was an accepted character in many of the plays based on *Frankenstein*. In his study of Frankenstein, Donald F. Glut observes that one of these adaptations, titled *The Devil Among the Players*, opened on October 9, 1826 at the Opera Glass. A poetic dramatization, it featured Frankenstein, Faust, and the Vampire.[12]

Of the numerous adaptations, two—both by J.R. Planche—are especially interesting to a study of nineteenth-century fiction because they reveal the growing emphasis on realistic settings and the desire for plausible human behavior. Planche, a writer of melodrama and farces, is now remembered—if at all—as a technical innovator, especially as the inventor of a new form of trap-door for the English stage. His desire for verisimilitude, however, was one of Planche's trademarks in his own day; and Stephen Weschhusen observes that Planche was a "serious student of art" who made numerous changes "in both costume and stage design." For example, plays were generally acted in contemporary costume until Planche "designed and supervised the costumes for John Kemble's revival of *King John* in 1823 making this the first recorded attempt at historical accuracy in a Shakespearian play."[13]

Despite his interest in historical accuracy, however, Planche's first vampire play, *The Vampire; or, the Bride of the Isles* (an adaptation of Nodier's version of Polidori's tale), which opened August 9, 1820 at the English Opera House, is guilty of a number of historical errors, as Planche confesses in his autobiography:

> Mr. Samuel James Arnold...had placed in my hands for adaptation a French melodrama, entitled "Le Vamprie," the scene of which was laid...in Scotland, where the superstition never existed. I vainly endeavored to induce Mr. Arnold to let me change it to some place in the east of Europe. He had set his heart on Scotch music and dresses—the latter, by the way, were in stock.... The melodrama had a long run, was often revived, and is to this day [1872] a stock piece in the country.[14]

Planche reveals that nine years later he was able to treat the subject according to his "own ideas of propriety." The result, he admits, is more realistic than the first version:

I was engaged to write the libretto, and consequently laid the scene of action in Hungary, where the superstition exists to this day, substituted for a Scotch chieftain a Wallachian Boyard, and in many other respects improved upon my earlier version. The opera was extremely well sung, and the costumes novel as well as correct, thanks to the kindness of Dr. Walsh, the traveller, who gave me some valuable information respecting the national dresses of the Magyars and the Wallachians.[15]

As Bram Stoker will do more than sixty years later, Planche researches the customs of Eastern Europe to provide a sense of authenticity to his extraordinary story. In addition, he is apparently somewhat familiar with the superstitions regarding the vampire. Although both plays, like many later works of literature, already confuse the creature from folklore with its literary offspring, Planche at least attempts to do justice to the folklore, as the following gruesome message from the 1820 playbill reveals:

THIS PIECE IS FOUNDED ON the various Traditions concerning THE VAMPIRES, which assert that they are *Spirits*, deprived of all *Hope* of *Futurity*, by the Crimes committed in their Mortal State—but, that they are permitted to roam the Earth, in whatever Forms they please with *Supernatural Powers of Fascination*—and, that they cannot be destroyed, so long as they sustain their dreadful Existence, by imbibing the BLOOD of FEMALE VICTIMS, whom they are first compelled to marry.[16]

Here Planche seems to confuse the vampire with that less corporal creature, the ghost, when he refers to vampires as spirits. In addition, as Polidori had done before him, Planche makes a moral connection that was not a part of folklore, when he emphasizes that the vampiric condition is a punishment for evil deeds; and he continues to emphasize that the vampire is a seductive figure. However, Planche adds the necessity of the vampire's marrying his victims, perhaps as a concession to his bourgeoise viewers, who may have already felt guilty about attending the theatre. In addition, Planche's vampire has none of the raw sexuality that is one of the vampire's trademarks in the twentieth century or even the aggression with which Polidori bestowed Lord Ruthven.

The rest of the play is watered-down Polidori. The vampire is named Ruthven, Earl of Marsden; and the plot focuses on an agreement not to reveal the vampire's death. However, because the characters in Planche's play are both less honorable and more pragmatic than Polidori's (the young woman's father suffers none of the agony that Aubrey does and simply breaks his oath), the vampire is destroyed. Thus, there is none of the despair one might associate with Polidori's *The Vampire*. In Planche's version, it isn't precisely virtue that triumphs, but audiences could leave the theatre confident in the overwhelmingly optimistic message that ordinary people could conquer the darkness of the Unknown.

The next major work to feature the vampire is *Varney the Vampire or, The Feast of Blood*, a work that was issued in serial form in the 1840s and reprinted in 1853 in penny parts. Written either by James Malcolm Rymer or Thomas Preckett Prest,[17] *Varney* was written at breakneck speed for an unsophisticated literary audience that was apparently more interested in fast pace and galloping suspense than in coherence or subtle character development. It was, despite its aesthetic flaws, one of the most popular works of the age, going on for 868 pages until Edwin Lloyd the publisher finally insisted that its author put Varney permanently to rest.

Naming a minor character in the second volume Count Pollidori [sic], the writer reveals his debt to *The Vampyre* when Varney, who is at least as interested in money as he is in blood, is prevented from marrying a young woman for her fortune:

> ...immediately afterwards, some officers, in the Venetian uniform, entered the chapel, among whom was the young count, Isabella's brother [Count Pollidori] and with him a young officer, into whose arms she instantly threw herself, and fainted.
> 'Father,' said the young count—'father, this must not be!... Because my sister loves another, and yon man is a monster.'[18]

There are other connections to both folklore and to the literary tradition. A brief preface written in 1847 and included with the Dover reprint reveals that the writer wants readers to believe in the authenticity of what he writes:

> A belief in the existence of Vampyres first took its rise in Norway and Sweden, from whence it rapidly spread to more southern regions, taking a firm hold of the imaginations of the more credulous portion of mankind.
> The following romance is collected from seemingly the most authentic sources, and the Author must leave the question of credibility entirely to his readers.

Thus the writer both bases the work on the actual beliefs of superstitious people and simultaneously draws those beliefs into question. There is no question, however, that the writer had the brutal creature from folklore in mind when he wrote the first chapter:

> It [the face] is perfectly white—perfectly bloodless. The eyes look like polished tin; the lips are drawn back, and the principal feature next to those dreadful eyes is the teeth—the fearful looking teeth—projecting like those of some wild animal, hideously, glaringly white, and fang-like. It approaches the bed with a strange, gliding movement. It clashes together the long nails that literally appear to hang from the finger ends. (Ch. I)

If Varney's bestial behavior owes a debt to folklore, his lasciviousness (reinforced by an accompanying illustration of him with his teeth at his victim's throat and his hand on her breast) follows the popular literary tradition. Varney, however, is able to accomplish what Squire B could not although he has to wait for his victim to sleep to do so:

> With a sudden rush that could not be foreseen—with a strange howling cry that was enough to awaken terror in every breast, the figure seized the long tresses of her hair, and twining them round his bony hands he held her to the bed.... The glassy, horrible eyes of the figure ran over that angelic form with a hideous satisfaction—horrible profanation. He drags her head to the bed's edge. He forces it back by the long hair still entwined in his grasp. With a plunge he seizes her neck in his fang-like teeth—a gush of blood, and a hideous sucking noise follows. *The girl has swooned, and the vampyre is at his hideous repast!* (Ch. I, p. 4, author's italics)

As Lord Ruthven had done with Ianthe, Varney simply takes what he wants—in this case, the blood of the appropriately beautiful and defenseless Flora Bannerworth. Thus his behavior in this scene combines the brutality of the creature from folklore (one significant exception is that Varney does not kill Flora) with the perverse sexuality of the rake and the Gothic villain.

Not only does *Varney* adapt existing material about the vampire, but it also adds to the popular concept of the vampire: it reinforces an idea begun by Polidori that the vampire is an aristocrat; suggests that the vampire represents the power of the past over the present; and emphasizes the perverse erotic attraction that the vampire has over its victims.

Like *Lord* Ruthven, *Sir* Francis Varney is an aristocrat; and the association of the literary vampire with the aristocracy will continue throughout nineteenth-century literature. (The approach differs from work to work, however. Carmilla, Countess of Karnstein, is so contemptuous of the peasantry that she doesn't even acknowledge their existence. Dracula, on the other hand, who refers to himself by the English title "count" as well as by more conventional military terms, prides himself on being a leader of his people. Thus his attitude is far different from Carmilla's.) While none of the writers develops a consistent rationale for the association between vampires and aristocrats, Polidori, LeFanu, and Stoker link the aristocrat's hereditary power over others and the vampire's supernatural power over human beings. Varney, however, is simply one of the many aristocratic villains in popular literature, for his title has little to do with either his evil nature or his power over others. A brief reference to Sir George Crofton, father of Clara—one of Varney's victims and a man who briefly believes himself to be a vampire, suggests that the writer may have associated aristocratic landlords with economic exploitation. At least the leader of the working class mob that goes off to destroy Clara perceives them all as potential victims of economic exploitation as well as potential victims of the vampiric Clara, who had already attacked and killed a sixteen year old girl: "Is we to be made into victims, or isn't we? What's Sir George Crofton and his family to us? To be sure he's the landlord of some of us, and a very good landlord he is, too, as long as we pay our rent" (Ch. CCIII). Here a mere reference, the economic relationship will be explored in greater detail in other works that feature the vampire.

More important is the fact that Varney, like many vampires in later literature, is a creature from the past who enters the present to influence it. In the case of Varney (who, depending on which chapter one happens to be reading, has either survived since the days of Henry IV or the Commonwealth), the author simply introduces problems of inheritance and the transmittal of property. Later writers—notably LeFanu, Stoker, Charlotte Bronte, and Dickens—will use the vampire to reveal the power that negative social values from the past often have over the present. However, neither Polidori nor any of the writers who adapted his work had presented the vampire specifically as a creature from the past; and *Varney*'s author is the first to make this connection even if he doesn't do more than suggest that Varney's swashbuckling behavior is the remnant of an earlier time.

The author of *Varney* also develops the sexual attraction between the vampire and his female victims and suggests that the vampire's touch becomes a kind of sexual initiation. (This attraction, merely suggested in *The Vampyre* and the two plays by Planche, will become much more explicit in later works.) Flora, for example, is drawn to Varney as both Mina and Lucy will later be to Dracula:

> But her eyes are fascinated. The glance of a serpent could not have produced a greater effect upon her than did the fixed gaze of those awful, metallic-looking eyes that were bent on her face.... The clothing of the bed was now clutched in her hands with unconscious power. She drew her breath short and thick. Her bosom heaves, and her limbs tremble, yet she cannot withdraw her eyes from that marble-looking face. He holds her with his glittering eye. (Ch. 1)

Despite her fear, Flora becomes even more intrigued by Varney; and, like Lucy, she becomes a sleepwalker whose unconscious desire will take her to the garden where he waits for her.

Both Frayling and Carter are confident that *Varney* had a direct influence on Stoker. Frayling cites several plot motifs including the sexual initiation of the heroine by the vampire, and the "incongruity" of a central European belief in England[19] while Carter argues that Chapter XX resembles "Dracula's attack on Mina.... The same perverse erotic content is present in both.... The charm exerted by the vampire over his unwillingly complaisant victim is breathtaking.''[20] Carter also compares the destruction of Clara Croftin (who is accused of attacking a sixteen-year old girl and taken to a crossroads and staked) to the destruction of Lucy Westenra in *Dracula*.

Clara's death is much less brutal than Lucy's, however; and she is destroyed by a mob rather than by her fiance and his friends. The similarities in the two works do not prove direct influence. Mutilation— staking, decapitation, burning—was a long accepted way to eliminate the vampire; and Stoker could have learned about it in his study of folklore, not necessarily by reading *Varney* or any other single treatment of the vampire.

However, despite a lack of proven direct influence (and I remain unconvinced by Carter's arguments), Chapter XX of *Varney* is important to our understanding of the way the literary vampire evolves during the nineteenth century, for it reveals a more human vampire, one who talks soothingly to Flora instead of attacking her in her sleep:

> There was a wonderful fascination in the manner now of Varney. His voice sounded like music itself. His words flowed...with all the charm of eloquence.
> Despite her trembling horror of that man—despite her fearful opinion,...Flora felt an irresistible wish to hear him speak on. (Ch. XX)

Not only does Varney talk to Flora instead of attacking her in her sleep and drinking her blood, but the subject of their conversation is surprisingly mundane and ordinary. Having quarreled with her brothers about purchasing Bannerworth Hall, Varney now discusses the subject with Flora. Thus, despite his brutality at the beginning of the work, Varney's perfectly ordinary behavior here and elsewhere anticipates the metaphoric treatments of the vampire by novelists, such as Charlotte Bronte and George Eliot.

Because of its numerous inconsistencies, including the inconsistencies in Varney himself, *Varney the Vampire* is almost as difficult to classify as a literary work as it is to read; in numerous scenes, such as the justifiably famous first chapter in which the reader sees Varney drink Flora's blood and others where either Varney himself or another character identifies him as a supernatural being, Varney is a character who might have come straight from folklore. However, in other scenes, there is even a question whether Varney *is* a vampire. For example, E.F. Bleiler's introduction to the Dover edition points out that Varney's nature and history are not consistently presented:

> Varney is identified...as a supernatural being who has lived since the days of Henry IV; as a turncoat from the days of the Commonwealth, sentenced to be a vampire because he had killed his son in a moment of rage; or as a modern criminal, not at all supernatural, who had been revived after being hanged.[21]

Furthermore, whether Varney himself is a supernatural being or not, the novel as a whole focuses on ordinary human evil, not on supernatural Evil.

In fact, much of the evil in *Varney* centers on money, for Varney is at least in some ways a perfectly ordinary economic parasite; and the author often links the fact that Varney is a bloodsucker to economic parasitism. For example, he makes elaborate plans to marry two young women but jilts them both at the last moment and leaves their mothers to pay the wedding expenses; and Twitchell observes that *Varney*'s working class readers would have "understood both the public embarrassment of the bride as well as the financial distress of her parents."[23] Certainly the author makes numerous connections between the parasitism of the vampire in folklore and economic exploitation although Varney, as Twitchell notes, is no more destructive than the other economic parasites in the novel:

...although Varney can be nasty, there are people like these highwaymen [who rob Varney and leave him for dead] or Mr. Marchdale [a "friend" of the Bannerworth family who plans to rob them], Mrs. Meredith, Mrs. Williams [two women who arrange for their daughters to marry Varney for his money], or the hangman [who, knowing Varney's story, attempts to blackmail him], who are worse. Varney is victimized by others as well as by his own uncontrollable thirsts, but these characters simply exploit others for financial gain.[24]

By focusing on Varney's economic parasitism instead of on his actual vampirism (with the exception of the first chapter, the reader rarely sees him actually drink his victims' blood), the author emphasizes Varney's human traits and makes him a more sympathetic character.

Moreover, by stressing the cruelty of human beings, the author makes Varney appear even less cruel. For example, after the mob's destruction of Clara, Varney alone mourns:

I thought that I had steeled my heart against all gentle impulses: that I had crushed— aye, completely crushed dove-eyed pity in my heart, but it is not so, and still sufficient of my once human feelings clings to me to make me grieve for thee, Clara Crofton, thou victim. (Ch. CCVIII)

If Varney's humanity comes to the forefront here and in his earlier treatment of Flora, he is never more human than at the conclusion, a conclusion that comes as a welcome relief for vampire and reader alike as Varney sums up his life for the guide who accompanies him:

You will say that you accompanied Varney the Vampyre to the crater of Mount Vesuvius, and that, tired and disgusted with a life of horror, he flung himself in to prevent the possibility of a reanimation of his remains. (Ch. CCXX)

It is a dramatic end for one of the nineteenth century's most popular literary characters as well as a conclusion that Bleiler argues had been prepared for the time that the audience finally tired of Varney and his exploits.[25]

Although Varney eventually becomes disgusted with his bloodthirsty deeds, the human characters seemingly never tire of their cruelty, either to Varney or to each other. The following passage, which appears in one of the numerous chase scenes that recur throughout *Varney*, is either a slip of the pen or a profound recognition that the vampire is as projection of humanity's cruelty: "...and as often was the miserable man [Varney] hunted from his place of refuge only to seek another, from which he was in like manner hunted by those who thirsted for his blood" (Ch. LXXXVII). The writer does not go on to develop this connection to any extent, but the metaphoric connection between the vampire's behavior and reprehensible human behavior will be made frequently by realistic novelists and by social writers later in the century.

Despite its movement toward the metaphoric treatment of the vampire's abilities, *Varney the Vampyre* maintains the belief begun in folklore that the vampire is a supernatural being, one that (at least in certain sections of the work) arises from the dead as well as one that requires blood to sustain that unnatural existence. Furthermore, *Varney the Vampyre* develops the literary characteristics established by Polidori and Planche by making the vampire an aristocrat who is sexually attractive to its victims, traits that will be developed later in the century by other writers. In addition, *Varney* introduces the vampire as an economic threat (a characteristic that will become a deliberate metaphor in *Bleak House* and in the works of various social writers), a creature from the past who nonetheless continues to have an impact on the present, and a being who is more human than animal.

Finally, *Varney the Vampyre* introduces one point that will continue to be developed in works that feature the vampire—the fact that certain human beings are ready victims. (Although Dickens will show that the young of both sexes are victimized by the old, the vampire's most frequent victim throughout the nineteenth century is a young, unmarried woman; and this point is especially important when one looks at the relationship between literature and culture and at the fact that numerous writers and thinkers in the nineteenth century were concerned with the role of women within their society.)

Whether young women in the novel—Flora Bannerworth, Clara Croftin, Helen Williams, and Margaret Meredith—are Varney's literal victims or the daughters and sisters of other characters, they have little control over their lives or their futures. As daughters of greedy and unscrupulous parents, they are pawns in arranged marriages; as sisters, they observe their brothers' blunders in silence; and as Varney's victims, they lie quietly waiting for him. In fact, the key to their characters is passivity. Later in the century, LeFanu, Stoker, and Charlotte Bronte will focus on this same passivity when they create the women victims of vampire attack; and all these writers will present a more consistent analysis of the way social conditioning makes women into victims. Here, as elsewhere, *Varney the Vampyre* is interesting because, in a rude, crude, and inconsistent way, it introduces characteristics that other writers will develop further. Equally important, it shows how overtly sensational works can reveal important social problems.

Varney the Vampyre is read today as an example of mid-Victorian popular culture rather than for any intrinsic literary merit, but such is not the case with Joseph Sheridan LeFanu's "Carmilla," a work first published in 1872. Not only is this elegant novella important to a discussion of the vampire in nineteenth-century English literature, but it is an interesting work in its own right.

Obviously conscious of working within a tradition, LeFanu picks up many of the characteristics of the vampire in earlier literature—Carmilla, for example, is an aristocrat, a sexual predator, and a creature from the past—as well as the more overt traits of the vampire from folklore. Instead of simply adapting the tradition, however, he takes these characteristics and develops them in his own unique way. Most important to our understanding of the literary vampire and its evolution is the fact that LeFanu is the first English writer to break with the tradition of the literary vampire as a Byronic figure by creating a woman vampire. (Despite Nethercot's often convincing arguments in *The Road to Tryermaine*,[26] Coleridge's mysterious Geraldine may not be a vampire; and Keats's Lamia and belle dame are not vampires in the strictest sense of the word either.)

Certainly, both Carmilla's femininity and her beauty are a distinct break with tradition. The vampire from folklore was usually thought to be monstrous—more bestial than human; and even Varney, who is not without his appeal to women, is often described as hideously ugly. Carmilla, on the other hand, appears as "the prettiest creature I ever saw" and as "absolutely beautiful."[27] In addition, she generally relies on seduction rather than on the direct attack so often associated with male vampires from Lord Ruthven on. During the day she woos Laura with words and actions, behavior that Laura describes as being "like the ardor of a lover":

...it embarrassed me; it was hateful and yet overpowering; and with gloating eyes she drew me to her, and her hot lips traveled along my cheek in kisses; and she would whisper, almost in sobs, "You are mine, you *shall* be mine, and you and I are one forever." (Ch. IV)

Carmilla's nightly visits are less subtle than her daytime attention although she never becomes as overtly aggressive as either Lord Ruthven or Varney:

Sometimes there came a sensation as if a hand was drawn softly along my cheek and neck. Sometimes it was as if warm lips kissed me, and longer and more lovingly as they reached my throat, but there the caress fixed itself. (Ch. VII)

In fact, this "attack," which is the most aggressive Carmilla ever gets, is described in terms of love instead of violence; and the reader need only contrast it to similar scenes in *Varney* or *The Vampyre* to see just how much Carmilla differs from these aggressive male vampires.

Despite the change in character, Carmilla is definitely a vampire— as the conclusion makes clear—not a human being that resembles the supernatural being; and, as such, she is responsible for the literal deaths of her victims, not just for the destruction of their reputations or fortunes. LeFanu might have taken the following account of Carmilla's destruction straight from folklore:

The features, though a hundred and fifty years had passed since her funeral, were tinted with the warmth of life...no cadaverous smell exhaled from the coffin...and the leaden coffin floated with blood, in which to a depth of seven inches, the body lay immersed.... The body, therefore, in accordance with the ancient practice, was raised, and a sharp stake driven through the heart of the vampire, who uttered a piercing shriek at the moment, in all respects such as might escape from a living person in the last agony. Then the head was struck off, and a torrent of blood flowed from the severed neck. (Ch. XV)

Such details might have come straight from Tournefort, Calmet, or any of the other reports of vampirism in the eighteenth century.

Despite his reliance on such details in the previous scene, however, LeFanu generally manipulates his source materials to stress the ordinary rather than the exceptional, and this emphasis includes attention to the details of setting, plot, and character. (Most of LeFanu's other works— even those that can be characterized as "Gothic"—avoid medieval settings or geographically remote locations and concentrate on plausible human motivation.) For example, although "Carmilla" is set in exotic Styria, where the superstition had flourished in the eighteenth century, LeFanu combines that exotic setting with attention to realistic social details:

In Styria, we, though by no means magnificent people, inhabit a castle, or schloss. A small income, in that part of the world, goes a great way. Eight or nine hundred a year does wonders. Scantily enough ours would have answered among wealthy people at home.... But, in this lonely and primitive place, where everything is so marvelously cheap, I really don't see how ever so much more money would at all materially add to our comforts, or even luxuries. (Ch. I)

The emphasis on financial security might have come straight out of Thackeray or Jane Austen; and the castle, or schloss, which has none of the mysterious underground caverns so familiar to readers of Radcliffe, Walpole, or M.G. Lewis, resembles the country houses found in Austen or George Eliot.

Besides using contemporary settings, LeFanu provides other evidence that he means to focus on realistic details. For example, the characters in "Carmilla" include Laura, the young narrator; her two governesses; and her father, a retired diplomat. Extremely ordinary people, all might have come from the pages of a realistic work; and even Carmilla initially appears only as an eccentric who likes to sleep late in the day and wander about at night.

This appearance of ordinary human motivation is standard in LeFanu's works, for his preface to *Uncle Silas*, his most famous novel, refutes the charge that he was a "sensation novelist" and reminds the reader that Scott's novels are not described as sensation novels, "yet in that marvelous series there is not a single tale in which death, crime, and, in some form, mystery, have not a place."[28] Distancing himself from the extremes of the sensation novelists (a group of popular novelists in the 1860s—the most famous being Wilkie Collins, Ellen Wood and Mary Elizabeth Braddon—who combined shocking subjects including adultery, bigamy, illegitimacy, murder, and disguise with attention to topical matters and realistic settings), LeFanu nonetheless reminds the reader that ordinary life is touched by death, crime, and mystery; and certainly Silas Ruthyn's attempts to murder his niece for her inheritance are almost as horrifying as the vampire's attack on its victims.

Events in "Carmilla" are less plausible, of course, for Carmilla *is* a centuries old vampire, not a wicked human being. However, because Laura and her father refuse to believe in the supernatural, the truth about Carmilla isn't revealed until the end of the book. Astute readers have probably already come to the conclusion that Carmilla is a vampire by that time, but they can still concentrate on the commonplace details that Laura observes (and on the similarities between the vampire's traits and ordinary human evil) up to that point.

LaFanu, for example, links the vampire's preying on all human beings to the treatment and occasionally the mistreatment of certain groups of people. Laura casually reveals her indifference to people outside her circle and her class when she describes the extremely small "party who constitute the inhabitants of our castle" (Ch. I) and admits that she doesn't include servants, who apparently don't even exist as human beings to her. There is no indication that Laura causes these "invisible people" to suffer, but the psychological distance from her indifference to Carmilla's predation is not so far as it might seem initially. Hearing that the daughter of one of the forest rangers had fallen victim to "the malady" (a condition that the reader suspects is caused by Carmilla or another vampire) that had been afflicting women, Carmilla is contemptuous: " '*She*? I don't trouble my head about peasants. I don't know who she is' " (Ch. IV). More extreme and certainly more overtly cruel (it is one of the few scenes in which Carmilla reveals the cruelty generally associated with the male vampire) is her reaction to the peddler who offers to file her sharp tooth: "My father would have had the wretch tied up to the pump, and flogged with a cartwhip, and burnt to the bones with the castle brand" (Ch. IV). By giving Carmilla anachronistic behavior, the cruelty of a bygone age, LeFanu thus reveals that she has the arrogance of a born aristocrat. In fact, she often pretends that the peasants do not exist even though she and the others depend on them for food (quite literally in the case of Carmilla and the other vampires.[29] There are degrees of cruelty, of course; and Laura's indifference to her servants, though analogous to Carmilla's literal feeding on the peasantry, is not equivalent. Nonetheless, if one thinks about the way that new vampires are created, one should remember that Laura is both Carmilla's easy victim and a victim who—more likely than not—will become a vampire in her turn and that Carmilla had been a victim of a vampire's attack when she too was young and susceptible.

Furthermore, that LeFanu establishes Laura as an "everywoman" character suggests that all women are potential victims. (It is important to note that Carmilla, besides being a woman vampire, also alters the strictly heterosexual behavior of Lord Ruthven and Varney by choosing only women as victims: Laura, the general's niece, and several peasant women.) For example, almost everything in Laura's character suggests her typicality. She is nameless for the first part of the story, and the reader never does learn her last name.[30] Because she has been educated only for a kind of social and sexual function, she has few interests except in the subjects that were expected to be the center of a young woman's life—parties and the opportunities they represented for meeting eligible young men. Furthermore, like many educated nineteenth-century people, she takes pride in her rationalistic education and mentions that she was "studiously kept in ignorance of ghost stories, of fairy tales" (Chapter I). Finally, even though she mentions that her father is English and that her mother is from an old Hungarian family, these concrete details about her background do not establish her as a unique individual. The only part of her life that makes Laura the least bit unique is her perverse relationship with Carmilla.

The relationship begins when Laura is a small child—too young to recognize either the sexual overtones of the vampire's embrace or the fact that such an embrace is ultimately deadly. Nonetheless, Laura is terrified by Carmilla's first visit and becomes even more frightened when her father (the source of power and authority in her world) laughs at her fears. She is so frightened in fact that the memory remains strong two decades later, when she finally tells her story:

> I remember my father coming up and standing at the bedside, and talking cheerfully, and asking the nurse a number of questions, and laughing very heartily at one of the answers: and patting me on the shoulder, and kissing me, and telling me not to be frightened, that it was nothing but a dream and could not hurt me.
> But I was not comforted, for I knew the visit of the strange woman was *not* a dream; and I was *awfully* frightened. (Ch. I, LeFanu's italics)

Such patronizing treatment of a young child is understandable even though most twentieth-century child care experts advise against laughing at a child's fears. However, the same kind of condescension becomes more disturbing to twentieth-century readers when Laura is a grown woman. In fact, continuing to laugh off her questions when she asks what the doctor had revealed about her illness (caused by Carmilla's repeated nocturnal visits), her father fails to give her information that might enable her to protect herself: " 'Nothing; you must not plague me with questions,' he answered, with more irritation than I ever remember him to have displayed before" (Ch. IX). His refusal to divulge the doctor's suspicions may result from his rationalistic upbringing or from a misguided desire to protect her. (Like Van Helsing's plan to protect Mina from Dracula, it backfires and leaves Laura vulnerable to another attack.) Lonely and ignorant, she is ready prey for Carmilla.[31]

Furthermore, by constructing a partial genealogy of Laura's family, one that includes only the female line, LeFanu suggests that other women have been similarly victimized. Laura reveals that her mother was from an old Hungarian family and that the picture of the Countess Mircalla (the real name of which Carmilla is an anagram) of Karnstein came from her mother's family. In addition, Laura's mother may also have been a victim of vampire attack, for Laura dreams—"Your mother warns you to beware of the assassin" (Ch. VII)—right before she awakes to discover a blood-drenched Carmilla at the foot of her bed; and Laura's father tells the general that his wife was "*maternally* descended from the Karnsteins" (Ch. X, my italics), a family now extinct. That Carmilla is a distant ancestor of Laura's mother, another woman who may have succumbed to vampire attack, leads the reader to infer that Laura is simply the last in a long line of victims.

The genealogy of victims seems to extend beyond Laura's mother, for Carmilla reveals enigmatically that she had been almost assassinated (her choice of words links her to the warning Laura receives), wounded in the breast after her first ball. (The literary presentation of the marriage market and the way that it exploits women was almost a cliche by the time LeFanu wrote "Carmilla.") Furthermore she seems to be surrounded by women who control her. For example, Laura observes that Carmilla's mother "threw on her daughter a glance which...was not quite so affectionate as one might have anticipated from the beginning of the scene" (Ch. II); and Laura's governess later mentions another woman who accompanied Carmilla, "a hideous black woman...who was gazing all the time from the carriage window, nodding and grinning derisively toward the ladies, with gleaming eyes and large white eyeballs, and her teeth set as if in fury" (Ch. II). These references suggest that others may hold the same kind of power over Carmilla that she holds over Laura.

The relationship between vampire and victim in "Carmilla" reveals a great deal about the power and powerlessness of women in the nineteenth century. Although the vampire does have the power of life and death over its apparently helpless victim, it is subject to a number of constraints: It is powerful only at certain times of day; it is immobilized by certain holy objects (the vampire's fear of religious artifacts is a commonplace in twentieth-century horror films, but Carmilla's discomfort when she hears the funeral hymns is the first literary example of the power that religious artifacts have over the vampire); and it has to use anagrams of its original name (apparently another of LeFanu's additions although one that has *not* become part of the tradition). On the other hand, the seemingly weak Laura has a significant kind of power—that of telling other women about their condition. Although the prologue implies that she tells her story to Dr. Hesselius, she actually tells it to another woman, "a town lady" (Ch. IV). It may be too late for Laura—the prologue reveals that she has died—but it may not be too late for the woman to whom she writes. (Waller is wrong to argue that Laura survives because "the old men of this rural world—doctor, father, General, scholar, Baron, priest—destroy the...creature who has threatened their young women" or that "through their alliance of social, religious, and scientific authority, these men reaffirm the power and the validity of a patriarchal ruling class that can only see female sexuality as an abberration."[32] If anything, "Carmilla" reveals that such patriarchal structures victimize women.) Her writing is an example of a relatively new kind of power for women, a way to manipulate people and events[33] that is metaphorical, not literal.

Although Carmilla is literally a vampire, the reader can see how the vampire becomes a vampiric character in more realistic nineteenth-century works. A dead body that drinks the blood of its human victims to sustain its existence, the vampire is linked in "Carmilla" to certain aspects of women's lives. Therefore it indirectly criticizes the way many women lived in the nineteenth century. For example, both vampires and women are parasitic creatures, the one by nature, the other by economic necessity. Both are dead, the one literally, the other legally. Both are defined primarily by their physiology rather than by their intelligence or emotions. Finally, however, both have a latent power to influence the lives of others. (Unlike their demonic counterparts, women also gained overt economic and political power as the century progressed, with the passage of the Married Women's Property Acts in the 1870s and 1880s, the opening of Girton College, and the entry of women into the professions.)

As a vampire, Carmilla is a literal parasite, one whom the reader sees standing at the foot of Laura's bed drinking the blood of her sleeping victim. However, LeFanu connects this biological parasitism and the economic dependence that was virtually mandated for women during most of LeFanu's lifetime by having Carmilla both a vampire and the idle guest of her victims' families. (This relationship will be used extensively as a metaphor of economic parasitism in *Jane Eyre*, *Wuthering Heights*, and *Middlemarch* and to a lesser extent in *Dracula*.) LeFanu, in fact, relates how she becomes the guest of General Spielsdorf and Laura's father; and in each case, the mother asks the head of the household to care for her daughter. Thus Carmilla becomes a non-contributing member of each family, both a welcome guest and a bloodsucker.

Although this kind of traditional feminine behavior might be justified in Carmilla who is after all an aristocrat as well as a woman from an earlier historical period, Laura—who admits that she and her father live in Styria because it is cheap—apparently has no plans for a life outside her father's home either.

LeFanu makes other connections between women and vampires. Besides being parasites, both can be described as dead, the one literally, the other metaphorically. Carmilla has been literally dead for more than a century, but Laura lives a kind of half-life because she has no intellectual or spiritual life of her own. Her conversation is full of the cliches and platitudes of her day, of sentimental beliefs in romantic love, of obligations to family and friends, and of the excitement of parties; and the reader infers that she has learned all of this from the two governesses who live with her and her father.

Finally both vampires and women are defined primarily by their physiology. The vampire is motivated exclusively by its physical need for blood, a substance it requires to maintain its unnatural existence. However, as a woman, Carmilla is also a physical being, one who is repeatedly described as being languid and frail. Carmilla also seems to be teaching Laura to be like her, for Laura becomes more and more languid as Carmilla's visits increase. Although a great deal of critical energy has been devoted to this lesbian relationship and also to LeFanu's supposed homosexuality,[34] it is equally likely that he uses the relationship between vampire and victim to represent the relationship between mother and child. (Both Dickens and Stoker will also use the fact that the vampire is a creature from the past to reveal how parents "feed" on their children, how the past influences the present.) This relationship is responsible for women's becoming languid and ornamental parasites. Isolated in their homes as women typically were in the early decades of the nineteenth century, they are trained (as LeFanu suggests, by other women—mothers and surrogate mothers, including Carmilla and the two governesses) to be ornamental and seemingly passive.

However, as LeFanu shrewdly reveals, some women were not as passive as they appeared. Having no power outside their homes and family circle, these women ultimately learn to manipulate others if only within that restricted circle. Carmilla, for example, may not have control over her own mother; but she knows that women can use their apparent passivity and the other traditional skills granted to women to manipulate others; and she is able to control Laura and her father and General Spielsdorf. Furthermore, she confesses to Laura that love, an emotion that many Victorians believed was traditionally associated with women, could be used to gain power over others:

You will think me cruel, very selfish, but love is always selfish; the more ardent the more selfish.... You must come with me, loving me, to death; or else hate me, and still come with me, and *hating* me through death and after. (Ch. VI, LeFanu's italics)

Furthermore, LeFanu shows that Laura's need for love and recognition enables Carmilla to gain power over the younger woman.

In fact, LeFanu reveals that women—though considered weak and frail—may have more real power than men. Although the men in the story use physical force, a skill traditionally associated with men, this skill is ultimately revealed as ineffectual. Laura's narrative concludes, not with the destruction of the vampire, but with the acknowledgement that Carmilla still exists: "...the memory of Carmilla returns to memory with ambiguous alternations...and often from a reverie I have started, fancying I heard the light step of Carmilla at the drawing-room door" (Ch. XVI). A preface at the beginning of the tale, which reveals that Laura has died, also suggests that Carmilla's violent destruction does not succeed in eliminating the vampire. It may also be LeFanu's way of saying that a situation that has evolved over centuries (Carmilla is, after all, a creature who has been around for more than a century) can not be eradicated in an instant—perhaps not at all.

LeFanu obviously works within a traditional notion of the vampire, one that originated in folklore and had been developed in earlier literary works. However, Carmilla is also a new kind of vampire, her "newness" a direct result of her femaleness. (This shift from men vampires to women vampires at mid-century, one of the most interesting characteristics of the vampire in nineteenth-century fiction, will be explored fully in Chapter VI.) A woman vampire, Carmilla is beautiful and seductive instead of violent and aggressive. In fact, the sexuality at which Polidori and the creator of Varney had hinted becomes overt in Carmilla, when Laura describes her memory of Carmilla's embrace:

Sometimes there came a sensation as if a hand was drawn softly along my cheek and neck. Sometimes it was as if warm lips kissed me, and longer and more lovingly as they reached my throat.... My heart beat faster, my breathing rose and fell rapidly and full drawn; a sobbing, that rose into a sense of strangulation, supervened, and turned into a dreadful convulsion, in which my sense left me, and I became unconscious. (Ch. VIII)

If this description of the vampire's embrace were not explicit enough, Baron Vordenberg specifically links sexual passion and vampirism:

The vampire is prone to be fascinated with an engrossing vehemence, resembling the passion of love.... It will never desist until it has satiated its passion, and drained the very life of its coveted victim. But it will, in these cases, husband and protract its murderous enjoyment with the refinement of an epicure, and heighten it by the gradual approaches of an artful courtship. (Ch. XVI)

Words, such as "fascinated," "passion," "love," and "courtship" underline the connection between love and the vampire's destructiveness. Moreover, one should remember that Carmilla's relationships to her female victims suggest two kinds of perverse sexual relationships— lesbianism and incest—relationships that the family-respecting Victorians regarded as especially destructive.

Carmilla thus becomes a new and powerful kind of vampire, one far removed from the hideous creature of folklore and one that threatens much that the Victorians revered. Nina Auerbach observes in *Woman and the Demon* that Carmilla resembles the Victorian ideal for good women, "Dickens' motherly angels...except that this angel proceeds to bite the child sharply in the breast" and adds that the "conceit of the Good Angel of the race has turned literal and become demonic, for Carmilla...has a vampire's power to survive generations, her cannibalistic loves keeping her face intact."[35]

Woman and the Demon focuses on powerful images of women in Victorian fiction, but it doesn't probe the real social reasons for this fear and awe or explore fully the relationship between literature and the culture that surrounds it. At the time LeFanu was writing, however, many people were insisting that women be given more power—economic, social, and political; and the issue of greater rights and responsibilities for women was constantly before the public eye. Others—including the group known as the sensation novelists—drew people's attention to the power that women already had. LeFanu's response was to distance himself from the sensation novelists, writers who sometimes let adultery, bigamy, and murder go unpunished and virtue unrewarded. LeFanu distinguished himself from the sensation novelists in the preface to *Uncle Silas*. In

"Carmilla," he also destroyed the "overreacher" for usurping the male domains of passion and power over others. There is a less orthodox reading, however, one that takes the ambiguous conclusion seriously and sees Carmilla as the "winner" in her struggles against men. This reading that takes the open ending seriously would link LeFanu with the sensation novelists.

Regardless of how one interprets the conclusion, it is impossible to see Carmilla as anything but a figure of immense power within her fictional world, power that she gains from her association with other literary characters and from the facts of social history. The same is true of *Dracula*. The last major work in the nineteenth century to feature a vampire and not a vampiric character, Stoker's novel, which was published in 1897, responds directly to both popular literature and to social events. Although there is no direct indication that Stoker was influenced by the Brontes, George Eliot, Dickens, or *Varney the Vampire*,[36] textual evidence suggests that he *was* familiar with "Carmilla."

The influence of LeFanu is particularly evident in the original first chapter, which Stoker later deleted. (Pressed for money, his widow published it in 1914 as a short story, "Dracula's Guest."[37] Because "Dracula's Guest" has Jonathan Harker discover the tomb of a vampire countess on his way to Dracula's castle, two of Stoker's biographers suggest that he had "Carmilla" in mind. Daniel Farson explains that the influence can be found in the inscription on the tomb:

COUNTESS DOLINGEN OF GRATZ
IN STYRIA
SOUGHT AND FOUND DEATH
1801

There is also a quotation from "Lenore" on the back, "The dead travel fast." Harry Ludlam, more specific about influence, cites that the women in both works are countesses who inhabit the exotic country of Styria.[38]

There are other influences as well. Dracula, for example, as Fry observes, is modeled on several well-known character types in popular literature:

Stoker establishes Dracula as a rake in large part by making him a "gothic villain," a derivative of the rake in English fiction. Like most gothic villains, Dracula lives in a ruined castle.... Dracula's physical appearance is that of the rake-gothic villain. He has a "strong—a very strong" face and "massive eyebrows." His face shows the pallor typical of Radcliffe's Schedoni, Maturin's Melmoth, and Lewis' Antonio, and, most impressively, he possesses the usual "glittering eye" of the villain.[39]

The women in the novel (discussed later in the chapter) are similarly modeled on characters from popular literature, including gothic novels, the sensation novels of the 1860s, the New Woman novels of the 1890s, and melodrama. (Stoker was, after all, manager of the Lyceum Theatre and friend to Henry Irving, one of the most famous actors of his day, an actor who was well known for his melodramas full of mystery and supernatural occurrences.)

Dracula is plainly a supernatural figure instead of a human one like Bronte's Bertha Mason or Eliot's Mr. Vincy. However, Stoker—like Polidori and LeFanu—doesn't reveal his character's supernatural abilities until the novel is well established, so the reader has an opportunity to look at Dracula as an aberrant human character and to see that he is condemned even before the narrators understand exactly how different he truly is.[40]

The reader is introduced to Dracula by Jonathan Harker's journal. As in *Varney* and "Carmilla," the vampire in *Dracula* is a threatening figure from an alien world, a world that the narrators perceive as violent and primitive. (He is also an aristocrat. Burton Hatlen observes Dracula's social status as a "threat to the *haute bourgeoise*, the threat posed by an aristocracy which, although moribund, might suddenly revive."[41] As such, he can be contrasted with the other aristocrat in the novel—Arthur Holmwood, Lord Godalming, a man who has internalized all the virtues associated with the middle class.) Even before he realizes that Dracula is a different kind of being, Harker is troubled by everything that Dracula represents. Journeying from London to Transylvania, Harker muses on the quaint customs he observes and notes in his journal that he must question his host about them. Harker, the product of a technological society where trains run according to schedule and life in general is neat and predictable, is as baffled by the lack of order in Central Europe as he is by the superstitious beliefs of the natives. Hoping to find someone like himself at the end of his journey, a person who can provide a rational explanation for these examples of non-English behavior, Harker finds instead a ruined castle, itself a reminder of bygone ages, and a man who, explaining that Transylvania is *not* England, is proud of being an integral part of his nation's heroic past:

...the Szekleys—and the Dracula as their heart's blood, their brains and their swords—can boast a record that mushroom growths like the Hapsburgs and the Romanoffs can never reach. The warlike days are over. Blood is too precious a thing in these days of dishonourable peace; and the glories of the great races are as a tale that is told. (Ch. III)

Because Dracula initially appears to be an anachronism—an embodiment of the violent past—rather than an innately evil creature, Harker's journal entries at the beginning merely reproduce his pride and his rugged individualism. In fact, Harker is almost willing to accept Dracula as a bizarre throwback to an earlier time until he remembers that he will be responsible for importing this anachronism to England.

Harker's fright indicates that on one metaphorical level Dracula represents a kind of reverse imperialism, this time with the primitive trying to colonize the civilized world. The reader, on the other hand, sees in the following response a profound resemblance between Harker and what he accuses Dracula of being:

This was the being I was helping to transfer to London, where perhaps for centuries to come he might...satiate his lust for blood, and create a new and ever-widening circle of semi-demons to batten on the helpless. The very thought drove me mad. A terrible desire came upon me to rid the world of such a monster. There was no lethal weapon at hand, but I seized a shovel which the workmen had been using to fill the cases, and lifting it high, struck, with the edge downward, at the hateful face. (Ch. V)

This scene is one of many that reinforce the similarities between man and monster. If the scene were taken out of context, it would be difficult to distinguish the man from the monster because the violent attack on a helpless victim, behavior generally attributed to the vampire is also the behavior of the civilized Englishman. Later in the novel, Mina provides an analysis of Dracula's character that ironically also describes the singlemindedness of his pursuers and reinforces the similarities between humans and vampires:

The Count is a criminal and of criminal type...and *qua* criminal he is of imperfectly formed mind. Thus, in a difficulty he has to seek resource in habit.... Then, as he is criminal he is selfish; and as his intellect is small and his action is based on selfishness, he confines himself to one purpose. (Ch. XXVI)

At this point as well as at numerous others Dracula appears as a human villain instead of a supernatural figure of Evil.

Although Dracula *is* a supernatural creature and not a vampiric character like those covered in the next two chapters, Stoker often uses the vampire as a metaphor for realistic social threats. Harker's journal introduces a being whose way of life is antithetical to theirs—a warlord, a representative of the past, an aristocrat, and the leader of a primitive cult who he fears will establish a colony in England. Van Helsing, on the other hand, sees Dracula as a moral threat, a kind of Antichrist. Yet, in spite of the narrators' moral and political language, Stoker reveals that Dracula is primarily a sexual threat, a missionary of desire whose only true kingdom will be the human body.[42] While he flaunts his independence of social restraints, Dracula adheres more closely to English law than his opponents in every area except his sexual behavior. (In fact, he invites Harker to Transylvania to teach him the subtle nuances of English law and business.) Neither a thief, a rapist, nor an overtly political threat, he is dangerous because he expresses his contempt for authority in the most individualistic of ways—through his sexuality. In fact, his thirst for blood and the manner in which he satisfies it can be interpreted as a metaphor for sexual desire that fails to observe any of society's attempts to control it—prohibitions against polygamy, promiscuity or homosexuality. More specifically, however, he is dangerous because of his influence on women. Craft observes, for example that "Dracula's mission in England is the creation of a race of monstrous women, feminine demons equipped with masculine devices."[43] Seducing them to his way of life, he causes them to abandon passivity and to become sexually aggressive and demanding. This altered behavior is perceived by the other characters as a defiance of religious tenets, social custom, and traditional masculine authority.

Stoker's emphasis on sexuality has been observed by recent critics, and much of the recent scholarship on *Dracula* notices that, despite the fact that the title character is male, the power of *Dracula* resides in its women characters. Auerbach observes that the novel focuses on "the vampiristic mutations Mina and Lucy undergo" while Dracula withdraws increasingly "except for intermittent stagy boasts."[44] Stephanie Demetrakopoulos describes Stoker as a feminist and states: "The novel falls clearly into two parts, each half centered around a different type of woman."[45] Judith Roth, Judith Weissman, and Gail B. Griffin, on the other hand, argue that Stoker is misogynistic. Roth observes that "hostility toward female sexuality" contributes to the popularity of the novel"[46] while Weissman explains that the "fight to destroy Dracula and to restore Mina to her purity is really a fight for control over women;"[47] and Griffin asserts that the "truly horrific scenes in the novel" are "consistently related to female sexuality."[48]

That Stoker is extremely interested in aberrant sexuality and uses the vampire as a metaphor for it are not at issue. For instance, Dracula is the single male vampire in the novel while four of the five women characters are portrayed as vampires—aggressive, inhuman, wildly erotic, and motivated only by an insatiable thirst for blood. Looking at the differences in men vampires and women vampires, Weissman argues convincingly that Dracula is "more interested in power and conquest than in the sensual pleasure of being a vampire which the women clearly enjoy."[49] The difference also stems from the popular literary figures on which Stoker models his characters. The rake, the Gothic villain, and the male vampire as presented in *The Vampyre* and *Varney* had been figures of extreme power, sexuality being only a small part of that power. However, in Carmilla and the women characters of both the sensation novels and New Woman fiction, sexuality is one of the chief characteristics.

Although the novel begins with Harker's trip to Dracula's castle, the emphasis on women begins early. The first half of the novel centers on the innocent Lucy Westenra's transformation into a vampire that must be violently destroyed; and Dr. Van Helsing destroys *three* women at the conclusion. If it were not for Mina Harker, the reader might conclude with Roth, Weissman, and Griffin that Stoker is a repressed Victorian man with an intense hatred of women or at least a pathological aversion to them. However, the second half of *Dracula* shifts from the presentation of women as vampires to focus on a woman who is the antithesis of these destructive creatures. Furthermore, Mina not only escapes the fate of the other women, she is also largely responsible for the capture and ultimate destruction of Dracula. Stoker's division of women into two distinct groups may partially stem from a literary tradition that divided women into good women and bad, angels and demons. However, *Dracula* suggests that Stoker's treatment of women may also stem from his ambivalent reaction to the changes taking place in his society, especially to the changing roles for women. This ambivalence can be seen most clearly in his response to the New Woman.

The first reference to the New Woman occurs early in *Dracula* when Stoker's heroine mentions it almost as an aside:

We had a capital "severe tea" at Robin Hood's Bay in a sweet little old-fashioned inn, with a bow-window right over the seaweed-covered rocks of the strand. I believe we should have shocked the "New Woman" with our appetites. (Ch. VIII)

The New Woman was a subject of controversy in journalism, fiction, and drawing rooms, so Mina's initial reference serves only to characterize her as a well-informed young woman of the 1890s[50] and suggests that she is familiar with the New Woman's insistence on greater freedom and physical activity, attributes that Gail Cunningham mentions in her discussion:

It was pointed out that women were likely to remain the weaker sex as long as they were encased in whalebone and confined their physical activity to the decorous movements of the ballroom, and the new 'doctrine of hygiene' as it was coyly termed advocated sports for women and Rational Dress. Many young women pedalled their way to undreamt-of freedoms on the newly popular bicycle; petticoats and chaperones were equally inappropriate accompaniments, and could be discarded in one go.[51]

Bicycle riding, bloomers, and badminton may have revealed women's increasing emancipation, but Cunningham adds that they were not responsible for the New Woman's becoming "a symbol of all that was most challenging and dangerous in advanced thinking. The crucial factor was, inevitably, sex."[52]

When it came to sex, the New Woman was more frank and open than her predecessors. She felt free to initiate sexual relationships, to explore alternatives to marriage and motherhood, and to discuss intimate matters such as venereal disease and contraception. In addition, a group of popular writers adopted the New Woman as a subject. These writers, according to Lloyd Fernando's study of the New Woman, emphasized "the role of women in society, the injustices women suffered in marriage, and the feasibility of free unions as a means of accommodating sexual relationships with greater fairness to both sexes."[53] Thus they chose to concentrate on explicitly sexual material.

The New Woman chose to explore many of the avenues recently opened to women, including education and the professions, instead of women's traditional roles as wives, mothers, and (one of the few professions open to the traditional woman) teachers. An educated woman with a career, Mina is comfortable with many of the characteristics associated with the New Woman, but her second reference indicates that she is uncomfortable with others:

If Mr. Holmwood fell in love with her [Lucy] seeing her only in the drawing-room, I wonder what he would say if he saw her now [as she lies sleeping]. Some of the "New Women" writers will some day start an idea that men and women should be allowed to see each other asleep before proposing or accepting. But I suppose the New Woman won't condescend in future to accept; she will do the proposing herself. And a nice job she will make of it too! There's some consolation in that. (Ch. VIII)

Here Mina rejects both the forward behavior and the sexual frankness of the New Woman writers. She never mentions the writers to whom she refers, but Stoker could have been thinking of Grant Allen, Emma Frances Brooke, Menie Muriel Dowie, George Egerton, Sarah Grand, Olive Schreiner, or even of Hardy, Meredith, Moore, or Gissing, all of whom created heroines who rejected aspects of the traditional feminine role. For example, the heroine of Schreiner's *The Story of an African Farm* (published in 1883 and therefore not technically a New Woman novel though it deals with many of the same issues and character types) proposes marriage to one man when she is pregnant by another. Angelica in Grand's *The Heavenly Twins* (1893) also proposes to her future husband, dresses in men's clothing, and states that, while she may be unusual, "'there will be plenty more like me by-and-by.'"[54] Evadne in the same novel refuses to consummate her marriage because she learns that her husband had kept a mistress and she fears that he may have a venereal disease. (New Women were not only aware of sexually transmitted disease, but they also refused to be their husbands' chattel; and Grand shows the wisdom of these decisions by having a more traditional woman, Edith, contract syphilis from a dissolute husband.)

Finally, Herminia Barton, the heroine of the 1895 best seller by Grant Allen, *The Woman Who Did*, like Hardy's Sue Bridehead, argues against marriage, the center of the traditional woman's life.

While Mina's statement on New Woman writers tends to lump them all together, the group did not have a consistent view of women. Although most of the writers can be rather loosely classified as realists, some wrote from a feminist perspective while others wanted "to portray the New Woman's dangerous limitations or self-delusion."[55] Some wanted women to be more informed, but others wanted them to be more experienced as well. However, as A.R. Cunningham states, there was one common bond: All wrote "of sexual behavior with a frankness which had previously been unthinkable; all employed as mouthpieces women unusually independent, intelligent, and free from convention."[56]

Stoker characterizes his heroine by her discomfort at this frankness. Of course, Mina is not the only person who objected to such openness. The novelist Mrs. Lynn Linton wrote to a younger woman of the "sweet womanly virtues which make women half divine," complaining that such virtues were not to be found in the works of the New Woman writers: "You don't find these qualities in The Heavenly Twins, Yellow Asters, and all the new women who set themselves to blaspheme nature and God and good."[57] Linda Dowling suggests that other Victorians shared this view:

The New Woman...was perceived to have ranged herself perversely with the forces of cultural anarchism and decay precisely because she wanted to reinterpret the sexual relationship...the heroine of New Woman fiction expressed her quarrel with Victorian culture chiefly through sexual means—by heightening sexual consciousness, candor, and expressiveness.[58]

While Dowling, Gail Cunningham, A.V. Cunningham, Fernando, and others who have studied New Woman fiction suggest that the heroines pave the way for a more realistic treatment of women in twentieth-century literature, Stoker allies himself and his heroine with a more traditional woman and uses the vampire as a metaphor to characterize the women that appeared in most New Woman fiction.

The reasons for these attitudes to women can be seen clearly by looking at both his life and his works. Born in Dublin in 1847, he was surrounded by strong women throughout his life. In fact, his grandnephew and biographer, Daniel Farson, reports that the "family were in awe of Charlotte [Stoker's mother] if not actually afraid of her."[59] Harry Ludlam, another biographer, also attests to her strong character and adds that she was a feminist who returned to "social welfare work and determined championing of the weaker sex"[60] when her children were quite small. Among her numerous volunteer duties was workhouse visitor; and she reported some of the shocking facts she discovered there to the Dublin newspapers. Revealing that "the idle and hopeless state of young women in a workhouse renders it the very hot-bed of vice," she explained that "only the poorest class of householders would take a servant from the workhouse." Her solution? "Equalise the sexes, both here and in our colonies, by encouraging emigration. In new countries there is a dignity in labour, and a self-supporting woman is alike respected and respectable."[61] Unfortunately neither biographer reveals more of Charlotte's character except to suggest that she continued to influence her children during her lifetime and to mention that Stoker retold some of her stories in his works.

An an adult, Stoker continued to be surrounded by capable professional women. He worked closely with the actress Ellen Terry during the years when he managed the Lyceum Theatre; and he often told people that he married Florence Balcombe because she was so intelligent. Nonetheless, while his relationship with his mother seems to have created no ambivalent feelings, his relationship with his wife may have. Farson states that Stoker's granddaughter believes that Florence refused to have sexual relations with him after the birth of their child;[62] and he adds the interesting fact that Stoker apparently died of tertiary syphilis:

When his wife's frigidity drove him to other women...Bram's writing showed signs of guilt and sexual frustration.... He probably caught syphilis around the turn of the century, possibly as early as the year of *Dracula*, 1897. (It usually takes ten to fifteen years before it kills.) By 1897 it seems that he had been celibate for more than twenty years, as far as Florence was concerned.[63]

Such conflicting information suggests several reasons for his ambivalence about the New Woman. Familiar with the feminist movement and apparently supportive of women's struggles for professional equality, he creates women characters who are the intellectual equals of the men in his novels; however, because his awareness of women's sexuality must have stemmed mainly from furtive encounters with prostitutes rather than from long-term loving relationships, he seems to have drawn the line at sexual equality. Therefore he has his heroines choose the traditional roles of marriage and motherhood instead of sexual liberation. In fact, he is so horrified at sexual openness that he chooses the female vampire as a shocking metaphor of the new liberated woman.

Dracula, which begins with Jonathan Harker's journal, focuses on aggressive sexuality quite early. While Harker often refers to his fiancee and censures the lack of modesty in the peasant women he sees on his journey, the first women in the novel are three vampire-women in Dracula's castle. A prisoner in that castle, Harker literally fears for his life; and he gains a brief respite from his terror by musing on the nature of woman:

The soft moonlight soothed, and the wide expanse without gave a sense of freedom which refreshed me. I determined not to return to-night to the gloom-haunted rooms, but to sleep here, where of old ladies had sat and sung and lived sweet lives whilst their gentle breasts were sad for their menfolk away in the midst of remorseless wars. (Ch. III)

The moonlit setting is conducive to Harker's romantic notions about women and to his belief in their sweetness, gentle mien, and passivity— behavior that he contrasts to that of their warlike menfolk. When his reverie is interrupted by three women, he believes that they are "ladies by their dress and manner" (Ch. III). However, their aggression and attempt to reverse traditional roles reveal them to be New Women; and Harker is openly ambivalent about this role reversal:

There was something about them that made me uneasy, some longing and at the same time some deadly fear. I felt...a wicked, burning desire that they would kiss me with those red lips.... I lay quiet, looking out under my eyelashes in an agony of delightful anticipation...till I could feel the movement of her breath upon me. Sweet it was in one sense, honey sweet...but with a bitter underlying the sweet, a bitter offensiveness.... There was a deliberate voluptuousness which was both thrilling and repulsive.... I closed my eyes in a languourous ecstasy and waited— waited with beating heart. (Ch. III)

This brief scene focuses on the reversal of sexual roles, a characteristic frequently associated with the New Woman.[64] Coyly watching from behind half-closed lashes, Harker describes his feelings when he is nearly ravished by three women.

The three later violate his preconceptions by having no maternal feelings, an absence that Stoker appears to associate with the New Woman. At least his novels seem to link female sexuality with cruelty to children. For example, the sensuous Lady Arabella in *The Lair of the White Worm* preys on children, and Lucy and the women in Dracula's castle are decidedly non-maternal. Instead of nourishing children, they prey on them:

...she pointed to the bag which he [Dracula] had thrown upon the floor, and which moved as though there were some living thing within it...there was a gasp and low wail, as of a half-smothered child...as I looked they disappeared, and with them the dreadful bag. (Ch.III)

The women do not harm him, but their aggression, voluptuous behavior, and treatment of the child cause Harker to conclude that they are monsters, not women: "I am alone in the castle with those awful women. Faugh! Mina is a woman, and there is nought in common. They are devils of the Pit" (Ch. IV).

The scene at the conclusion, when Van Helsing prepares to destroy the three women, reinforces Harker's views:

She lay in her Vampire sleep, so full of life and voluptuous beauty that I shudder as though I have come to do murder.... She was so fair to look on, so radiantly beautiful, so exquisitely voluptuous, that the very instinct of man in me, which calls some of my sex to love and to protect one of hers, made my head whirl with new emotion. (Ch. XXVII)

Van Helsing also emphasizes her sensuality. In addition, even though she is passive at this time, he reveals that women who renounce their traditional feminine roles must be destroyed.

The three vampire-women appear in a mere half-dozen pages, and their primary function is to introduce attitudes and beliefs that can be explored more fully in Lucy Westenra and Mina Harker. Lucy, the first of Dracula's English conquests, is introduced by a series of letters she writes to Mina, letters that suggest that she is a most unlikely candidate for the aggressive behavior that Stoker associates with the New Woman. Her first letter recounts the pursuits of a middle-class Victorian girl and her love for the unexceptional Arthur Holmwood; and her second confirms that she is the kind of woman so romantically envisioned by Harker. Admitting that she had received three proposals, she confesses that she chose Arthur because "we women are such cowards that we think a man will save us from fears, and we marry him" (Ch. V).

Stoker reveals another side to Lucy's character, however. Outwardly rather dull and compliant, she has a covert desire to escape these constraints. Her second letter provides the first clue to this other side: "Why can't they let a girl marry three men, or as many as want her, and save all this trouble?" The thought is immediately suppressed with the recognition that it is "heresy, and I must not say it" (Ch. V), but her desire for three husbands suggests a latent sensuality that connects her to the New Woman of the period. It also implies that Lucy is unhappy with her social role and that she is torn between the need to conform and the desire to rebel. Mina's journal and its revelation of Lucy's sleepwalking confirm this division. By day, Lucy remains an acquiescent and loving Victorian girl. By night, her other side asserts itself; and Mina describes her as restless and impatient to get out. This restlessness ultimately leads her to Dracula and to emancipation from her society's restraints.

After she meets Dracula, the conflict between conformity and individual desire becomes more apparent:

...the moment she became conscious she pressed the garlic flowers close to her...whenever she got into that lethargic state, with the stertorous breathing, she put the flowers from her...when she waked she clutched them close. (Ch. XII)

The garlic flowers are a familiar charm to ward off the advances of the vampire, and the reader witnesses in Lucy's reaction to the garlic a symbol of a struggle between two alternatives. While her conscious side feels guilty for her liaison with Dracula, her unconscious side desires the freedom that the vampiric condition seems to promise.

As Lucy's rebellious nature gains strength, this change is mirrored by an alteration in her physical condition:

Whilst asleep she looked stronger...her open mouth showed the pale gums drawn back from the teeth, which thus looked positively longer and sharper than usual; when she woke the softness of her eyes evidently changed the expression, for she looked her own self, although a dying one. (Ch. XII)

Dr. Seward's analysis of the change in Lucy reveals certain preconceptions about women's nature. Believing that the true Lucy is characterized by her soft eyes, docile nature, and tenderness, he cannot recognize the increased strength or the sharp white teeth and the potential for pain, aggression, and violence that they suggest as part of her character. As yet he attaches no moral significance to her physical transformation.

Stoker's contemporaries, however, would have been aware of the significance of this physical transformation, an alteration that suggests the dangers of venereal diseases. More likely to accompany promiscuity in the days before the discovery of antibiotics, venereal diseases were known to alter the appearance of victims. Moreover, these diseases had captured the imagination of New Woman writers. For example, the innocent Edith Beale in *The Heavenly Twins* marries a profligate, contracts syphilis, and dies in agony; and Evadne in the same novel explains that fear of venereal disease keeps her from consummating her marriage. As Elaine Showalter indicates, such caution was not excessive because about "fifteen hundred infants died annually of hereditary venereal infections" between 1880 and 1900; and she adds that medical experts "confirmed that syphilis (incurable at the time) was almost invariably transmitted to innocent wives and children."[65] Perhaps Florence Stoker was sensible, not frigid.

Many of the New Woman writers illustrated the ravages of venereal diseases on innocent women and children; and even the most conservative insisted that women be informed of potential dangers. Stoker continues this argument by showing the impact on the innocent Lucy and carries the argument one step further by showing that she might also infect innocent men. Dr. Van Helsing, the father figure as well as the spokesman for the Church and the scientific community, is the only character who is aware of the dangers of contagion. Therefore he turns Lucy's body into a moral battlefield and eventually convinces the others that her awakened sexuality and attempt to reverse traditional sexual roles threaten them all:

> In a sort of sleep-waking, vague, unconscious way she opened her eyes...and said in a soft, voluptuous voice..."Arthur!...Kiss me!" Arthur bent eagerly over to kiss her; but at that instant Van Helsing...dragged him back with a fury of strength which I never thought he could have possessed, and actually hurled him almost across the room. (Ch. XII)

Here Arthur is punished for almost succumbing to the New Woman, but both he and Seward (who narrates the preceding episode) are perplexed by Van Helsing's hostility and uncharacteristic violence. Apparently familiar with the aggression of the New Woman, neither seems particularly troubled by Lucy's seductive behavior or by her refusal to wait passively for Arthur's kiss. However, after being initiated by Van Helsing, they come to believe that such attempts to reverse traditional sexual roles are evil. The following passage reveals the change:

> When Lucy...saw us she drew back with an angry snarl.... At that moment the remnant of my love passed into hate and loathing; had she then to be killed, I could have done it with savage delight...the face became wreathed with a voluptuous smile.... With a careless motion, she flung to the ground...the child that up to now she had clutched strenuously to her breast.... There was a cold-bloodedness in the act which wrung a groan from Arthur; when she advanced to him with outstretched arms and a wanton smile, he fell back and hid his face in his hands. (Ch. XVI)

Both Seward and Arthur had been surprised by Van Helsing's hostile reaction to Lucy's seductive behavior, but they quickly become his obedient pupils. After being punished for responding favorably to Lucy's advances, Arthur now dutifully hides from temptation; and Seward's more articulate response parallels Harker's horror at the vampire-women's aggressive sexuality and their treatment of the child that Dracula brought to them. What troubles Seward most is Lucy's callous treatment of the child and her unexpectedly aggressive behavior. The Lucy he had loved was sweet and gentle; she had endured Van Helsing's medical treatment and had allowed herself to be the passive victim of whatever was done to her. Now, when she rejects her former passivity and deference to male authority, the usually tender Seward responds with violence and admits that he could kill her "with savage delight."

Convinced by Van Helsing and by their own perceptions of Lucy's behavior, the three men (who had previously wanted to marry her) now decide to destroy her. On September 28 (the day after what would have been *their* wedding day and Lucy's initiation to a more traditional sexual role), Arthur plunges a stake into her breast and ends her vampiric "marriage." It is a vicious attack, but it succeeds in destroying the New

Woman and in reestablishing male supremacy. Only when that traditional order has been restored does Van Helsing allow the kiss that both Arthur and Lucy had desired during her lifetime.

Craft offers a fascinating reading of Lucy's destruction and the blood transfusions that are Van Helsing's first attempts to save her as examples of "gang rape":

> Yet beneath this screen or mask of authorized fraternity a more libidinal bonding occurs as male fluids find a protected pooling place in the body of a woman. We return...to those serial transfusions which, while they pretend to serve and protect "good women," actually enable the otherwise inconceivable interfusion of the blood that is semen too. Here displacement (a woman's body) and sublimation (these are medical penetrations) permit the unpermitted, just as in gang rape men share their semen in a location displaced sufficiently to divert the anxiety excited by a more direct union.[66]

While the first half of the novel concludes with the destruction of a character who illustrates the aggression and sensuality associated with the New Woman, the second centers on a more traditional kind of woman—Mina Harker.

Stoker introduces Mina by the letters that she and Lucy exchange. The two have been friends since childhood, but their letters reveal profound differences in the two adult women. Lucy, a perpetual child, pampered by everyone around her, writes about social events and the thoughtless pursuit of her own pleasure. Mina, on the other hand, has had to take care of herself. At the beginning of the novel, she is an assistant schoolmistress, a productive and conscious member of her society; and the intelligence and capacity for independent action and judgment that appear in these initial letters remain the predominant elements in her character throughout the novel.

By providing Mina with a responsible profession but one that had been acceptable for women throughout the nineteenth century and a means of economic independence, Stoker reveals that she is *not* a New Woman (at least, not the most extreme version, for New Woman writers favored non-traditional professions, such as medicine, nursing, and business for their heroines). Furthermore, her decision to marry and her subsequent relationship with her husband, her desire to nurture and protect children, and—most clearly—her response to Dracula himself link her to more traditional feminine figures. Before her marriage, Mina resembles the New Woman in some ways, but she adopts a more traditional role afterwards. She does everything she can to help Jonathan in his work. (For example, she learns shorthand and memorizes train schedules for his benefit and generally remains supportively in the background until he asks for assistance.) Of course, as she admits, she has prepared herself for this role: "...you can't go on for some years teaching etiquette and decorum to other girls without the pedantry of it biting into yourself a bit" (Ch. XIII).

In addition to accepting the traditional view that wives should defer to their husbands, Mina also believes in women's traditional role as mother. While both the vampire-women and Lucy prey on children, Mina believes that motherhood is an important responsibility. In fact, she becomes a "mother" to all the other characters:

I felt an infinite pity for him, and opened my arms unthinkingly. With a sob he laid his head on my shoulder, and cried like a wearied child, whilst he shook with emotion.

We women have something of the mother in us that makes us rise above smaller matters when the mother-spirit is invoked; I felt this big, sorrowing man's head resting on me, as though it were that of the baby that some day may lie on by bosom, and I stroked his hair as though he were my own child. (Ch. XVII)

Roth, Wolf, and Griffin use scenes such as this to focus on the contrast in the two women. Roth stresses that Lucy and Mina are both mother figures and demonstrates that Lucy is the evil and devouring mother while Mina is the nourishing mother.[67] Griffin calls Lucy "a demonic mother-parody, taking nourishment from children instead of giving it, as do the three women at the Castle."[68] Wolf describes Mina's treatment of the men as "a matronly parallel to the scene in which Lucy receives three proposals, accepts one, and wishes she could accept all."[69] Although Stoker may be manipulating the mythic figure of the Mother, it is also possible that he is consciously contrasting the sexually liberated New Woman with a more traditional kind of woman. In fact, Mina finally gets her wish at the conclusion, when she appears with an actual baby at her breast, a baby that is named for all the men who had participated in the quest. It is almost as though Stoker is suggesting that the child is the product of an asexual social union rather than the result of a sexual union between one man and one woman.

Leatherdale provides this fascinating commentary on the child's background:

He is linked to the band of Dracula's adversaries in more than just their names: he also has their blood. Worse, he has that of Dracula flowing through his veins. His mother has sucked the blood of Dracula, who had previously sucked that of Lucy, who had already received transfusions from Seward, Van Helsing, and Holmwood. The only blood *not* in the boy is that of Quincy Morris, his nominal 'father,' for Lucy died before she could transmit his blood to Dracula.[70]

Similarly Craft refers to little Quincy as the "unacknowledged son of the Crew of Light's (Craft's name for the group that follows Van Helsing) displaced homoerotic union."[71] Stoker, however, does not show us how little Quincy lives up to his "bloodlines" though his allusion to a second generation also makes *Dracula* more open-ended than many critics give it credit for being.

Mina's acceptance of a traditional feminine role distinguishes her from the other women in the novel. These differences are revealed most clearly by her response to Dracula and her utter repudiation of her sexuality. Unlike Lucy who remembers only the bitter-sweet sensation of yielding to Dracula, Mina is horrified by her brief tryst even though Dracula had overpowered her in her sleep. She also seems to recognize (as Lucy had not) the sexual nature of her clandestine relationship, and she fears that she will spread that contagion: "Unclean, unclean! I must touch him [Harker] or kiss him no more. Oh, that it should be that it is I who am now his worst enemy, and whom he may have most cause to fear" (Ch. XXI). Later confessing that she had succumbed because Dracula had threatened to kill Jonathan, she is nonetheless horrified that, because she "did not want to hinder him" (Ch. XXI), she is somehow linked with him and with the increased sexuality that the vampiric condition entails.

If Mina is isolated from the group before her encounter with Dracula, she becomes even more isolated afterwards, as Van Helsing observes:

I can see the characteristics of the vampire coming in her face.... Her teeth are some sharper, and at times her eyes are more hard...there is to her the silence now often; as so it was with Miss Lucy...we must keep her ignorant of our intent, and so she cannot tell what she know not. (Ch. XXIV)

Again, Mina's silence reinforces the fact that, like Dracula, she is an outsider, an alien distrusted by the dominant group.

However, if Dracula accepts being an outsider who is never seen objectively, who is never permitted to speak for himself, Mina does not. Her silence is temporary. Remembering that Dracula had told her that their brains would be linked and her will subject to his, she offers to be hypnotized so that Van Helsing and his followers can trace Dracula's escape to Transylvania and trap him before he reaches sanctuary. Furthermore, by meticulously duplicating the rational process by which she discovers the route that Dracula will take, Stoker reveals that her intelligence is superior to that of her male companions. She studies maps of the area and analyzes both Dracula's previous behavior and the information she had revealed under hypnosis. Thus it is her perception and analytical skills that enable her companions to trap and destroy Dracula.

By emphasizing Mina's intelligence, her ability to function on her own, and her economic independence before marriage, Stoker focuses on characteristics that were associated with the New Woman; but, by negating Mina's sexuality, having her adopt a traditional feminine role, and showing her decision to abide by the group's will instead of making an individual decision,[72] he also reveals that she is not a New Woman. Van Helsing, after first meeting Mina, best captures the essence of her character:

> She is one of God's women, fashioned by His own hand to show us men and other women that there is a heaven where we can enter, and that its light can be here on earth. So true, so sweet, so noble, so little an egoist—and that, let me tell you, is much in this age, so skeptical and selfish. (Ch. XIV)

The same self-sacrifice and spirituality are typical of Stoker's other heroines. Stephen Norman (*The Man*, 1905), Teuta Vissarion (*The Lady of the Shroud*, 1909), Mimi Watford (*The Lair of the White Worm*, 1911), and Margaret Trelawny (*The Jewel of Seven Stars*, 1912) are strong and independent women who choose marriage and motherhood instead of careers. Moreover, they display a sexual reticence uncommon in novels after 1890. For example, Margaret shares Mina's spirituality: "There were refinement and high breeding; and though there was no suggestion of weakness, any sense of power there was, was rather spiritual than animal."[73] In Margaret there is the hint of sensuality under control, a hint that is in keeping with Stoker's other heroines. For, despite their spirituality, they believe in knowing the existence of evil so that they can choose virtue consciously. The following conversation between Stephen Norman and her spinster aunt reinforces the message in *Dracula* by pointing to the difference between ignorance and informed innocence, between the traditional woman and a newer woman:

> 'Necessary!' the old lady's figure grew rigid as she sat up, and her voice was loud and high. 'Necessary for a young lady to go to a court house. To hear low people speaking of low crimes. To listen to cases of the most shocking kind; cases of low immorality; cases of a kind, of a nature of a-a-class that you are not supposed to know anything about....'
> 'That is just it, Auntie. I am so ignorant that I feel I should know more of the lives of those very people!'[74]

Whether people liked it or not, there would be no return to the innocent (and one-dimensional) heroines of the early Gothic novel or to the female villains who were their antithesis (and, one should add, to the real women on whom these fictional women were thought to be modeled,). Even though the appearance of *Jude the Obscure* and *The Woman Who Did* "brought about the final daunting attack on the 'New Woman' both in actual life and in the polemical fiction she had inspired,"[75] the heroines of the New Women writers heralded a more realistic portrayal of women in twentieth-century fiction. A contemporary of these writers, Bram Stoker combines some of the realism of the New Woman writers with the innocence of an earlier age.

A novel with a contemporary setting, plausible human characters, and a narrative structure that reinforces that the events are ordinary, *Dracula* combines the Gothic emphasis on awe and mystery with the realistic emphasis on mundane human life. Furthermore, despite its fantastic elements and the presence of supernatural characters, *Dracula* is a novel that—like *Jane Eyre*, *Wuthering Heights*, and *Middlemarch*—often focuses on the social issues of its own day, including the growth of imperialism, the rise of science, and the development of an increasingly assertive feminism.[76]

In such a novel, the vampire is a character that combines both a Gothic and a realistic dimension and, therefore, becomes a social metaphor. Expected to hold both dimensions in mind at once, the reader recognizes that the creature from folklore symbolizes forces that are a genuine threat to England at the turn of the century. To create such a metaphor, Stoker chooses to emphasize certain elements of the vampire's character. To show that Dracula is an anachronism, Stoker has him come to civilized England from a primitive country, where he has sustained his existence for over four hundred years. Furthermore Stoker emphasizes Dracula's erotic nature by focusing on both his gross corporality and his power over women and on his irrationality by emphasizing his reliance on habit. Although these characteristics are an integral part of Dracula's character, Stoker also focuses the reader's attention on contemporary society by showing that these characteristics are more serious in ordinary women than they are in the vampire. Dracula, for example, is permitted a dignified death in a battle that is appropriate for a former warlord. However, his three women companions and Lucy Westenra are destroyed like animals because they are not just evil but unfeminine, unmotherly, and parasitic as well.

Although the vampires in *Dracula* are transitional figures who occasionally anticipate the more sympathetic portraits of the vampire in twentieth-century literature, they also resemble vampires in other nineteenth-century literature. Dracula is a seducer like Lord Ruthven and Sir Francis Varney, an aristocrat like Ruthven, Varney, and Carmilla. Furthermore, like Coleridge and LeFanu, Stoker de-emphasizes Dracula's supernatural powers by revealing the vampire's inability to enter a dwelling without the express invitation of one of the inhabitants. Thus Dracula's weakness is one of the vampire's traditional weaknesses while his strength is the power of temptation, the awareness that many Victorians may have wished to shed their conventional social lives to be free and independent like Dracula—free from moral strictures and free from prohibitions against unlimited sexuality and violence.

Furthermore, like Sir Francis Varney, Bertha Mason, and Carmilla, Dracula is a creature from the past. Over four hundred years old, he is a warlord, a magician, and a representative of an entirely different culture; and Van Helsing and his English followers fear him as a barbarian who is attempting to take over their civilized world. Moreover, Dracula is a figure from the past who is finally overcome by the power of the present—by the modern industrial state (especially by the more rapid means of communication and transportation that are part of that modern state), by scientific experimentation (including Van Helsing's multiple transfusions on Lucy), and the power of the group. Clearly—at least in Stoker's eyes—the day of the rugged individual is over.

Dracula is an outsider because he is literally a foreigner, but his connection with women in the novel reveals the extent to which women are outsiders even within their native cultures. For example, Seward, Arthur, and Quincy Morris can kill Lucy with relative detachment; and even Mina Harker, who represents the values that Stoker associates with his society, temporarily becomes lonely and silent, a being outside her society—like Sir Francis Varney, like Bronte's Bertha Mason, and like Heathcliff.

Dracula in some ways is the last of its kind—the last nineteenth-century fictional work in which characters identify "real" vampires (creatures who return from the dead and who actually suck the blood of their victims) within their fictional world. Whether or not one accepts the argument that Stoker was familiar with specific works that featured the vampire—especially with "Carmilla," *Varney*, or the numerous dramatic versions—one can see that he was influenced by the general tradition regarding the vampire in the nineteenth century. In particular he saw that he could turn an East European superstition into a metaphor to describe troubling aspects of his own society and to enable his readers to see that there were horrors in everyday life.

However, although *Dracula* and the other works covered in this chapter—works that are outside the mainstream of English fiction in the nineteenth century—combine the supernatural figure of the vampire with realistic settings and characters, it is up to realistic nineteenth-century writers—the Brontes, Eliot, and Dickens—to fully explore the metaphoric richness of the vampire. Furthermore, by transforming the supernatural creature from folklore into the vampiric character, these writers focus their readers' attention on the almost hidden horrors of ordinary life.

Chapter Four
Suspicions Confirmed, Suspicions Denied

Rupert Sent Leger, protagonist and chief narrator of Bram Stoker's *The Lady of the Shroud* (1909), writes in his journal about the visits of a mysterious woman. Attempting to discover whether or not she is a vampire, he analyzes her behavior according to what he has read and heard of these supernatural beings:

My having to help my Lady over the threshold of my house on her first entry was in accord with Vampire tradition; so, too, her flying at cock-crow.... Into the same category came the facts of her constant wearing of her Shroud...her lying still in the glass-covered tomb; her coming alone to the most secret places in a fortified Castle where every aperture was secured.... But then came the supreme recollections of how she had lain in my arms; of her kisses on my lips; of the beating of her heart against my own; of her sweet words of belief and faith breathed in my ear.... No! I could not accept belief as to her being other than a living woman of soul and sense, of flesh and blood, of all the sweet and passionate instincts of true and perfect womanhood.[1]

The mysterious woman who ultimately will become Rupert's wife, is finally revealed to be as human as he suspects in this passage. Nonetheless, the question of whether she is a vampire, a supernatural creature of immense power, is central to the first three-quarters of *The Lady of the Shroud*.

Similarly, the question of whether Emily Bronte's Heathcliff and Catherine (*Wuthering Heights* [1847]) are vampires or ordinary human beings is central to the interpretation of that novel. Telling Lockwood of Heathcliff's behavior right before his death, Nelly Dean compares him to several supernatural beings:

"Is he a ghoul, or a vampire?" I mused. I had read of such hideous, incarnate demons. And then I set myself to reflect how I had tended him in infancy; and watched him grow to youth; and followed him almost through his whole course; and what absurd nonsense it was to yield to that sense of horror.[2]

Just as Stoker's hero, who is an amateur occultist, has learned about the vampire from books, Mrs. Dean mentions that she has learned about the vampire through reading (presumably the same kind of works that had influenced Bronte). Furthermore, like him, she quickly replaces the horrors of literature with known reality—in this case, not a loving woman but the cruel though ultimately human Heathcliff she has known as boy and man.[3]

Despite their obvious similarities, *Wuthering Heights* and *The Lady of the Shroud* are very different kinds of novels. Stoker's novel is a typical mystery and adventure story in which the reader is most interested in acting as a detective to unravel a complicated plot. In *Wuthering Heights*, on the other hand, a novel that combines Gothic horror with psychological interest and attention to ordinary social details, characterization is most important. However, the two works are similar enough to be treated together here. In both works a character suspects another character of being a vampire, and the suspicion is strong enough to make the reader interested in the question of *whether* the supernatural exists within the fictional world. Furthermore, the question of whether the supernatural exists helps the reader to concentrate on the difference between supernatural power and actual power, between the Gothic world and the real world, and between characters of almost mythic dimensions and ordinary human beings.

Thus, these works are different from the works treated in the previous chapter, works in which characters accept or come to accept the existence of the supernatural in the fictional world and in which the reader is expected to take pleasure in the existence of this Gothic dimension. Furthermore, *The Lady of the Shroud* and *Wuthering Heights* differ from the realistic works discussed in the next chapter, works in which both writer and reader accept the vampire as a metaphor for plausible human behavior. Thus, they are especially interesting to this study of the vampire, for they are "transitional" works that reveal how realistic novelists incorporate gothic elements. Finally, both Stoker and Bronte expect their readers to be familiar with the tradition of the literary vampire and therefore to be able to pick up the most subtle allusions to that figure; and Stoker may have even hoped that his readers would be familiar with his own extremely popular *Dracula*, published more than ten years earlier. At least, sections of his second vampire novel read almost like a parody of his earlier one.

Of the two works, *The Lady of the Shroud* is a much less interesting treatment of the vampire, for the suspected vampire in this novel is eventually revealed to be a woman pretending to be a vamprie to protect her country from being overtaken by the Turks. Because Teuta is "the only child of the Voivode Vissarion, last male of his princely race" and a woman who represents "the glory of the old Serb race," (Book VI) she pretends to be a vampire to avoid being kidnapped—an event that finally happens in the last quarter of the book. Thus she is more like the characters in Jules Verne's *Carpathian Castle* or the historical individuals that Stoker will examine in *Famous Imposters*, a non-fiction work published the following year, than the supernatural temptresses of "Carmilla," *La Morte Amoureuse,* or *Dracula.*[4] (*The Lady of the Shroud* is interesting, however, because of the insights it provides about *Dracula* and about Stoker in general, for it contains many of the same characteristics that preoccupy him in other works: the juxtaposition of primitive superstition and modern technology [the rescue of Teuta and her father, who had also been captured by the Turks, depends on Rupert's airplane and bullet proof suits—both a far cry from the power of the vampire], multiple narrators who focus on slightly different aspects of the same problem, the confusion of sexual roles, the obsession with strong women [Rupert is accompanied by his spinster aunt Janet MacKelpie, who is gifted with second sight], and a complicated rescue that reveals the power of the community over the isolated individual.) In fact, Archbishop Steven Palealogue, one of the minor narrators of the novel, ultimately reveals that the Lady Teuta, Voivodin of the Blue Mountains, merely pretended to be a vampire to protect herself from being captured by enemies of her family and her people. This revelation, however, occurs late in the novel; and the reader's main interest in Teuta for most of the novel is in determining whether or not she is a vampire.

As with *Dracula,* Stoker uses the superstition of the vampire to focus on the question of power. Because of her father's position, Teuta has access to political power over the fiercely independent residents of the Blue Mountains, who have a long history of rebelling against their own kings and other countries. Moreover, she clearly has intellectual power of her own. When the mountaineers try to recapture her father from the Turks, Rupert notes that "her woman's quick wit was worth the reasoning of a camp full of men" (Ch. VI) and that "the whole plan of action, based on subtle thinking, had mapped itself out in her mind" (Ch. VI). Thus, like Mina Harker, Teuta is clearly an intelligent woman though like Mina, she uses her power primarily to support husband and family rather than in her own interests. Although she initially meets Rupert when she comes to his bedroom for warmth and is apparently unaware of the impropriety of her action (Stoker seems to suggest here that merely pretending to be a vampire gives Teuta certain power over social conventions), she soon learns that proper womanly behavior includes obedience to her husband; and the novel concludes with Teuta totally domesticated and any hint of the vampire's power totally exorcised.

The Lady of the Shroud, much like *Dracula,* asks readers to look at women's power. Teuta informs Rupert, "I am not as other women are" (Book V); and both Rupert and the reader quickly recognize that pretending to be a vampire and lying quietly in the grave require a great deal of courage. However, Stoker quickly eliminates the exceptional nature of Teuta's power. Once safely married, Teuta becomes diminished, a support figure to her husband. There is, however, one exception to this elimination of female power: Aunt Janet. She had, after all, been responsible for rearing Rupert; and she is recognized as a significant force in his life. However, by making her a spinster, Stoker assures us that women's power as mother (in this case, surrogate mother or maiden aunt) is totally separate from their sexual power.

Although the vampire turns out to be a hoax in Stoker's novel, *Wuthering Heights* never answers the question of whether vampires exist; and Mrs. Dean's hurried change from assuming that Heathcliff is a vampire to accepting him as a cruel man to later mentioning that superstitious country people see him walk is a crucial part of Bronte's narrative strategy. Like other Victorian novelists, she uses gothic materials as metaphors to focus on certain aspects of reality. (Even George Eliot, that most realistic of novelists, compares Gwendolyn Harleth to a lamia and Maggie Tulliver to a witch while Thackeray, Dickens, and Charlotte Bronte often rely on gothic materials.)[5] Aware of her readers's familiarity with gothic motifs, Bronte can expect them to understand the allusions to a mysterious—even forbidden—power beyond that usually experienced by ordinary human beings but also to suspect that she is using these gothic allusions to describe a plausible situation. Moreover, to reinforce the realism, she locates *Wuthering Heights* at a specific historical time— the first word in the novel is the date 1801—and refers to actual locations: Mr. Earnshaw finds Heathcliff in Liverpool; Isabella escapes to the south near London, where her son is born; and Lockwood suggests that Heathcliff may have been to America, where he could have picked up revolutionary ideas. Other references are less specific, but the reader knows that Lockwood is also from the south and that he has vacationed at the seacoast. Thus because *Wuthering Heights* is not set in the timeless never-never land so characteristic of the Gothic novel of her day and of our own,[6] readers understand that it is not a continuation of the romantic Gondal saga, but a work which links together elements of both realism and romance. Using the romantic vampire motif as a metaphor to describe ordinary human life is simply part of her narrative strategy.

Unlike the works discussed in either the previous chapter or the next chapter, however, *Wuthering Heights* relies on a certain ambiguity about the possibilities posed by the vampire. Unlike *The Vampyre* or *Dracula*, works that accept the actual existence of supernatural characters and implausible events in their fictional worlds, *Wuthering Heights* depends on the reader's continued uncertainty about the existence of a supernatural dimension. On the other hand, despite her reliance on real places and social problems, *Wuthering Heights* is still less rooted in everyday nineteenth-century social concerns than the novels of Elizabeth Gaskell, *Jane Eyre*, *Middlemarch* or even *Bleak House*; and Bronte's metaphoric use of the vampire—if indeed it *is* a metaphor— is clearly different. In the latter three novels, the writers use the vampire to focus on perfectly ordinary social conditions—unbridled sexuality and the restrictions placed on unconventional women in *Jane Eyre*; the exploitation of the proletariat by the new capitalist class and the more general dangers of unrestrained egoism in *Middlemarch*; and the predatory nature of the law in *Bleak House*. Both writers and readers in these three works (and in the polemical works of Marx and Engels) accept the comparison only as metaphor. In *Wuthering Heights*, on the other hand, they must recognize that the metaphor may also be the reality.

Heathcliff is literally described as both a vampire and as a human being; and the reader infers that Catherine, who initially appears as a ghostly presence and only later as a human being, is also a vampire. Furthermore, the novel concludes with the two of them walking the moors. However, because Lockwood may have only dreamed about Catherine and because the report of the young shepherd *may* be unreliable, the reader is never certain whether these haunting characters are preternatural bloodsuckers or the victimized human beings so capably analyzed by Bernard Paris's psychological study, a work that treats Heathcliff's revenge as the perfectly understandable result of the abuse he suffered as a child.

The metaphoric possibilities of the vampire are just as striking in Catherine Earnshaw. Heathcliff's becoming a vampire at the conclusion of the novel—even if he is a vampire only in the metaphoric sense rather than the literal—depends on the reader's awareness that literary characters—even extremely wicked ones—rarely become vampires spontaneously. (Even in folklore, people rarely become vampires without first being attacked by another vampire. The exceptions, of course, are witches and suicides.) Therefore, the novel requires someone to fulfill the vampiric role. That someone is Catherine who returns to Wuthering Heights after twenty years. More important, seeing Catherine as a vampire (a creature who has considerable power over others but also a creature who suffers from severe constraints) helps the reader to focus on a subject that was of great interest to Bronte: the unique condition of women during the period in which she wrote, a condition that made them alternately powerless and powerful.

Seeing the vampire motif as a way of exploring power in nineteenth-century fiction helps to answer why the motif is so important. First, the vampire motif is one that appealed to a number of influential writers—far more than similar gothic motifs. Furthermore it enabled these writers to emphasize and articulate different kinds of power (for example economic and political power in *The Vampyre*, *Varney*, and *Dracula*, sexual power in "Carmilla" and *Dracula*). Finally, because the vampire becomes a predominately female image at mid-century and because it becomes a character in realistic fiction at about that same time, focusing on the vampire helps us to explore the relationship between gender and genre, between mythic power and actual power.

A great deal has been written recently of women's lack of political and economic power during previous historical periods. However, Judith Newton, who evaluates women's writing during the nineteenth century, reminds modern readers of something that Bronte knew instinctively: Women, although deprived of political and economic power over their culture, nonetheless had a great deal of subtle power over their society:

> The debate over the "women question," in addition to its mass production of theories about women's "mission," "kingdom," or "sphere," gave an emphasis to the subject of women's power, and in particular to their influence, which was historically unprecedented. One has only to take manuals addressed to genteel women in the late eighteenth century and lay them alongside those written for middle-class women some sixty to seventy years later to see a deepening tension over women's power begin to manifest itself like footprints in a flower garden.[7]

Bronte, who wrote at roughly the period that Newton describes in the second part of the quotation, was certainly aware of women's unique condition; and her portrait of women in *Wuthering Heights* reveals both their power and their powerlessness.

Before looking at the metaphoric richness of the vampire in *Wuthering Heights*, however, it is necessary to *see* Catherine as a vampire; and that means to see her both as a passionate young woman who loves two men, marries the more socially respectable of the two,[8] and dies giving birth to their child *and* as a dead body that destroys its victims by drinking their blood and that turns at least one of them into a vampire like herself.

The suggestion that Catherine is a vampire occurs the first time she enters the novel. While the typical ghost is supposed to be a disembodied spirit, Lockwood discovers that Catherine is decidedly corporeal; and he is horrified, when he rubs her wrist on the broken glass to keep her from entering the room, to see that "the blood ran down and soaked the bed-clothes" (Ch. III). Furthermore, Bronte stresses Catherine's lack of spirituality throughout the novel. While Catherine is a mere teenager, she tells Mrs. Dean that she would be unhappy in a more spiritual world. Recording a dream that she had had, she explains that she was so unhappy in heaven that the angels angrily flung her out "into the middle of the heath on the top of Wuthering Heights; where I woke sobbing for joy" (Ch. IX). In recording this dream, Catherine herself draws an implicit comparison between herself and the vampire by admitting that she doesn't want to leave this world behind; and she later makes an additional comparison by promising to haunt Heathcliff after her death and to turn him into a creature like herself:

> "I'll not lie there by myself: they may bury me twelve feet deep, and throw the church down over me, but I won't rest till you are with me. I never will."

She paused, and resumed with a strange smile, "He's considering—he'd rather I'd come to him! Find a way, then! not through that Kirkyard. You are slow! Be content, you always followed me!" (Ch. XII)

Thus Catherine rejects the conventional Christian afterlife when she advises Heathcliff not to come "through the Kirkyard" and also when she promises to return to him. The conclusion implies that Heathcliff does ultimately follow Catherine even though he first undertakes a perfectly plausible social revenge on the families who had abused him.

Bronte relies on other traditional views of the vampire. A reanimated corpse, the literary vampire must seek out human victims and drink their blood to sustain its unnatural existence. Moreover, in many literary versions, the victim must invite the vampire into a dwelling for it to have any power over him or her. Finally, once the vampire has gained entry, the victims become more pale and listless before they finally die (and sometimes become vampires in turn.) Bronte hints at the parasitic relationship between vampire and victim early in the novel when Ellen Dean mentions that the elder Lintons die soon after Catherine joins their household, but the suggestion of a vampiric relationship is most evident in her description of Heathcliff's final days. After hearing Lockwood prevent Catherine from entering, Heathcliff begs her to come in. (The reader may wonder why it takes so long for her to return since most fictional vampires return within days of their deaths. However, Bronte clarifies this mystery at the end of the novel, when Heathcliff admits that he had had Catherine's grave opened a month or so earlier while the sexton was digging Edgar's grave. It is this act that apparently unleashes Catherine's vampiric power.) Working with the literary view that vampires have no power over unwilling victims, Bronte suggests Heathcliff's further complicity in his eventual destruction by having him start sleeping in the bed where Lockwood had dreamed of Catherine. Eventually his dream of being reunited with Catherine is realized, for Nelly observes that he seems to see someone in the room:

Now, I perceived he was not looking at the wall, for when I regarded him alone, it seemed exactly that he gazed at something within two yards distance.... The fancied object was not fixed, either; his eyes pursued it with unwearied vigilance, and, even in speaking to me, were never weaned away. (Ch. XXXIV)

Furthermore, right before his death, Heathcliff begins to resemble the literary vampire physically—it is at this point in the novel that Mrs. Dean describes him as a vampire—for his appearance begins to change. Mrs. Dean keeps referring to this physical change, observing "the same unnatural...appearance of joy under his black brows; the same bloodless hue, and his teeth visible, now and then, in a kind of smile" (Ch. XXXIV). His "bloodless hue" suggests that he has been drained of blood; and the reference to prominent teeth implies that he is being transformed as well. The transformation is apparently complete at his death, for the teeth become even more vulpine then, as Mrs. Dean observes: "I tried to close his eyes.... They would not shut...and his parted lips and sharp, white teeth sneered too" (Ch. XXXIV). Finally Bronte completes the portrait of a vampire by having people around Wuthering Heights imply that Heathcliff is not really dead:

> But the country folks, if you asked them, would swear on their Bible that he *walks*. There are those who speak of having met him near the church, and on the moor, and even within this house. (Ch. XXXIV, Bronte's italics)

If these allusions to the vampire were not enough Bronte even has the professedly unromantic Nelly Dean confess her apprehension about staying at Wuthering Heights at night, the time when the vampire supposedly left its grave to seek victims.

The above discussion reveals that Emily Bronte was familiar with the vampire motif, and Twitchell observes accurately that she could rely on contemporary readers being able "to supply what was missing—they had to know enough about vampires to fill in the blanks about Heathcliff's unexplained character." However, Twitchell goes on to generalize unnecessarily "that the myth was current in Yorkshire."[9] A more plausible assumption would be to acknowledge that the literary vampire was known throughout England—indeed throughout Europe. In fact, the immensely popular *Varney the Vampire* was going through serial publication at the time Bronte was writing *Wuthering Heights*; and Bronte, who probably was unfamiliar with *Varney*, was certainly familiar with Byron's works and with the German Romantic literature of the previous century.[10]

More revealing than identifying Bronte's sources, however, is recognizing the consistency with which she uses the vampire to characterize both Heathcliff and the elder Catherine. Her treatment of the two, however, is somewhat different, for Heathcliff—as a vampire— is derivative of earlier literary types, including the eighteenth-century rake, the Gothic villain and the Byronic hero. Thus, one can easily see his resemblance to Lovelace, to Schedoni, and Manfred as well as to actual literary vampires—Lord Ruthven and Sir Francis Varney. Like these literary types, he is a seducer of young women; and his erotic attraction can be seen in his relationships with both the elder Catherine and Isabella. Indeed, though both women see his destructive nature, they are unable to reject his advances. In addition, Heathcliff's revenge is clearly modeled on the behavior of the Gothic villain who is fatal to himself and others; and the implicit reference to the vampire serves to underline the similarities in literal bloodsucking and plausible economic behavior. Finally, when she outlines his revenge on the younger generation, she reveals that Heathcliff, like the typical Gothic villain or Byronic hero, is an inscrutable figure from the past that continues to wield his power on the present.

Catherine, on the other hand, is a new kind of vampire as well as a new kind of Gothic heroine.[11] While Heathcliff's character derives largely from a literary tradition of masculine physical and economic power, Catherine's character asks the reader to look at women's lives rather than at a literary tradition. Furthermore, the metaphor of the vamprie enables Bronte to focus on the unique position of women during the nineteenth century and to reveal both their lack of political and economic power and their very real power; and other writers throughout the nineteenth century will continue to emphasize this curious combination in the woman vampire.

As a new kind of vampire, Catherine has none of the animal traits found in the vampire from folklore or even in literary versions, such as Hoffman's "Aurelia" or even Polidori's *The Vampyre*. In addition, because her behavior for the most part is plausible and realistic, she foreshadows characters like Rosamond, Lucy Westenra, and even twentieth-century vampires like Sterling or Valan.

Although Catherine is a new kind of vampire, she is even more interesting as a new kind of Gothic heroine. Unlike the frail and pallid heroines of Walpole, Lewis, and even Radcliffe, Catherine has traits previously associated with the Gothic villain. Assertive, strong, intelligent, and independent, she clearly wants to control her own life although that desire often brings her into conflict with those who wield authority within her society.

Despite the changes she makes in the vampire motif, Bronte relies on the fact that the literary vampire is a creature that is strangely powerful and powerless. Its power lies in its immortality and in its ability either to confer that power on its victims or to destroy them completely by drinking their blood. Furthermore, many of the literary vampires that might have served as models for Bronte are characterized by their physical power, not their moral or intellectual influence, a fact that is underlined by the emphasis on their teeth and by the eroticism that appears in so many versions, including *Christabel*, *Lamia*, and "Aurelia." On the other hand, its lack of power lies in the peculiar constraints of vampiric existence. For example, although Bronte does not utilize this characteristic specifically, the literary vampire was typically confined to the grave during the day and, therefore, had power only at night; and the ghostly Catherine appears to Lockwood at night. Moreover, that Catherine has no power over Lockwood also stems from the fact that the traditional vampire had no power over an unwilling victim and from the fact that certain symbols offer protection against vampires. To prevent Catherine from entering, Lockwood piles books, including her own Testament, against the broken window. These symbols of authority—both sacred and secular—are used in the same way that Van Helsing uses the Host against Dracula and that the contemporary vampire film uses the ubiquitous crucifix. Moreover, the following scene reinforces the fact that the vampire was often at odds with traditional religious authority:

...but they can't keep me from my narrow home out yonder, my resting place where I'm bound before spring is over! There it is, not among the Lintons, mind, under the chapel-roof; but in the open air with a head-stone.... (Ch. XII)

Catherine thus distinguishes herself from the socially conventional Lintons and also establishes herself as a creature of earth, not spirit. Moreover, the scene is a reminder that the vamprie, although powerful, has power only within certain well-defined bounds. (Catherine's apparent desire for death in this scene should also remind the reader that the vampire—both in folklore and in earlier literature—was often a suicide.)

If the literary vampire is an odd hybrid creature that both wields tremendous power over others and suffers from severe constraints, the position of women at the time Bronte was writing is no less peculiar. (Heathcliff too shares this peculiar hybrid existence, for—though he is apparently a foundling with no legal rights to the Earnshaw fortune— he gains a tremendous amount of economic and personal power over two families and over the entire community of which he is a part.) The historian Gerda Lerner observes that women have traditionally been both powerful and powerless:

Women at various times and places were a majority of the population, yet their status was that of an oppressed minority, deprived of the rights men enjoyed. Women have for centuries been excluded from positions of power, both political and economic, yet as members of families...they often were closer to actual power than many a man.[12]

Although Lerner is referring to women at all historical periods, the sense of women's being both powerful and powerless can have been no more evident than it was during the Victorian Period, when a queen ruled England and its empire yet other women lost political and economic power. Winifred Gerin, who has written biographies of all the Bronte children and who therefore understands the forces that influenced them, observes that Emily's interest in powerful women characters began at the time that Victoria become queen:

The subject [of Victoria as queen] evidently stimulated and excited the growing Emily.... While Charlotte applied all her talents to creating the Byronic 'Zamorna'...Emily chose a woman for her protagonist, an emancipated woman, a queen, and a rebel round whose fatal destinies she raised a whole complex of plots that took her permanently outside the orbit of her sister's and brother's influence.[13] Later, when she wrote the more realistic *Wuthering Heights*, she continued to focus on a strong, rebellious heroine.

However, if Bronte was aware of women's power as queens and as members of the ruling class, she also knew that women were often second-class citizens who could neither vote, enter a university, nor choose a profession and who (if they were married) could not own property. For example, Charles Percy Sanger's classic essay on *Wuthering Heights* demonstrates that Bronte was familiar with the laws governing inheritances and wills,[14] so she knew that women did not receive the same legal treatment as men. In addition, because she was a daughter in a family that gave preferential treatment to the only son, she knew from first-hand experience that women often had less power over their lives than men. Aware of the complexities of women's existence, Bronte wrote a novel that uses the gothic image of the vampire as a metaphor to evoke both women's lack of overt power and their very real power over their own lives and the lives of others.

Catherine's lack of power can be seen in the following ways: Bronte presents her and other women as children, reveals that Catherine's identity is established by her relationship to men, and emphasizes that she has no socially acceptable way to escape from her circumscribed role.

Although a significant portion of *Wuthering Heights* focuses on literal childhood—Heathcliff, Edgar and Isabella Linton, the two Catherines, Hareton, Hindley, Linton Heathcliff and even the sober Ellen Dean are all children during most of the story—women with the exception of Mrs. Dean never seem to mature. The novel, however, is most emphatic about the effect that perpetual childhood has on the older Catherine.

The early sections of the novel focus on Catherine's wild youth and adolescence before her marriage to Edgar Linton. Still a young hoyden, Catherine remains unfettered by any social restrictions. In fact, Bronte succinctly reveals Catherine's childhood character by the gift she asks her father to bring her from Liverpool. While her brother requests a fiddle (a musical instrument often used in harmony with other musical instruments), the six-year old Catherine, who—as Mrs. Dean informs Lockwood—could already ride any horse in her father's stable, demands a whip, an appropriate symbol of control and independence. After the death of her father, she becomes even more headstrong and unruly. Rebelling against Hindley's power and Joseph's religious teaching, she likes nothing better than escaping with Heathcliff to the moors. In fact, accepting no authority other than her own will, Catherine is literally free to create herself, for there seems to be no social authority over her.

Although Catherine's freedom from external authority might suggest a kind of power, Bronte reveals that Catherine is free only because those with more power choose not to use it against her. Hindley and his wife are too indifferent to attempt to control her very often. Finally, however, the freedom—both literal and figurative—concludes when Catherine reaches puberty. Having reached twelve, Catherine and Heathcliff are separated; and when they escape to the moor for one of their Sunday outings, they are attacked by the Linton watchdogs. Bitten by one of them, Catherine is invited to stay with the Lintons until she recovers. Although she remains at Thrushcross Grange for only five weeks, Catherine becomes socialized within this brief period and thus abandons the freedom of her childhood:

> The mistress visited her often...and commenced her plan of reform by trying to raise her self-respect with fine clothes and flattery...so that, instead of a wild, hatless little savage jumping into the house...there alighted from a handsome black pony a very dignified person with brown ringlets...and a long cloth habit which she was obliged to hold up with both hands that she might sail in. (Ch. VII)

In growing up and becoming a lady (a *social* construct rather than a biological one), she learns to control much of her wildness, but she also loses much of her unique character. In this way Bronte reveals what socialization does to women.

Although the untamed side of Catherine's character continues to prefer Heathcliff, the socialized side comes to accept the Edgar Linton she ultimately marries. (Mrs. Dean informs Lockwood that the first six months of Catherine's marriage to Edgar are happy, but she inadvertently suggests that the happiness may be only on the surface.) Certainly her desire to be wild and free intensifies when Heathcliff's return reminds her of her previous life:

> I wish I were a girl again, half savage, and hardy, and free, and laughing at injuries, not maddening under them! Why am I so changed.... I'm sure I should be myself were I once among the heather on those hills. Open the window again wide, fasten it open! (Ch. XII)

At this point, Catherine has not only abandoned her social freedom in marrying Edgar Linton, but she has also lost the little physical freedom granted to married women by becoming pregnant. (The same word, 'confinement,' describes both imprisonment and childbirth in the nineteenth century.) Bemoaning the changes that have taken place, she might be referring merely to physiological changes or to the enormous social changes that motherhood would bring. Emily Bronte, whose own mother died before she was old enough to remember her, well understood that motherhood restricted women by asking them to conform to a highly important social role.

Unwilling to accept the changes—both physical and spiritual that accompanied motherhood—Catherine longs to return to childhood—to be *herself* rather than a socialized view of what she should be. This desire is finally achieved when she returns to Wuthering Heights twenty years after her death. Lockwood describes his ghostly visitor as a child, but Bronte makes sure that the reader recognizes that the child is Catherine Linton:

> "Catherine Linton," it replied, shiveringly (why did I think of *Linton?* I had read *Earnshaw* twenty times for Linton). "I'm come home, I'd lost my way on the moor!" (Ch. III, Bronte's italics)

Why does Bronte link the child to the name acquired only by the adult woman? According to Margaret Homans, this scene is one of the "novel's indications that the dream is a genuine apparition."[15] More important to our understanding of the scene, however, is the emphasis here on Catherine as a child, a being that appears powerless but that—like the vampire—is actually powerful because it is free from many of the social restrictions that impede ordinary adult human beings.

In fact, Bronte uses the childhood motif much as she uses the vampire motif—to demonstrate the complicated status of women. In the nineteenth century women were often treated as minors, as people with no rights of their own and therefore with no legally recognized power over their lives or over the lives of others. (This fact is revealed by several scenes in the novel. Hindley treats his young wife like a child—treatment of which both Catherine and Heathcliff are contemptuous—and both Isabella and the younger Catherine lose all rights to their own property after their marriages.) Furthermore, she points to the emotional reality that would be associated with being a legal minor by showing Catherine's happiness as a real child and her distress at being a woman who, although treated like a child, does not have the child's freedom from social constraints.

Catherine, however, does not remain a child forever. Nelly Dean reveals that the living Catherine always behaves like a spoiled child, and Lockwood sees Catherine Linton return as a child. However, country people see Heathcliff walking with a *woman.* Bronte uses this subtle shift to suggest that women have an alternative to being treated like children and that that alternative is to take control over their own lives. (The younger Catherine—discussed later in this chapter—does choose to control her own life after the deaths of her father and Linton Heathcliff.) Thus, when Catherine returns to haunt Heathcliff, she makes a conscious choice between the freedom that he represents and the spiritually confined life of the chapel, the grave, and a conventional afterlife. She also chooses the rough, wolfish Heathcliff she had always desired rather than the socially acceptable Edgar she had been taught to admire. That conscious choice and its concomitant refusal to allow others to continue to govern her is a sign of maturity.

In addition to revealing that women are treated like children, Bronte emphasizes that they are treated as outsiders whose only source of identity is their relationship to men. The scene in which Heathcliff and Catherine are found staring in the window at Thrushcross Grange reveals that both are treated as outsiders by the powerful Lintons. Accused initially of being gypsies and thieves, they are attacked by the watchdogs before Edgar recognizes that Catherine is Miss Earnshaw, the daughter of a respectable father. Moreover, the names that she carves on the windowsill of her old bedroom reinforce the fact that her only identity is through her relationship to men. She can thus remain Catherine Earnshaw, the spinster who is dependent on her drunken brother for charity; she can marry Heathcliff and be a beggar or she can marry Edgar and gain some access to power and prestige through that relationship.

Although she takes the choice that would seem to offer the most power, Catherine nonetheless does not gain a sense of personal identity with her marriage to a powerful man; and her lack of identity is reinforced by the fact that, when she is near death, she cannot recognize her face in the mirror.[16] Terrified by her lack of identity, she lapses into memories of childhood, becomes in Nelly's words "no better than a wailing child" (Ch. XII), and desires to become a child again. Finally, dying in childbirth, she can be said literally to become a child again, in this case a new Catherine.

Although Bronte reveals that women could take control over their lives, she also focuses on the limited options available to demonstrate why the majority failed to do so. Moreover, in *Wuthering Heights*, these limitations are made to stand out in stark relief by the geographical isolation of the area and by other special circumstances, including Catherine's haphazard education. While the Bronte sisters, like many other women at the time, explored teaching as an alternative to economic dependence on father, brother, or husband, this option is apparently not available to Catherine because she lives in a geographically remote area and because she has not been trained to do anything productive. Unlike the Bronte sisters who were thoroughly trained by their father and who eventually went to school in England and Belgium, Catherine is left to fend for herself. Thus, although she is certainly intelligent, she has not received any systematic training, as Lockwood's description of her books reveals:

Catherine's library was select, and its state of dilapidation proved it to have been well used, though not altogether for a legitimate purpose; scarcely one chapter had escaped a pen and ink commentary—at least, the appearance of one—covering every morsel of blank that the printer had left.

Some were detached sentences; other parts...a regular diary, scrawled in an unformed, childish hand. At the top of an extra page...I was greatly amused to behold an excellent caricature of...Joseph, rudely yet powerfully sketched. (Ch. II)

Lockwood here recognizes her native intelligence and creativity. However, Mrs. Dean's discussion of Catherine's childhood and youth reveals nothing but the most haphazard education, an emphasis that becomes almost a parody of the sort of training that passed as education for most women in the late eighteenth century and even during the period when the Brontes themselves were being educated. That Bronte has her story take place in the previous century, however, permits her to explore a time when women's roles were even more circumscribed. The point is that, because Catherine—indeed most women at the time—was not trained for work outside the home, her options were extremely limited and her genuine talents wasted.

Although Bronte reveals women's lack of overt power over their culture, however, she also reveals their indirect power. For example, even though women as a whole had no legal rights, some women were members of powerful families. Catherine, for instance, gains some protection from the Linton watchdogs when Edgar recognizes her. Moreover, Isabella is able to escape from an unhappy marriage because of the power and protection of her family's position. Clearly despising her, Heathcliff is careful nonetheless not to be too abusive and can tell Edgar "to set his fraternal and magisterial heart at ease, that I keep strictly within the limits of the law" (Ch. XIV). Moreover, in moving to London, Isabella is free from both her husband and her brother, for the money that Edgar sends her apparently has no strings attached. Thus Isabella has more power than other women with unhappy marriages.

In addition to the limited power that women sometimes gained as members of powerful families, Bronte reveals that some women have power as individuals. Because Catherine, for example, clearly exercises erotic power over both Edgar and Heathcliff, she can manipulate the two of them, but she cannot persuade Isabella to forget Heathcliff. Through this subtle contrast, Bronte reveals that Catherine's power stems not from intelligence or family background but from her sexual charms and perhaps also from the moral influence so often granted to women during the nineteenth century. Judith Newton, who examines literature by other nineteenth-century women writers, demonstrates that influence of the kind that Catherine uses with both Heathcliff and Edgar was one of the main sources of power for women during the time in which Bronte wrote:

This same tension and counterinsistence in relation to women's power leave traces on periodical literature.... In 1810, for example, an author for the *Edinburgh Review* makes only one reference to women's influence, giving far more emphasis to the dignity, the delightfulness, and the ornamental quality of women's character and to the importance of their personal happiness. But by 1831, in literature of the same kind, power and influence are frequent subjects of concern.... [17]

In fact, Catherine's moral influence on Heathcliff continues even after her death, for he confesses to Ellen Dean that he avoids harming Hareton and Cathy because they remind him of his lost love—his better self:

> In the first place, his startling likeness to Catherine connected him fearfully with her. That, however, which you may suppose the most potent to arrest my imagination, is actually the least, for what is not connected with her to me?... The entire world is a dreadful collection of memoranda that she did exist, and that I have lost her! (Ch. XXXIII)

Thus, Catherine's influence continues to temper and modify Heathcliff's revenge.

Finally, Catherine has the power traditionally associated with women—that of giving birth and, therefore, of conferring a kind of immortality. Thus, women's power, like the power of the vampire, lies in their influence—both direct and indirect—on others and in their ability to perpetuate existence. And both have power to influence the present even though people pretend that they do not exist. The conclusion, for example, reminds the reader of the continued existence—even power—of ghostly presences. When Ellen Dean informs Lockwood that Wuthering Heights will be boarded up, he observes that it will remain for "the use of such ghosts as choose to inhabit it." Mrs. Dean replies piously that "the dead are at peace, but it is not right to speak of them with levity" (Ch. XXXIV). Nonetheless she refuses to sleep at the Heights at night, and she also tells Lockwood the story of the shepherd boy who had told of seeing Heathcliff and Catherine on the moors. Through her confused and inconsistent response to their ghostly presences, Mrs. Dean overtly denies and indirectly acknowledges the continued power of Catherine and Heathcliff. Like the vampire from folklore and earlier literature, Heathcliff and Catherine—outsiders who are theoretically far removed from conventional sources of power—continue to influence their world if only in relatively minor ways. They thus reveal both the power and the powerlessness of the people that history ignores—of women and of other outsiders like Heathcliff.

Despite the ghostly presences at the conclusion, the second half of the novel is in many ways a more plausible retelling of the first; and the younger Catherine is a more realistic version of her Gothic mother. Moreover, the younger Catherine gains a more socially acceptable kind of power. While her mother and Heathcliff continue to haunt the moors and the consciousness of whatever people continue to believe in their existence, the younger Catherine is shown at the conclusion planning to return to her father's home and to the overt economic power of the Lintons. Therefore, the metaphor of woman as vampire—overtly powerless but surreptitiously powerful—does not work for her at all.

Furthermore, Bronte suggests that her anticipated marriage to Hareton Earnshaw will be far different from the marriages that had preceded.

To understand that difference fully, the reader must see that Hareton and the younger Catherine differ from their predecessors in several important ways. When Cathy enters his life, Hareton is what Heathcliff terms "a personification of my youth, not a human being" (Ch. XXXIII). Thus Bronte underlines the fact that Hareton is in the same state of graceless nature that Heathcliff was when Catherine said that it would degrade her to marry him. However, the boorish and occasionally violent Hareton seems to have no plans for the kind of systematic revenge that occupies so much of Heathcliff's time. The younger Catherine is similarly different from her mother and from her two aunts. True heir to the Lintons and therefore conscious of social rank and power, she initially treats her boorish cousin like a servant and attempts to make both him and the servants subject to her commands. However, disinfranchised from her economic and social heritage, Catherine soon learns to see beyond these arbitrary social distinctions and to recognize Hareton's human worth. The scene in which she makes peace with him is proof of these changes. Instead of responding with the Earnshaw violence or the Linton manipulation, Catherine plants a friendly kiss on his cheek to make peace. When this gesture fails to elicit the desired response, she wraps a book as a present and asks Mrs. Dean to be her messenger: "And tell him if he'll take it, I'll come and teach him to read it right...and, if he refuse it, I'll go upstairs, and never tease him again" (Ch. XXXII). Rather than try to dominate him or seduce him (an attempt to gain power that is typically used by those without overt power), Cathy leaves Hareton free to choose.

Hareton chooses to accept her offer, and the two become as oblivious to Heathcliff's threats as the first Catherine and Heathcliff had been to the violence of Hindley and Joseph. Despite the apparent similarities, however, the two love relationships are quite different. The love between Heathcliff and Catherine had been primitive, violent, elemental, and frequently as cruel and inscrutable as the natural elements to which they so often compare it. The love between Hareton and Cathy, on the other hand, is more conscious, mature, and plausible, partially because it begins when they are older, partially because it develops over books and partially because Bronte has replaced the Gothic model with a more realistic one.

Here too Emily Bronte reveals a significant change in the younger generation, for unlike the other "readers" in the novel, Cathy and Hareton use these written texts to establish a relationship that extends far beyond anything they might have learned directly from either the texts or from the human models around them. For example, the pragmatic Mrs. Dean learns to understand the power she sees around her by reading books.

The romantics, Lockwood and Isabella, attempt to model their lives on the material they find in popular romances and fairy tales; and Sandra Gilbert and Susan Gubar demonstrate that these romantic fictions reinforce the traditional sexual roles that give power to men. Thus while Lockwood pretends to worship women, his "phrases, like most of his assumptions, parody the sentimentality of fictions that kept women in their 'place' by defining them as beneficent fairies or amiable ladies"[18] and that label women who violate this role as demons or vampires. Moreover, they argue that the same works that have taught Lockwood to exert power over women have also prepared Isabella to be a victim (or—as I am suggesting—to exert power over others in indirect or devious ways):

Ironically, Isabella's bookish upbringing has prepared her to fall in love with (of all people) Heathcliff. Precisely because she has been taught to believe in coercive literary conventions, Isabella is victimized by the genre of romance. Mistaking appearance for reality, tall athletic Heathcliff for an 'honourable soul'...she runs away from her cultured home in the naive belief that it will simply be replaced by another cultivated setting.[19]

Another reader, Edgar Linton asserts his power over his wife by escaping to his library and therefore ignoring her needs for human warmth and recognition; and Joseph uses the printed word to justify his harsh behavior. In a marvelous scene, which briefly hints at the direct social and economic power given even to a factotum like Joseph and denied to virtually all women and other outsiders, he "solemnly spread his large Bible on the table, and overlaid it with dirty bank-notes from his pocketbook, the produce of the day's transactions" (Ch. XXXII). The scene beautifully reveals a combination of two sources of power during the nineteenth century—economic power and moral power (and indirectly suggests that the economic—and almost exclusively male—is more important). However, despite their power (or—in Isabella's case—lack of it), these people are hardly healthy role models for a new generation.

Bronte has Cathy and Hareton sensibly refuse to live according to the human role models around them, models that had made both Catherine and Heathcliff into vampires or vampire-like creatures, or even according to the models they might have found in books. Although she is silent about the titles the two discuss, practically any book would have reinforced the negative role models they saw around them. What is important, however, is their refusal to blindly follow any of the models available to them. Thus the younger Catherine and Hareton—strong individuals nonetheless—use their strength to support rather than to manipulate the other. In this way, they are unlike their equally strong ancestors, who can exist happily only on a supernatural plane.

Despite its reliance on supernatural characters and gothic materials,

Wuthering Heights is a work that refuses to leave the real world behind. Therefore it falls on the boundary of the mainstream in English literature; and Bronte's use of the vampire motif is one example of a general movement toward greater realism in English literature.[20] This study examines one gothic image, the vampire, but readers could as easily examine other gothic or mythic images and the way that nineteenth-century writers incorporate them into realistic fiction.

In fact, by combining the exaggeration that is common to all types of Gothic literature with the details of ordinary human life, Bronte produces a novel that focuses on the lives of women and other outsiders and uses the literary vampire as a metaphor to reveal both their lack of social and economic power and their tremendous personal power. Thus *Wuthering Heights* reveals that women and other outsiders are not waiting obediently on the periphery of history. Instead, Heathcliff and Catherine are powerful beings who refuse to die and who exert their influence on the lives of both present and future generations. Members of the younger generation go even further, for they discover how to gain legitimate power over their own lives and over the lives of others. Planning their move to Thrushcross Grange—the locus of Edgar Linton's magisterial power—reveals their access to traditional power.

Wuthering Heights uses the literary vampire to explore different kinds of power in the nineteenth century and to reveal who has it. Because her novel is located in the reality of the nineteenth century with its emphasis on wills and inheritances, it is tempting to say that her vampiric characters are simply metaphors like those used by her sister Charlotte and later by Dickens and George Eliot. Nonetheless, because Emily Bronte refuses to abandon the awe and mystery and asocial power of the gothic novel, it is more accurate to look at *Wuthering Heights* as a kind of transitional work, one that incorporates aspects of realism—an interest in surface details, plausible human behavior, identifiable settings, and legitimate social concerns—with the overwhelming and often incomprehensible power associated with the gothic. Most important, the reader can never say for certain that those larger-than-life characters, Heathcliff and Catherine, are ever displaced to the world of memory or legend, for they continue to exert an indirect influence on the lives of others at the same time that their more ordinary offspring gain power in more humanly comprehensible ways.

Similarly, the memory of gothic power exerts its control over much of the reading experience of *The Lady of the Shroud*. Even after realizing that a hoax has been played on him/her, the reader continues to feel some of the overwhelming power associated with the gothic in this novel. This sense of the overwhelming will not be the case in the novels discussed in the next chapter—*Jane Eyre, Middlemarch,* and *Bleak House*—or in the various polemical works that use the vampire as a social metaphor. In these works, the mystery and awe of the gothic are simply a memory.

Chapter Five
Myth Becomes Metaphor in Realistic Fiction

The fictional works discussed in this chapter—*Jane Eyre, Bleak House*, and *Middlemarch*—use the vampire in more obviously metaphoric ways than the works discussed in the previous two chapters; and the difference is revealed most clearly by the fact that a character or characters uses the term "vampire" as a significant metaphor for destructive human behavior and shows, therefore, that he or she is aware of the literary tradition and of the social or historical resonance of the vampire motif.[1] In addition, because these three novels are also more or less within the realistic tradition of English fiction, *Jane Eyre, Bleak House*, and *Middlemarch* feature ordinary human beings who behave in psychologically plausible ways instead of having implausible plots and supernatural characters; and the authors' use of the vampire motif serves primarily to emphasize the horror that is sometimes part of ordinary human life.

However, despite the obvious difference in approach and the greater subtlety, the difference is not immediately apparent, especially in the early sections of *Jane Eyre*, where Bronte consciously manipulates the tradition handed down to her by her Gothic predecessors.[2]

The first specific reference to the vampire, which seems to be solidly within the Gothic tradition, focuses on the mystery and terror that are characteristic of the Gothic. The day before Jane is to marry Rochester, she tells him that she had been awakened the night before by a strange woman who entered her room, tore her bridal veil, and trampled the pieces beneath her feet. Afterwards, she moved to the bed where Jane lay and stared intently into her face. Jane admits that she fainted; but before losing consciousness, she looked closely at the woman's face, which she describes to Rochester in frightening detail: savage, with rolling red eyes, a face which reminded her "of the foul German spectre—the Vampyre" (Ch. XXV). Aware of the eerie laughter that frequently issues from the third floor, the nocturnal attacks on Rochester and Mason, and the presence of the mysterious Grace Poole, the reader is prepared for this disclosure.[3] However, Bronte drops the Gothic connection when she reveals that Thornfield's secret is not a supernatural evil but something much more horrifying. The strange and violent woman whom Jane first sees in the mirror and then face to face is neither the mysterious Mrs.

Poole nor an inhabitant of the grave, but a living woman, Rochester's mad wife.

Given Jane's superstitious nature and what she had already seen of Bertha's violence, her initial conclusion is understandable. Like the vampire in folklore and in earlier literary accounts, Bertha had appeared only at night, once to set fire to Rochester's bed, once to attack her brother and suck his blood. Called to the third floor to nurse Mason after this attack, Jane is frankly perplexed by his semi-delirious references to Bertha: "She bit me.... She worried me like a tigress, when Rochester got the knife from her.... She sucked the blood: she said she'd drain my heart" (Ch. XX). Jane cannot understand such inhuman violence; and when she finally sees Bertha herself, she ignores the fact that Bertha is a woman too and distances herself even further from the mad woman by attributing her behavior to a supernatural cause.

That Jane's supernatural solution is negated and replaced by a natural one suggests that Bronte is deliberately manipulating the conventions of the Gothic novel, conventions that had enabled writers like Walpole, Lewis, and Radcliffe to liberate extra-rational qualities, expose hidden motives, and explore the more perverse elements of human behavior; and choosing the vampire to illustrate Bertha's incomprehensible behavior is clearly within the Gothic tradition. What distinguishes Bronte from the Gothic novelists, however, is her emphasis on the psychological and social elements of Bertha's past rather than on the fantastic and lurid aspects of her present existence. This re-emphasis moves Bronte beyond most of the Gothic novelists in that it brings to the foreground elements that were usually only suggested in Gothic novels. In fact, Bronte reveals that characteristics such as violence, irrational behavior, and aggressive sexuality should not be displaced to remote and mysterious regions or buried in the exotic past. These qualities are part of human life even though human beings may try to evade and repress them. In fact, Edith Birkhead observed over half a century ago that all three Brontes adapt Gothic conventions to focus on real life:

In *Jane Eyre*, many of the situations are fraught with terror, but it is the power of human passion, transcending the hideous scenes that grips our imagination. Terror is used as a means to an end, not as an end in itself.... The Brontes do not trifle with emotion or use supernatural elements to increase the tension. Theirs are the *terrors of actual life*.[4]

Bronte's retrospective comments on Bertha suggest that she meant to make her character natural and immediate rather than "Gothic":

I agree with them that the character is shocking, but I know that it is but too natural. There is a phase of insanity which may be called moral madness, in which all that is good or even human seems to disappear from the mind and a fiend-nature replaces it....

It is true that profound pity ought to be the only sentiment elicited by the view of such degradation, and equally true is it that I have not sufficiently dwelt on that feeling; I have erred in making *horror* too predominant.[5]

Agreeing with Bronte's analysis, most twentieth-century criticism has seen only the horrible aspects of Bertha's character, ignored the past with which Bronte provides her, and overlooked the very important connections between Bertha and Jane.[6] Not only does the revelation of Bertha's presence and her relationship to Rochester prevent the bigamous marriage, but it alters the course of Jane's life and forces her to see herself more clearly. Whereas Bertha is mad, imprisoned, enslaved by her passions, and parasitic, Jane describes the forces that threaten her as madness, imprisonment, enslavement, and death. To reinforce this comparison, Bronte dramatically links Jane and Bertha throughout the novel. Seeing the multiple connections between the two women, the reader understands that Bertha's existence is a possibility for Jane, her vampiric condition a provocative symbol of everything that Jane must overcome. Thus the vampire is not a gratuitous bit of Gothicism, but a profound symbol of the kind of personal existence that Jane must escape and a vehicle for criticizing the treatment of women in nineteenth-century England.[7]

That Bronte is combining a Gothic motif with a realistic social situation becomes quickly apparent, for, despite the Gothic conventions, Bertha's progress as a woman is carefully presented. Although she appears in the novel's present only as a blood-sucking animal, she had once been a beautiful and accomplished woman, the pride of Spanish Town, whom Rochester describes as a "fine woman, in the style of Blanche Ingram; tall, dark, and majestic." In fact, he confesses that he married her because he was blinded with desire: "I was dazzled, stimulated: my senses were excited; and being ignorant, raw, and inexperienced, I thought I loved her" (Ch. XXVII). By this comparison, Bronte reveals that Blanche is a dramatic incarnation of Bertha's past; and Blanche—despite her superficiality, insensitivity, and greed—is a plausible representation of an upper class woman in the nineteenth century: beautiful, accomplished, and determined to use her physical charms to make a wealthy marriage. Shallow and conniving though she appears to the reader, Blanche is respected—even admired—by the society in which she lives. In fact, of the characters in *Jane Eyre*, only Jane and Rochester appear to penetrate her gorgeous exterior and expose the barrenness beneath. Jane's comments on Blanche's character are as precise as they are devastating:

Miss Ingram was a mark beneath jealousy: she was too inferior to excite the feeling.... She was very showy, but she was not genuine: she had a fine person, many brilliant attainments; but her mind was poor, her heart barren by nature.... She was not good; she was *not original*: she used to repeat sounding phrases from books: she never offered, nor had, an opinion of her own. She advocated a high tone of sentiment; but she did not know the sensations of sympathy and pity; tenderness and truth were not in her. (Ch. XVIII, my italics)

Jane's portrayal of a superficial and acquisitive upper-class woman also suggests several reasons why Bronte chose the vampire to depict this kind of woman. If the vampire in folklore and German literature was a dead body masquerading as a living one, a creature with neither love nor hate nor anything approximating human motivation, then Blanche, the mindless and heartless woman, is a type of social vampire; and her determined pursuit of a husband with an attractive rent-roll is only slightly less parasitic and aggressive than the vampire's insatiable thirst for blood. Furthermore, while the leap from social and economic parasitism to vampirism may at first appear forced, it becomes more clear when one remembers that Bertha initially desired Rochester because of his respectable family background—his "good blood."

Although Jane's descriptions of Blanche and Georgiana and Rochester's memories of life with Bertha reveal examples of social and economic parasitism, what turns a socially acceptable emphasis on surface polish and seductiveness into drunkenness, aggressive sexuality, and violent madness is merely suggested. Georgiana's whining superficiality and Blanche's cold materialism, although reprehensible, at first seem to have only the most superficial connection to the vampire's violence; and it is difficult to imagine either of them becoming like Bertha. Nonetheless, the logic of the novel leads to this conclusion, for Jane's dreams link them irrevocably together; and Rochester specifically compares Blanche and Bertha. The difference is one of degree, not of kind. In Blanche, the violence and insatiable hunger of the vampire remain hidden beneath a social mask that is charming and physically appealing, just as Bertha's madness had once been concealed. In fact, it was only after the marriage that Rochester discovered the hidden aspects of her history and character—her family's madness and her own coarseness and perversity—and found that he was "bound to a wife at once intemperate and unchaste" (Ch. XXVII). Finally, these excesses led to violence and madness so extreme that he was forced to conceal her from the world.

The connections between Blanche and Bertha become more clear if one looks at Jane and discovers how she avoids the qualities that doom Blanche to a parasitic, non-human existence and the qualities that destine Bertha to imprisonment, madness, and death. Among these are certain tendencies within Jane herself: a streak of irrationality in her nature and an affinity for allowing her will to be engulfed temporarily in the wills of those around her. Reinforcing these personal tendencies, however, are social conditions that affect all the women in the novel; and it is as a metaphor of the social problems that confronted women that Bronte's choice of the vampire becomes most clear. Rather than simply condemn Blanche and Bertha for being "vampires," Bronte examines the social forces that encouraged women to be seductive, aggressive, less than human. As her sister had done in *Wuthering Heights* and as George Eliot will later do in *Middlemarch* (again using the vampire to characterize this type of woman though without most of the Gothic overtones), Bronte focuses on the generally low level of women's education, on their limited possibilities for employment, and on nineteenth-century notions of marriage—in short, on a wide spectrum of social forces that kept women parasitic, inferior, and confined. Through Jane's description of her education, she criticizes the paucity of women's practical training: a "narrow catalogue of accomplishments" that includes the "usual branches of a good English education, together with French, Drawing, and Music" (Ch. X). Not only is this training limited, but also it prepares women only to be beautiful ornaments rather than independent human beings, prepares them only with the arts that were believed necessary to attract husbands. It is Bronte's artful characterization that makes Jane's condemnation of Blanche's conventionality and artifice both a criticism of what upper-class women were expected to be and a *personal* reaction to these expectations. In her childhood, Jane had been the outcast while she heard Georgiana Reed praised for her beauty, for looking "as if she were painted;" and, during her adulthood at Thornfield, Jane feels like an outsider in the presence of the beautiful Blanche even though she recognizes Blanche's personal inferiority. Through her portrayal of Blanche, Bertha, and Georgiana, Bronte reveals that, whatever other qualities her society may have expected women to possess, it admired women who were false, conventional, less than fully human.

Bertha is the extreme, of course, for she is the woman in whom any human characteristics have totally disappeared. Although Bronte's presentation of Bertha's past reveals that she had the potential for extreme behavior even when she married Rochester, her careful revelation of Bertha's present existence provides additional reasons for choosing the vampire motif, reasons that stem directly from the social position of women in the nineteenth century. Imprisoned on the third floor of Thornfield, Bertha is on the periphery of the novel's history, which she can enter and influence only by furtive midnight attacks. She is a parasite, not only because she sucks Mason's blood, but because she—like most married women at the time—is entirely dependent on her husband. His refusal to send her to Ferndean where the damp and unwholesome climate might cause her literal death, is thus a compassionate gesture that simply prolongs her bodily existence. In short, Bertha's past is an exaggerated version of the hollow and non-human lives that upper-class women were expected to lead; and her present existence is a horrible parody of what marriage could mean for women in the nineteenth century: death in the eyes of the law, imprisonment both within their homes and within their physical bodies, and a dependent, parasitic, vampiric existence, governed entirely by their husbands.

Although it is only comparatively recently that twentieth-century critics have begun to study the social and historical elements of Bronte's work, her personal correspondence reveals a deep concern with the condition of women in her society and a profound questioning of the restrictions placed on them. Many of Bronte's concerns about the condition of women stem directly from her own life and from that of her sisters, and she incorporates many of these concerns directly into *Jane Eyre*: her struggles for a profession, her resentment of the treatment she and Anne had received as governesses, and her desire for a marriage between equals.[8] Her choice of the vampire to portray the woman who permitted social conventions to determine her life casts in a new (although certainly exaggerated) perspective the character of the heroine in both sentimental and Gothic fiction and provides a harsh criticism of the Victorian myth of the Angel in the House and the myth of domestic bliss. Instead of emphasizing the desire for economic and emotional dependence, the coy flirtatiousness, and the reliance on piety and conventional standards of behavior that form an element in the character of the sentimental heroine from Pamela onwards, Bronte stresses parasitism, seductiveness, and thoughtless obedience to social standards. Moreover, if the fate of the sentimental heroine was generally marriage, Bronte emphasizes the social and legal reality that was frequently obscured by the myth: legal death, restriction of movement, and the acceptance of an inferior status. Instead of being pampered, protected, and adored by loving husbands, women might be confined, rejected, and detested by men who saw them as inferior, less than human creatures.

In Jane Eyre, Bronte creates a woman who, by questioning nineteenth-century standards of feminine behavior, becomes a new kind of heroine, a woman who achieves a kind of minor triumph over her inferior education, her poverty, and most importantly over the stereotyped notions of what a woman should do and be. (She thus becomes a more successful version of Catherine Earnshaw and a more self-conscious version of the younger Catherine in *Wuthering Heights*.)[9] Unlike Blanche, who is confined by the social role she chooses to play, and unlike Bertha who is literally imprisoned, Jane is constantly in motion, a quality suggested by both the plot and by her last name.[10] First Bronte has Jane progress through the social roles permitted to an impoverished gentlewoman in the nineteenth century. Then she has her move from an inarticulate reaction to the forces that oppress her to a conscious rebellion against them.

To help the reader understand the extent of Jane's triumph—both over the external conditions that restrict her freedom of movement and over the impediments in her own nature—Bronte repeatedly links Jane and Bertha. Of these scenes, only a few reinforce the Gothic tradition of the vampire. The others emphasize the social condition of women in the nineteenth century.

One of the numerous scenes linking Bertha and Jane occurs on the morning of Jane's wedding, when she looks at herself in the mirror, the same mirror in which she had seen the hideous and (she believes) supernatural face of Bertha Rochester two days earlier, and remarks, "I saw a robed and veiled figure, so unlike my usual self that it seemed almost the image of a stranger" (Ch. XXVI). Although Jane draws no overt connection between this scene and the earlier one when she had seen the hideous bloated face of Bertha in the mirror, the reader should see at least a potential similarity between the two veiled figures, between the old bride and the new.[11] In each scene, the veil suggests Bertha's identity to the reader and conceals it from Jane; and Jane, generally so observant of signs and portents, ignores such an obvious sign and avoids seeing any likeness to herself, first by fainting, then by placing Bertha in the realm of the supernatural. Furthermore, the veil in the second scene almost hides Jane from herself; and Bronte suggests that Jane is a naive young woman who is not quite conscious of her motives and intentions. Believing that her happiness will be assured by marriage to Rochester, she falls blindly into a romantic trap; and more important, although she had been highly critical of Rochester's reasons for marrying Blanche, she fails to question his desire for her or her own reasons for wanting to marry him.

In fact, Bronte's presentation of Jane's courtship suggests to the reader many difficulties of which Jane is only partially conscious. She protests the clothing that Rochester buys for her, clothing that she feels is a subtle attempt to change her or at least to misrepresent her, and accuses him of trying to mask his "plebian bride in the attributes of a peeress (Ch. XXV). However she doesn't quite understand the extent of his power over her or why she is so apprehensive about the marriage. Bronte, however, is aware of what marriage could mean for women, who gave up their legal status as single women and became totally dependent on their husbands; and the mature narrator's reflection on her relationship with Rochester suggests that marriage might have resulted in her absolute renunciation of self:

My future husband was becoming to me my whole world: and more than the world: almost my hope of heaven. He stood between me and every thought of religion, as an eclipse intervenes between man and the broad sun. I could not, in those days see God for his creature: of whom I had made an idol. (Ch. XXV)

Later, when Jane accompanies Rochester to the third floor where she is confronted by her predecessor, she begins to realize the existence that she had fortunately escaped: the loss of self, a voluntary confinement, a vampire-like state. To be saved from Bertha's fate, Bronte reveals that Jane must flee temptation; she must refuse an unequal marriage in which she would become a parasite and a dependent just as she must avoid the other aspects of the vampire's existence—death and madness.

The reader first becomes aware of Jane's determination to avoid death when Brocklehurst asks her what she must do to avoid damnation; in reply, Jane informs him and the reader of one of the guiding principles of her life: "I must keep in good health and not die" (Ch. IV). Although naive and unpremeditated, Jane's insistence on health and life takes on powerful resonance in a novel in which death of one form or another is so all pervasive[12] and in which the vampire is used as a metaphor of a way of life for many women. More important than the many literal deaths in the novel, however, are the half-lives of many characters who either ignore or voluntarily destroy part of their being: Helen Burns seeks death as a child seeks a beloved parent and admits that she is avoiding future errors; St. John Rivers sacrifices emotion, sexuality and finally life itself in pursuit of his ambition; finally the vampire Bertha allows any recognizably human qualities she may have possessed to be destroyed. Unlike these characters who in one form or another are death-oriented, Jane seeks life in all its spiritual, intellectual, and physical fullness. Throughout the novel, she clearly articulates her will to live, most vehemently when she is confronted with people who attempt to alter her consciousness, to force her into a mold, to destroy her or force her to suppress part of her life.[13] For example, she describes the Reed family's tyranny, Rochester's emphasis on her passionate nature, and St. John's insistence that she abandon herself to a life of religious martyrdom, as death. Aware that the tropical climate of India might cause her literal death, she nonetheless reveals a stronger concern with St. John's effect on her mental and spiritual life. Thus she describes his proposal as an "iron shroud" that contracts around her and her entire relationship to him as a loss of self, a kind of death:

By degrees, he acquired a certain influence over me that took away my liberty of mind; his praise and notice were more restraining than his indifference. I could no longer talk or laugh freely when he was by.... I fell under a freezing spell. (Ch. XXXIV)

When the mature narrator reveals how close she was to accepting his proposal, she again describes how close she was to a kind of death:

I was tempted to cease struggling with him—to rush down the torrent of his will into the gulf of his existence, and there lose my own. I was almost as hard beset by him now as I had been once before, in a different way, by another. I was a fool both times. To have yielded then would have been an error of principle; to have yielded now would have been an error of judgment. So I think at this hour, when I look back to the crisis through the quiet medium of time: I was unconscious of folly at the instant. (Ch. XXXV)

For the mature narrator, loss of self, folly, and the power of unconscious forces are synonymous with death; and she presents the alternatives to these destructive forces as struggle, adherence to principles, and rational judgment. Although the shift from the passive voice to the active in this paragraph reveals the triumph of life over merely passive existence, the change in Jane can be seen more clearly by looking at her struggles to live fully and independently and at her confrontations both with the people who try to confine her and with madness.

Telling Rochester that she will not become his mistress, she compares her desire to stay with him to madness:

I will hold to the principles received by me when I was sane, and not mad—as I am now.... They have a worth—so I have always believed; and if I cannot believe it now, it is because I am insane—quite insane: with my veins running fire.... (Ch. XXVII)

Jane had just seen the horror of Bertha's existence; and her argument is an implied comparison to that creature of fire and madness. What prevents Jane from becoming Bertha's successor, both in love and in a kind of mad renunciation of self, is an intense struggle. Her conscious beliefs in herself war with her unconscious desires and with a social heritage that makes her desire to abnegate her will in her love for another. The result is that she begins to distrust her sanity. It is only later, when she is at the Riverses, that she understands that life with Rochester would have made her perpetually at war with herself. It would have been a "fool's paradise"—part ecstasy, part conscious awareness of degradation and loss—in which she would have been "fevered with delusive bliss one hour—suffocating with the bitterest tears of remorse and shame the next." Conscious of her narrow escape, she congratulates herself for being a "village schoolmistress, free and honest" and for crushing the "insane promptings of a frenzied moment" (Ch. XXXI). Again, the alternatives Jane poses reveal how far she has moved from the vampire's existence. She has chosen freedom and independence over passion and parasitism.

Jane's ability to keep her passionate feelings under control does not mean that she is totally cold, rational, unfeeling like her cousin Eliza Reed, however. In fact, it is her familiarity with passion that first causes her to pity Bertha and to want to hear her story. By revealing Jane's passionate feelings, Bronte shows that Jane understands the pressures—personal as well as social—that make women abandon their independence and become engulfed in the wills of the men they love. And even after she had escaped the temptation of Rochester's presence, she is still affected by feelings for him:

...I still again and again met Mr. Rochester, always at some exciting crisis; and then the sense of being in his arms, hearing his voice, meeting his eye, touching his hand and cheek, loving him, being loved by him—the hope of passing a lifetime at his side, would be renewed, with all its force and fire. Then I awoke. Then I recalled where I was, and how situated. Then I rose up on my curtainless bed, trembling and quivering; and then the still, dark night witnessed the convulsion of despair and heard the burst of passion. By nine o'clock the next morning I was punctually opening the school; tranquil, settled, prepared for the steady duties of the day. (Ch. XXXII)

These are Jane's nocturnal wanderings and her continued temptations; and it is primarily her struggle to avoid being overwhelmed by them that distinguishes her from the insane frenzy of Bertha.

The question of passion and its association with madness raises several provocative questions with regard to Bronte's choice of the vampire motif and her portrayal of Jane. Often the literary vampire was associated with aggressive and unreflecting sexuality; and Bronte's portrayal of Bertha's amoral passion and desire is consistent with this. That Bertha ultimately destroys herself while Jane repeatedly fights against her own passionate feelings suggests one conclusion: the necessity for exorcising passion.[14] That Jane rejects St. John, the absolutely spiritual man, compares his power over her to death, and ultimately returns to Rochester suggests a different conclusion. Perhaps the clearest response to these questions can be discovered, not in Jane's comments on her relationships with the men in her life, but in the mature narrator's comments on Georgiana and Eliza Reed:

True, generous feeling is made small account of by some: but here were two natures rendered, the one intolerably acrid, the other despicably savourless for the want of it. Feeling without judgment is a washy draught indeed; but judgment untempered by feeling is too bitter and husky a morsel for human deglutition. (Ch. XXI)

While it is feeling and judgment that are opposed here rather than passion and reason, the passage nonetheless suggests Jane's inner struggle and her need to find a personal balance between reason and passion. It is, after all, the same beliefs that cause her to choose Rochester instead of St. John.[15] Thus Bronte reveals that Jane must avoid becoming like Bertha whose passion and violence have deteriorated to madness and the death of all human qualities without becoming Bertha's opposite, a being also dead and inhuman.[16] Her choice involves a degree of passion that is unusual in a Victorian heroine.

Even without relying on the Gothic figure of the vampire, Bronte could have made the reader aware of Jane's search for a balance in her life, her need to overcome excessive passion, irrational behavior, and self-destructive tendencies. However, *Jane Eyre*, although it is a fictional autobiography of an individual woman, is also a comment on the position of women in nineteenth-century England; and Bronte's juxtaposition of her heroine and the vampire-like Bertha helps the reader to understand Bronte's attitudes toward the problem. In fact, the first connection between Jane and Bertha has decidedly social overtones. Having gone up on the roof of Thornfield to escape her feeling of confinement, Jane broods about her life:

> ...I longed for a power of vision which might overpass that limit; which might reach the busy world, towns, regions full of life I had heard of but never seen: that then I desired more of practical experience than I possessed; more of intercourse with my kind, of acquaintance with variety of character, than was here within my reach. (Ch. XII)

From feelings of personal discontent, Jane's thoughts wander to the way most women are forced to live. Thus, she places her personal trials within a definite social context:

> Millions are condemned to a stiller doom than mine, and millions are in silent revolt against their lot.
> ...Women are supposed to be very calm generally: but women feel just as men feel; they need exercise for their faculties and a field for their efforts as much as their brothers do; they suffer from too rigid a restraint, too absolute a stagnation, precisely as men would suffer; and it is narrow-minded in their more privileged fellow creatures to say that they ought to confine themselves to making puddings and knitting stockings, to playing on the piano and embroidering bags. It is thoughtless to condemn them, to laugh at them, if they seek to do more or learn more than custom has pronounced necessary for their sex. (Ch. XII)

Jane's reverie is interrupted by Bertha's wild laugh. Although Virginia Woolf considered this laugh an "awkward break" that disturbs the continuity of the novel,[17] it is not a break, but Bronte's way of providing a connection between Jane, the eminently sane and healthy young governess, and Bertha, the imprisoned mad woman. Both Jane's brooding and Bertha's laugh are responses to confinement. True, there are significant differences in their conditions, for Jane *feels* imprisoned because she is a woman in a society that places numerous restraints on women and because she is poor in a society that equates wealth and merit while Bertha *is* imprisoned because her violent and irrational behavior threatens herself and the lives of others. Nonetheless suffering and the response to suffering merge for a moment, and the comparison provides the reader with a quick insight into Bronte's feelings about the condition of women, feelings that Jane describes as doom, stagnation, suffering, and a stifling half-life. That Bertha is portrayed as a vampire—dead, imprisoned, non-human—is simply a Gothic metaphor of a way of life that affects millions of women.

Although the two women join in a mutual response to their confinement, the important point of this passage and of the novel as a whole is the difference in the response. Bertha's reaction is a laugh, a meaningless gesture, which, like her revolt against her keepers, is primitive, violent, irrational, a regression into a bestial state rather than a transcendence of limitations; and comparing her to a vampire emphasizes the irrational nature of her revolt. However, the difference can be seen even more clearly later in the novel when Bertha stands on the roof in Jane's place, then plunges to her death when Rochester calls to her. The fire that ends her death-in-life existence and leaves Rochester permanently scarred is the logical culmination of Bertha's violence, her passion and orientation toward death.[18] It is only by a hideous death—her blood and brains smashed over the pavement—that Bertha can renounce her vampiric existence and be acknowledged by Rochester as his wife and as another suffering human being. On the roof, Jane's response to confinement is already indicative of the kind of rebellion that will free the human potential both in herself and in Rochester. Her ability to respond to restraint with reason prevents her from succumbing to Bertha's fate.

Although Jane has to learn socially acceptable ways to rebel against restraint, even her childhood classes her as a kind of rebel against authority; and the first scene in the book, as Kathleen Tillotson suggests, provides the reader with the "double impression of constraint and freedom,"[19] confinement and the rebellion against that confinement that will motivate Jane's adult behavior. Tillotson, however, like most critics of *Jane Eyre*, sees this constraint on an entirely personal level and ignores the social implications of this scene. Bronte, on the other hand, is careful to present Jane's problem as being both personal and social. At the Reeds, she is not only a child in a world controlled by adults, but—as her cousin John keeps telling her—a member of an inferior social class who should be forced to keep in her place. Thus her childhood is not simply a reenactment of the familiar fairy tale story of the persecuted child, the cruel stepmother and the jealous stepsisters/stepbrothers. In fact, she deemphasizes the fairy-tale aspect of her childhood by comparing it to a real historical period. (Like her use of Gothic conventions elsewhere in the novel, Bronte uses fairy tale elements here only to replace them by a socio-historical reality.)[20] However, caught off guard when John Reed strikes her and draws blood, she rebels and responds to him with more violence. Although there is just enough violence and irrationality in her behavior to suggest that Jane could succumb to Bertha's fate, this scene also foreshadows the adult woman who understands her position and acts accordingly. Before she strikes, she shows that she recognizes John as a tyrant and an oppressor, a representative of the ruling class as well as her bad-tempered cousin. And she is a "rebel slave," an articulate spokesman for the downtrodden.

Although Jane occasionally speaks out in behalf of the poor, her concern for the rights of women takes priority over her interest in strictly economic problems, and Bronte often portrays the restraints placed on women dramatically—as she does in this initial scene—by Jane's relationships to the men in the novel. In fact, all the men in the novel are determined to alter Jane in accord with their needs as Martin S. Day argues: "The Rochester from whom Jane flees and the Rivers she refuses are both domineering males. Both strive to overpower her will and to rule her."[21] Day is correct in his analysis of Rochester and Rivers, but his analysis could be (and I believe it should be if we are to understand Bronte's views on the condition of women) extended to include Brocklehurst and John Reed also. The men in the novel are far more than Jane's immediate antagonists, for all four are representatives of the established authority and are, therefore, indirectly responsible for the oppression of women: Brocklehurst and St. John are members of the clergy, Rochester and John Reed, members of the gentry.[22] As such, they are directly responsible for Jane's problems and indirectly responsible for the problems that affect all women.

Recording her first official meeting with Rochester, Jane portrays him as a tyrant who warns her, " 'Excuse my tone of command; I am used to say "Do this," and it is done: I cannot alter my customary habits for one new inmate' " (Ch. XIII). While his tone of command may be justified while he is her employer, Jane finds it degrading and humiliating when he becomes her lover. And equally degrading is his paternalistic treatment of her. Although she does not rebel against him, she compares their engagement to the relationship of a sultan to "a slave his gold and gems had enriched" (Ch. XXIV). Her choice of metaphor reveals that she understands both the political and sexual sources of his power. That she senses a need to rebel long before she actually does so is suggested by her response to Rochester's gifts. Its difference from her earlier reaction to John Reed is an indication of her growth:

I'll be preparing myself to go out as a missionary to preach liberty to them that are enslaved—your harem inmates amongst the rest. I'll get admitted there, and I'll stir up mutiny; and you...shall in a trice find yourself fettered amongst our hands: nor will I, for one, consent to cut your bonds till you have signed a charter, the most liberal that despot ever yet conferred. (Ch. XXIV)

Unwilling to be totally dependent on Rochester, Jane had already asked to continue as Adele's governess after the marriage; and her desire for employment is an attempt to replace the master-slave relationship with a contract based on mutual responsibility.

Although obviously uneasy with Rochester's fanciful treatment, Jane does not recognize the full extent of his power until after she has seen Bertha. Then the fairy tale becomes a nightmare with the princess transformed into a wild beast howling in the attic; simultaneously the Gothic nightmare is replaced by the historical reality.

The painful knowledge that Bertha is a woman like herself rather than a supernatural figure of evil forces Jane to look at her own position, to distrust her feelings of passion and her belief in herself and temporarily to seek refuge in external systems of belief. Looking back at that time, she describes her tyrannical conscience which "held passion by the throat, told her tauntingly she had yet but dipped her dainty foot in the slough" (Ch. XXVII). Conscience, however, is not a tyrant she can rebel against, particularly when Rochester's account of his past confirms her own sense of possible degradation:

...if I were so far to forget myself and all the teaching that had ever been instilled into me as—under any pretext—with any justification—through any temptation—to become the successor of these poor girls, he would one day regard me with the same feeling which now in his mind desecrated their memory. (Ch. XXVII)

The point is, of course, that Jane had forgotten herself and all she had ever learned, had forgotten the reality of her position, had almost succumbed to the tyrant's power and to her own feelings. Her decision to leave him is partially motivated by a reawakened conscience, partially by her identification with Bertha and her realization that Bertha's fate might be hers. In fact, Bronte underlines the identification by having Jane dream that night of her former imprisonment in the red room and hear a voice that urges her to flee temptation.

Jane's emphasis on moral law appears highly conventional, a predictable response to the man of passion, not an act of rebellion or self-assertion. And so it would be if she did not move beyond a refuge in accepted religious beliefs that is essentially an evasion of the truth and a negation of consciousness to a reaffirmation of her self and her life. Again it is a kind of mirror image that forces her to see the truth about herself. Looking at St. John, she recognizes that he is using religion to escape from Rosamond Oliver, just as she had used religion to escape from Rochester:

I was sure St. John Rivers—pure-lived, conscientious, zealous as he was—had not yet found that peace of God which passeth all understanding: he had no more found it, I thought, than I had; with my concealed and racking regrets for my broken idol and lost elysium—regrets to which I have latterly avoided referring; but which possessed me and tyrannised over me ruthlessly. (Ch. XXX)

In spite of Jane's critical judgment, she almost succumbs to St. John's power over her and the strength of his moral arguments. Having promised to marry him if she is convinced that God wills it, she again hears the voice; and this time she describes her reaction to it in terms of renewed energy, vitality, and motion: "My powers were in play, and in force"

(Ch. XXXV). It is with a renewed sense of life that she rejects the man of stern obligation and cruel self-sacrifice and returns to Rochester.

She returns before she knows that Bertha is dead and that Rochester has been reborn. Whether she returns to become his mistress or simply to be his neighbor and companion is perhaps an irrelevant question. It is certainly a question that the text makes no attempt to answer. All the reader knows is the Gothic metaphor of the supernatural voice and the realistic social fact that Jane tells Rochester when they meet: "I told you I am independent, sir, as well as rich: I am my own mistress" (Ch. XXXVII). Her legacy of five thousand pounds has made her an independent woman who can afford to build a cottage near his door: a woman who is free to be his friend, his neighbor, his companion, and his equal.

Jane's economic independence is only part of Bronte's realistic conclusion, however. Another and equally important part is the man Jane finds at the end of her journey, a man who is greatly changed from the proud tyrant he had once been. Too frequently, critics of *Jane Eyre* regard Rochester's altered condition merely as a form of punishment: the result of his giving way to unrestrained passion, a "symbolic castration," a dramatic portrayal of the Biblical punishment for adultery, and a symbol of Jane's vengeance.[23] True, one should not forget that Rochester himself sees it as a form of divine punishment. However, it is also, as he himself comments, a stage in his regeneration:

You know I was proud of my strength; but what is it now, when I must give it over to foreign guidance, as a child does its weakness? Of late, Jane—only—only of late.... I began to experience remorse, repentance; the wish for reconcilement to my Maker. (Ch. XXXVII)

Rochester's altered condition is a way of portraying dramatically his need for Jane, not simply in the physical sense that she acts as his sight and his right hand, but as a kind of spiritual and emotional guide.

Thus, like her sister Emily's novel, *Jane Eyre* ends with a marriage that differs significantly from the other marriages in the novel, a marriage that eliminates both the Gothic horror and the real social problems present in so many nineteenth-century marriages. For Jane, marriage is not a prison; nor does she become a parasite, a dependent, an inferior—at best condemned to silent revolt, at worst condemned to a horrible half-life, a life so horrible that Bronte uses the Gothic motif of the vampire to characterize it. In fact, marriage enables Jane to rediscover the happiness she had first known at Lowood so many years before. Then a small child, she had first experienced contentment when she learned to conjugate *etre* and sketched her first cottage. Now, as an adult woman, she experiences contentment by "be-ing" a woman who does not have to suppress the intellectual, physical, or emotional parts of her nature.

The conclusion thus provides Jane, for the first time since Lowood, with a congenial living space and an end to her wandering.

The conclusion provides a happy ending for Jane and Rochester. However, is the conclusion appropriate? Ruth Bernard Yeazell, in an article that centers on Jane's mysterious summons to return to Rochester, argues that it is:

> If an Austen novel, in Charlotte Bronte's terms, is "more *real* than *true*, Jane Eyre can be said to be more true than real." For while the miraculous events which conclude this novel are scarcely realistic, they *are* "true"—true to the vision of human experience which informs Bronte's world, and true to the internally consistent laws by which that world is governed.[24]

Others—myself included—disagree. The problem with Yeazell's analysis—and to a lesser extent, with the conclusion of *Jane Eyre* as well—is that the world that the novel portrays is not governed by internally consistent laws. Thus, one should not expect "harmony between the individual psyche and the world which it confronts."[25] Jane's problems are not only individual and personal (the kind of areas so often scrutinized by the Gothic albeit in an exaggerated manner) but social and historical as well (and therefore the kinds of problems on which realistic fiction focuses); they are the result of Jane's being an impoverished gentlewoman; and Rochester's tyrannical treatment of Bertha and his paternalistic treatment of Jane had been reinforced by his privileged social position. These problems cannot be solved by miraculous legacies or by supernatural voices or even by fire. The novel as a whole rejects such Gothic responses and fairy tale solutions that obscure the truth of human experience and moves toward an analysis of a social and historical reality; but the conclusion retreats back to wish-fulfillment and dream. Thus, while the conclusion is Edenic and may satisfy the reader's desire for a happy ending, it ignores the very basis of Jane's and Rochester's happiness. Their ability to live in seclusion (away from society's corrupting influence) is at least partially dependent on their economic status. Their bower of bliss has been purchased with money Rochester acquired when he married Bertha, the rents from Rochester's family estates, and the money that Jane acquired from her uncle's imperialistic ventures. As a result, Jane and Rochester remain very much a part of the world that they think they have rejected, a world that continues to oppress the poor and imprison women.

Given Charlotte Bronte's life and the world in which she lived, happiness for a few lucky individuals may have been all she could imagine. In a letter to William Smith Williams, her publisher and friend, written May 12, 1848, Bronte focused specifically on the condition of women *and* on her inability to discern a solution to the problems she saw:

I often wish to say something about the 'condition of women' question, but it is one respecting which so much 'cant' has been talked, that one feels a sort of repugnance to approach it.... One can see where the evil lies, but who can point out the remedy?

In fact, Bronte's inability to point out a solution to the problems that oppressed women may help to explain why the resolution of Jane's predicament is as much due to good luck as it is to her strengths and desires for independence.

Despite Bronte's occasional reliance on the supernatural, however, there is no question that her use of the vampire motif is metaphoric rather than literal and that she expects her readers to be sophisticated enough to see the similarities between Gothic excess and ordinary human behavior. Dickens and George Eliot will expect the same kind of sophistication from their readers though they will make the vampire both more ordinary and more metaphoric.

Published in book form in 1853, a mere five years after *Wuthering Heights* and *Jane Eyre*, *Bleak House* is much more obvious in its metaphoric use of the vampire.[26] Unlike Charlotte Bronte, who carefully sets her Gothic stage before she reveals that her vampire is a human being, Dickens opens *Bleak House* with a London fog. Moreover, his parasitic characters—no matter how extreme their behavior may be— are clearly human beings rather than supernatural monsters.

Probably Dickens's most despairing portrait of a world gone wrong, *Bleak House* is peopled with a horrible assortment of predatory individuals and decadent institutions that destroy the happiness and occasionally the lives of those around them; and Dickens uses the vampire motif to illustrate his characters' exploitative and unnatural behavior and his world's gradual evolution toward death in a particularly graphic and disturbing manner.

While many characters in *Bleak House* manifest the parasitic and amoral qualities of the vampire, only Krook and Vholes are specifically compared to this preternatural creature. In fact, Esther's perception of Vholes might have been taken directly from folklore: "So slow, so eager, so bloodless and gaunt, I felt as if Richard were wasting away beneath the eyes of this adviser, and there was something of the Vampire in him" (Ch. LX). Unlike Jane Eyre, Esther does not seem to believe that Vholes is actually a supernatural figure, but she uses his funereal appearance, "lifeless manner" (Ch. XXXVII), and apparent hypnotic power over Richard to remind the reader of the vampire from folklore. In fact, so much of her description is designed to remind the reader of certain similarities between the predatory attorney and the supernatural figure. His office, for example, suggests the native soil in which the vampire rested when he was not seeking his next victim:

The name of Mr. Vholes, preceded by the legend Ground Floor, is inscribed upon a door-post in Symond's Inn, Chancery Lane: a little, pale, wall-eyed, woe-begone inn, like a large dust-binn of two compartments and a sifter. It looks as if Symond were a sparing man in his way, and constructed his inn of old building materials, which took kindly to the dry rot and to dirt and all things decaying and dismal.... (Ch. XXXIX)

Moreover, the office itself has the cramped feeling of a tomb, for the chambers are "on so small a scale, that one clerk can open the door without getting off his stool" (Ch. XXXIX). When Vholes raps on his desk, "it sounds as hollow as a coffin" (CH. XXXIX). Finally, Vholes himself draws a final connection when he alludes repeatedly to his impaired digestion and consequent need for a liquid diet: "I am but a poor knife and fork at any time. If I was to partake of solid food at this period of the day, I don't know what the consequences might be" (Ch. XLV).

Although Dickens adheres closely to the characteristics of the vampire when he describes Vholes's physical appearance and personal habits, he nonetheless makes it clear to the reader that Vholes's closest resemblance to the vampire is in his predatory and amoral behavior. Instead of being a dead body who returns from the grave at night, he is a parasite who eventually destroys the weak-willed and susceptible Richard Carstone, not by literally sucking Richard's blood, but by encouraging him to believe in a successful outcome to the Chancery suit.

While Vholes illustrates the harmful influence that one individual can have over another, Krook (because of his association with the Court of Chancery) represents the harmful effect that decadent institutions have over the people who continue to believe in them. Initially presented as sadistic, amoral, and destructive, he too is explicitly compared to the vampire when the narrator describes him "with his lean hands spread out above the body [of Captain Hawdon] like a vampire's wings" (Ch. XI). As with Esther's descriptions of Vholes, however, the third-person narrator clearly does not expect the reader to see Krook as a vampire, only to see how his behavior resembles that of the supernatural figure.

Although Dickens obviously doesn't expect the reader to see Krook as a supernatural figure, he does focus attention on certain points of similarity. When William Guppy and Tony Jobling discuss Krook's drunkenness, they reinforce his "deadness":

"Did you ever see such a stupor as he falls into, between drink and sleep?" says Mr. Guppy.... It's always more like a fit than a nap.... Open your eyes!"

    After much ado, he opens them, but without appearing to see his visitors, or any other objects. Though he crosses one leg on another, and folds his hands, and several times closes and opens his parched lips, he seems to all intents and purposes as insensible as before. (Ch. XX)

Thus Dickens reinforces certain physical similarities in Krook and the vampire from folklore. Other similarities are more relevant though. Living amid the dead relics of the past, Krook resembles the vampire in his total indifference to the sufferings of others and in seeing other human beings only as components that may be useful to him. For example, when he admires Ada's hair, it is evident that he thinks of it only as a means of filling another sack for his shop instead of something contributing to her beauty. And he admits that, much as the vampire absorbs the blood of its victims, he absorbs the physical possessions of others:

"And I can't abear to part with anything I once lay hold of (or so my neighbors think, but what do they know?) or to alter anything, or to have any sweeping, nor scouring, nor cleaning, nor repairing going on about me. That's the way I've got the ill name of Chancery." (Ch. V)

A complete parasite, Krook absorbs everything around him without giving anything in return. It is this characteristic that, by his own admission and by the consensus of his neighbors, causes him to be equated with the most evil and destructive institution within *Bleak House*, the Court of Chancery.[27]

Krook is described as a vampire; and Chancery becomes, by analogy, a kind of macro-vampire that draws all people under its control. Both a symptom of the evil that plagues individuals and institutions and a symbol of it, Chancery lies at the center of the novel and manages to cast its malignant influence over many of the minor characters in *Bleak House*. Cursed by Gridley, Boythorne, and the narrator, it is actually compared to a vampire by the half-crazed Miss Flite:

"But, my dear," she went on, in her mysterious way, "there's a dreadful attraction in the place. Hush! Don't mention it to our diminutive friend when she comes in. Or it may frighten her. With good reason. There's a cruel attraction in the place. You can't leave it.... Draw people on, my dear. Draw peace out of them. Sense out of them. Good looks out of them. Good qualities out of them. I have felt them even drawing my rest away in the night. Cold and glittering devils!" (Ch. XXXV)

Although Miss Flite's perceptions of the world are clouded by her madness, Dickens lets the reader know that her personification of Chancery as a kind of demonic force is accurate by having it confirmed by other characters in the novel. For example, though other characters do not describe Chancery as a vampire, they show that, like the vampire, the court robs people of their health, their sanity, and eventually of life itself. Furthermore, like the vampire in both folklore and literature, Chancery gains control over people by a peculiar kind of hypnotic attraction.

There are other, more subtle resemblances between Chancery and the vampire that are only implied in *Bleak House* though Dickens may have had these similarities in mind when he wrote the novel. Both are relics of the past that refuse to abdicate their power over the present; and both are perversions of their former selves: the vampire a human body with none of the human capacities for love and compassion and tenderness, Chancery an agent of law and justice no longer capable of delivering either. Although the court had evolved in the fourteenth and fifteenth centuries because the Common Law was too rigid to handle civil suits such as trusts, wills, contracts, and disputes over property and had originally been instituted to decide cases on their merits rather than on the technicalities of the Common Law,[28] it had degenerated by the time Dickens wrote *Bleak House.* Cumbersome, inefficient, and overburdened with cases, it had become a travesty of its former self.

In addition, the vampire enables Dickens to explore one of his favorite themes—the way parents exploit their children.[29] The vampire in folklore was believed to return from the dead particularly to prey on the still-living members of its family. In similar fashion, Chancery, originally conceived as a protective institution for the wards under its authority, now exploits and destroys the people under its care; and a similar kind of exploitation occurs within individual families. Everywhere in the novel, parents feed upon their children, the dead upon the living, the old upon the young.[30] Thus, the hideous Smallweed family, which lives in a narrow street that is "closely bricked in on all sides *like a tomb*" (Ch. XXI, my italics) becomes a kind of caricature of all the families in the novel.[31] The only "child" in several generations, Grandmother Smallweed suffers all the indignities usually inflicted upon the naturally young. Mrs. Jellyby and Mrs. Pardiggle are committed to abstract values rather than to the immediate needs of their children. Chancery and old Turveydrop fail as parents because of their commitment to the past: Turveydrop to the Regency style and Chancery, because of its concern with wills and trusts, to the desires of the dead rather than to the needs of the living.

Although the Chancery suitors are particularly cursed by the demands of their ancestors, orientation to the past is a universal malaise in the novel. Lady Dedlock, John Jarndyce, and the Chancery suitors are all trapped by a past whose effect they cannot escape, their every action determined either by their own previous actions (in the case of the appropriately named Lady Dedlock) or by the action of some long-deceased ancestor. This predisposition results in inertia and the general inability to act, which are, according to Dickens, largely responsible for the gradual deterioration of the world. The final culmination of the world's evolution to filth and corruption is Tom-All-Alone's, Dickens's graphic symbol for man's failure to act.

If Vholes, Krook, and Chancery are actually described as vampires, *Bleak House* is also peopled with countless others who resemble the vampire because they are parasites or because their allegiance to the past obscures their perceptions of present needs. Simple parasites like Harold Skimpole and the ravenous Smallweed family merely rob others of their property while more complex parasites like Tulkinghorn—significantly described as never having been young[32]—seem determined to destroy their victims' will to live. On the other side of the coin are the perpetual victims like Caddy Jellyby's deaf-mute baby and the ignorant Jo. The world as Dickens portrays it in *Bleak House* seems to be divided into oppressors and oppressed, into parasites and those on whom the parasites feed. Thus, with a few exceptions, the vampire-victim relationship is an appropriate symbol of Dickens's view of society.

Though he is more concerned with describing a realistic social and moral state than with reproducing folklore, Dickens nonetheless maintains a close analogy between his predatory characters and the vampire from folklore. The analogy breaks down, however, when he attempts to provide an alternative to the exploitation he depicts. Vholes simply disappears from the story though not until after Richard's death. Krook's fiery death is a fine example of poetic justice, as well as a kind of magical attack on Chancery, but Dickens clearly does not expect the evils of his society to destroy themselves miraculously, by spontaneous combustion or by any other means. In fact, the beginning of the novel suggests that someone will have to destroy the evil that is Chancery:

If all the injustice it has committed, and all the misery it has caused, could only be locked up with it, and the whole burnt away in a great funeral pyre,—why so much the better for other parties than the parties in Jarndyce and Janrdyce! (Ch. I)

Just as it supposedly took someone with the appropriate ritual knowledge to exorcise the vampire, Dickens suggests that it will take someone with courage and fortitude to tackle all the evils that plague his society.

In *Bleak House*, no one is capable of destroying the dead past and setting up a new and fresh present as far as institutions such as Chancery are concerned. People in authority are corrupt and inefficient: the men who interpret the law are more concerned with technicalities than with justice; the men who make the laws are ineffectual; religion and philanthropy have forgotten the ideals of charity and seem bent on paper work rather than on desperately needed assistance; and families no longer have feelings of love and kindness for their weaker members.

Only on the individual level is there a glimmer of hope through characters who are capable of taking positive action—Mrs. Bagnet, Sir Leicester Dedlock, John Jarndyce, Allen Woodcourt, Esther, and Trooper George. However, they exert their influence on such a limited scale that the reader wonders whether they can make any lasting impact on the larger society.

Nonetheless, it is with these loving individuals that Dickens seems to place his faith, for they offer the only real alternative to the predation of the vampiric society. In fact, the scene in which Esther looks in the mirror after her illness suggests one way she differs from the vampire as it had been presented in folklore and earlier literature:

Then I put my hair aside, and looked at the reflection in the mirror.... I was very much changed.... At first, my face was so strange to me.... Very soon it became more familiar, and then I knew the extent of the alteration in it better than I had done at first.... I had never been a beauty, and had never thought myself one; but I had been very different from this. It was all gone now. Heaven was so good to me, that I could let it go with a few not bitter tears, and could stand there arranging my hair for the night quite thankfully. (Ch. XXXVI)

It is a scene very much unlike the mirror scenes in either *Wuthering Heights* or *Jane Eyre*, for Esther almost immediately recognizes herself despite significant physical changes.[33] Furthermore, unlike the vampiric Catherine Earnshaw, Esther is almost immediately reborn to a new life as a feminizing force within the novel. She is like Jane Eyre, who also escapes becoming a vampire, in that she gains strength by recognizing who she is and what she has to offer to the world.

What she has to offer are an orientation to the present instead of the past and a feminizing influence[34] that undermines some of the predation in the world immediately around her. Given both the lack of nurturing she received during her childhood and her illegitimacy, Esther should be either an outsider or a predator. However, because Dickens wants to demonstrate an alternative to the predation that surrounds her, Esther is neither. Unlike the third-person narrator, who remains a spectator and who sees only the death and decay of the present moment, Esther actively participates in the actions she describes. Moreover, she is committed both to the forces of life and to a future that is better than the present.

Even the names that she is given point both to her willingness to work for the future and to her femininity. Thus, she is Dame Durden, Old Woman, Little Old Woman, Mrs. Shipton, and Mother Hubbard— all names that imply domesticity rather than eroticism. There is, of course, more than one negative side to these names. As Michael Ragussis indicates, these names point to her lack of individual identity: symbolic names "no matter how appropriately they point to characteristics in Esther, seem finally to make more apparent that her true name is unknown."[35] Valerie Kennedy points to the fact that Esther's multiple names tend to obscure her identity completely:

Esther has no existence. Indeed Esther's identity, her very self, has a tendency to be totally absorbed by her role as Jarndyce's housekeeper, a state of affairs indicated by the fact that her own name is replaced by a variety of others....[36]

Certainly both Kennedy and Ragussis are correct to point to the significance of Esther's multiple names. However, because both are interested in her unique character, neither indicates how these names relate to her femaleness. Esther's lack of identity is compounded by her illegitimacy, but her apparent lack of identity is not far from the Victorian ideal. Women in the mid-Victorian period when Dickens wrote *Bleak House* were not expected to have too strong a sense of self, and they were expected to care for homes that they did not own. In fact, had Esther been legitimate, she would have carried her father's name, Hawdon, rather than one uniquely her own; and she apparently is known by her husband's name at the conclusion. Moreover, she admits that people know her as "the doctor's wife," a title that in one important way resembles all those nicknames, for it too emphasizes her function instead of her identity. Dickens, therefore, manipulates Esther's nicknames to highlight a common fact: women's names always deny their independent existence.

In addition, Esther's emotional responses to others (or her repeated attempts to repress emotional responses when her own life is concerned) help her fit the Victorian stereotype of femininity. She underlines the head/heart split by drawing the reader's attention to her lack of analytical skills, and she confesses that she is not clever except when her feelings are involved. While many critics have taken Esther's admission to mean that she is stupid or dishonest or lacking self-awareness, Dickens suggests that she is quite perceptive as far as individuals are concerned. (For example, she penetrates Harold Skimpole's mask and sees the kindly Boythorne beneath the gruff exterior.) Furthermore Esther's femininity (and George Eliot will explore the same behavior in Will and Dorothea, Mirah and Daniel Deronda) offers a positive alternative to the predation around her. While the third-person narrator sees only the dirt and squalor that the poor inhabit and thinks of them as a slightly higher form of dumb animal, Esther sympathizes with the human suffering she witnesses. While he merely describes the misery around him and provides no solution for it, Esther admits that she has difficulty keeping herself out of the narrative and attempts at all times to alleviate the pain she encounters. For example, she covers the dead child with her handkerchief and tries to soothe the grief-stricken mother; she nurses Jo in his illness; and she performs such homely tasks as washing Peepy and teaching Caddy how to bring order to her disorderly life. In all these cases, she sees only the individual's unhappiness instead of the universal misery that the third-person narrator describes;[37] and in each case she does what she can to eliminate the unhappiness she sees.

From beginning to end, Esther's narrative revolves around a small group of people. Because Dickens models her character on the Victorian ideal of womanhood, she is oriented to her various homes—her godmother's, the school where she learns to be a governess, John Jarndyce's Bleak House, the second Bleak House where she and Woodcourt set up housekeeping, and the *Bleak House* that she narrates—and to the people in the immediate environment. Hers is thus a restricted point of view that, as Leonard W. Deen explains, is "primarily about parents and children and their impoverished relationships."[38] Deen is accurate in his assessment, for Esther certainly does describe the bad families in the novel—the Jellybys, the Pardiggles and the Turveydrops, for example—and she even observes that the Lord Chancellor "appeared so poor a substitute for the love and pride of parents" (Ch. IV). Thus Esther rarely sees past the small family unit to the society beyond. However, because her point of view is restricted to the family and to individuals within the family, she also sees warmth and potential for growth: Caddy's love for her lame husband and her deaf-mute child, her Guardian's kindness, and the love that Ada and Richard share. It is a blissful (and somewhat simplistic) view of the world, one that sees only the beauty in the people she loves and that is therefore totally oblivious to the continuing misery in the surrounding society. Nonetheless, it does provide a kind of answer to the predation in the world around her.

Despite the simplicity of Esther's conclusion, a number of critics have argued that it resolves the problems depicted in *Bleak House*. John Kucich, for example, sees the conclusion as a type of progress:

...through Esther the novel builds a kind of attitudinal potency by developing a sexual transition that was hopelessly blocked in the beginning. Rather than merely repeating Lady Dedlock's frigidity, Esther has broken with it—warmly, generously—and has made her life what her first chapter title called it: "A Progress."[39]

Angus Wilson argues that "the contemporary idea of domestic happiness as the resolution of, or perhaps more fairly one should say, the counterpoise to social evil, was a strongly held personal conviction."[40] Wilson's view, though partially accurate, is an oversimplification of the world created by Dickens, however. Many of his novels do conclude with a happy domestic scene and with a woman who is responsible for ordering it (for example, Little Dorrit, Agnes in *David Copperfield*, Bella in *Our Mutual Friend*, and Esther). However, Dickens also indicates that this happiness is merely a personal solution for the privileged few rather than a "counterpoise to social evil." No other Dickens novel reveals this duality more clearly than *Bleak House*, with its two narrators and their separate stories. The notion of domestic happiness applies only to Esther and to the small group of people who are intimately connected to her. The social evil and grim despair described by the third-person narrator remain untouched by this domestic serenity.

In addition to combining the perceptions of two such radically different narrators, Dickens also combines realistic details—the surface texture of ordinary human life, social manners and customs, and plausible behavior—with fairy tale or Gothic elements—mystery, psychic intensity, and violent extremes of behavior.[41] In this respect, he employs much the same narrative strategy as Charlotte Bronte though Dickens's reliance on contemporary matters and realistic social details—his descriptions of London and his use of people and institutions that contemporary readers could readily recognize—rather than on the timeless is much more obvious. Moreover, as Harry F. Stone observes, Dickens weaves his unrealistic elements into what is "usually part of a captivating and compelling realism."[42] Thus, in the case of the vampire motif in *Bleak House*, he uses an exaggerated Gothic metaphor rather than a photographic description to reveal the social horrors of his own time.[43]

Certainly the "Author's Preface" to *Bleak House* suggests Dickens's interest in a recognizable social world, one that he expects his readers to comprehend. In fact, he is careful to point out that his depiction of Chancery is truthful rather than fictional:

...everything set forth in these pages concerning the Court of Chancery is substantially true, and within the truth. The case of Gridley is in no essential altered from one of actual occurrence, made public by a disinterested person who was professionally acquainted with the whole of the monstrous wrong from beginning to end.

However, the "Author's Preface" further explains Dickens's narrative strategy, for he also admits here that he "purposely dwelt upon the romantic side of familiar things."[44] In other words, Dickens clearly states that, despite his interest in truthful representation, he is offering more than photographic realism. In fact, the "Author's Preface" suggests that he intends to demonstrate to his readers that wonder and mystery and terror—all the excesses usually associated with the Gothic—are indeed part of their ordinary, everyday worlds.

Despite Dickens's own statements, the question of whether he *is* a realist has been much debated. Kucich, though he does not deal with the question specifically, seems to imply that he is. However, the best discussion of the issue is John Romano's *Dickens and Reality*, a work that begins by addressing the fact that Dickens is not generally regarded as a realist:

The question of what world Dickens drew upon has become moot in our consensus that the world he created and ceded to us in such bulk is an unreal and imaginary one.... There are real things in it, but they have been transmogrified in having gone the distance from the real world to Dickens' own.... His influence on writers normally regarded as realists...has been acknowledged for a long time. But the high critical estimate of Dickens' novels today is largely based on an appreciation of those aspects which are least realistic in the ordinary sense: their grotesquerie and "expressionism," their self-conscious symbolism and "myth-making" or their spiritual and artistic affinities with the "higher realism" of Dostoyevsky or the frank irreality of Kafka.[45]

Having commented on the current critical climate regarding Dickens, Romano goes on to argue that Dickens is a realist. One of the first bits of evidence he cites is Dickens's characters—often labeled caricatures or exaggerations rather than realistic depictions of ordinary human beings. To counter this view, Romano points to something the common reader is likely to sense: "More often than is commonly admitted, Dickens' 'exaggerations' are faithful imitations of reality's own exaggerated specimens."[46] Proof of this realism is the fact that Forster asked Dickens to modify his portrait of Harold Skimpole (modeled on Leigh Hunt) so that readers would not "attribute his moral qualities to Hunt as well." As a result, "Dickens toned down the portrayal, introduced traits which were not those of Leigh Hunt, and changed Skimpole's first name from Leonard to Harold."[47]

However, Romano argues that the most important characteristics of realistic fiction are not "verisimilitude or mimetic exactness" but "something teleological instead":

...their desire to suggest incrementally...the actuality of the outlying, formless real world.... The teleology has specific, recognizable consequences for the form of realist novels. The animating spark which eludes Venus' creations and the spiritualizing halo which Jenny cannot copy...suggest still more about the reality that form excludes. They suggest that what is excluded has, if recognized or "confessed" by form, the power to actualize, to vitalize, to "animate" what is contained; and, conversely, that where the exclusion of form is not confessed, what is contained is dead, inert, unreal, whatever its degree of verisimilitude. This is so because the excluded is precisely the locus of the larger, essential or primary reality on which the contents are dependent for their own reality.... It is recognition of this dependence, rather than verisimilitude, that constitutes the realism of the artistic whole.[48]

In other words, Romano demonstrates that Dickens solves the problem that, according to George Levine, "plagued realism from the start" and that is the "incompatibility of tight form with plausibility."[49] Thus Romano locates Dickens's realism in his artistic manipulation of details rather than in his ability to merely recreate nineteenth-century English society. Moreover, in attempting to convey the formlessness of the actual world, Dickens communicates a world of chaos and disorganization like the world that the reader knows.

Finally, Romano comes close to explaining the way that Dickens's use of Gothic metaphors actually contributes to his realism:

The real is only apprehended by art where its actuality is not diminished or swallowed up by a tedious exactitude of imitation, a tediously reasoned appropriateness of context...and we are not greatly wrong if we are reminded of it [Dickens's representation of reality] by Marianne Moore's metaphor for one relation of art to reality, "imaginary gardens with real toads in them," or of Lionel Trilling's incisive rejoinder to it: "Indeed, we have come to believe that the toad is the less real when the garden is also real."[50]

Thus Dickens chooses the vampire figure from folklore and Gothic literature to depict the horrors surrounding his ordinary middle-class readers, the horrors of economic exploitation and individual victimization—the material reality of their everyday lives—and to encourage them to *see* the reality of their own lives. It is the kind of transformation of Gothic details that George Levine argues is characteristic of nineteenth-century realism:

The monstrous, domesticated by Austen, exorcised by Scott, is, in Thackeray, transformed into banality (which occasionally, as in the story of Colonel Newcome, achieves an almost tragic intensity again). If Becky Sharp is occasionally perceived as a mermaid with skulls wound within her submerged tail, she is more often a clever social climber, an occasion for minor scandal, as she is seen, glancingly, even in *The Newcomes*.[51]

Transforming the monstrous figure of the vampire from folklore into a lawyer or the proprietor of a rag and bottle shop is precisely what Dickens does in *Bleak House*. As a result, Gothic details become an integral part of his realism.

Moving from *Bleak House* to *Middlemarch*, it is not difficult to see why George Eliot is generally classified as a realist, for her novels meet most of the characteristics ordinarily associated with realism: the emphasis on ordinary human life and commonplace characters—what D.A. Williams describes as "the undramatic, uneventful nature of the lives lived by the greatest number;"[52] the attention to the "physical and historical setting as well as to the social context;"[53] the attempt at scientific objectivity; the emphasis on content rather than form; and the translation of monstrous excesses into banalities. In fact, Patsy Stoneman, who discusses *Middlemarch* as an example of realism, observes that Eliot's narrative strategy was influenced by Lewes's scientific work:

Under the influence of this zoologizing [during a scientific holiday she spent with Lewes at Ilfracombe in 1856], she noted 'a tendency that is now constantly growing in me to escape from all vagueness and inaccuracy into the daylight of distinct, vivid ideas.' One of the articles written during this holiday was a review of two works by the German writer Wilhelm Heinrich Riehl...and George Eliot roundly praises his patience and accuracy in recording detailed observations.[54]

The result of Eliot's desire to "escape from all vagueness and inaccuracy" is a work that Stoneman likens to sociology with all characters chosen "as if they were a part of a sociological survey."[55]

Nonetheless, there is a growing tendency to see George Eliot as a different kind of realist and sometimes not as a realist at all. John McGowan begins his discussion in "The Turn of George Eliot's Realism" by referring to the current critical climate:

> George Eliot called her novels "realistic," but what she meant by "realism" and how successfully she practiced what she preached have been matters of controversy since her novels first appeared. In *George Eliot's Early Novels: The Limits of Realism*, U.C. Knoepflmacher offers the most extended consideration of Eliot's break with her own "realistic" dicta to present "ideal" characters shaped to serve the author's moral concerns. For Knoepflmacher, realism, defined as a writer's presentation of the actual and commonplace, is still a possible undertaking; he only wishes to argue that George Eliot is not one of the writers who is most faithful to the task realism sets itself.[56]

McGowan, who goes on to discuss various deconstructionist views of Eliot, nonetheless argues that Eliot is a realist who was "well aware that the work of art is not reality itself, and yet she still believed that something which she called realism was not only possible but was the proper task of the novelist."[57]

Nonetheless, many of the people who discuss Eliot as a realist are forced to confess that she is a particular kind of realist, one for whom the standard categories do not fit. Stoneman, for example, argues that "what seems to be the Realists' first priority—'rigorous objectivity'— will not take us very far in understanding *Middlemarch*:

> George Eliot's 'objectivity' is itself motivated by an ethical intention, and even historically formulated problems in the novel are given an ethical solution, in terms of inter-personal relations, of the individual's 'heroic effort' towards an objective/subjective balance, and an integration of disparate experience.[58]

In fact, both Williams and Stoneman discuss the way that Eliot's emphasis on morality influences her narrative strategy:

> Both George Eliot and Balzac break with the Realist canon of impersonal detachment by allowing themselves the same freedom as Fielding who, in George Eliot's words, 'seems to bring his armchair to the proscenium and chat with us in all the lusty ease of his fine English.'[59]

In fact, Stoneman even coins a phrase—'moral' Realism—to characterize Eliot's unique narrative strategy:

> In practice, this 'moral' Realism differs from a supposed photographic Realism mainly in the selection of material, not in its treatment, although it certainly predisposed George Eliot to retain the intrusive method of narration, which allowed her to draw attention to the morally important aspects of her story.[60]

This emphasis on morality rather than on objectivity distinguishes Eliot's novels from novels in the Continental tradition of realism.

Eliot's work within the realistic tradition and the way she differs from the often somber or disillusioned realists at the end of the century is most easily seen, however, in a careful analysis of *Middlemarch*. Outlining her plans for *Middlemarch* in a letter to John Blackwood, Eliot explains that she intends to "show the gradual action of ordinary causes rather than exceptional;"[61] and the novel that she subtitled "A Study of Provincial Life" depicts a cross-section of English society in the years that precede the 1832 Reform Bill. However, into this realistic world she introduces a Gothic motif, the vampire, four times—twice specifically and twice by rather pointed suggestion. Although the vampire initially seems out of place—a mythic figure in an otherwise realistic novel,[62]—by looking carefully at Eliot's use of the vampire motif, the reader quickly discovers that she ignores the vampire's supernatural traits and focuses on its predatory nature and amoral behavior as specifically human possibilities. Thus, she uses the vampire to achieve a heightened realism, provides the reader with a glimpse into the darkness that lies within the most prosaic characters, and enables the reader to see that horror, cruelty, and the exploitation of others are a part of daily existence. In fact, Levine illustrates the horrors of ordinary life when he observes that *Middlemarch* is an extremely violent novel, full of "murders, riots, blackmail and briberies, political rhetoric, deaths,"[63] in other words, the ordinary kind of violence that fills the daily newspaper.

This section will study Eliot's use of the vampire motif and show how the power of the original mythic image is altered in *Middlemarch*. Furthermore, it will demonstrate that Eliot transfers the "once objective world of myth and romance into the subjective consciousness of man," thereby achieving what J. Hillis Miller calls the "change from traditional literature to a modern genre like the novel," which is the result of man's growing disbelief in anything greater or more powerful than himself.[64] Finally, it will focus on Eliot's concern with the world in which she lived: her preoccupation with the destructiveness of egoism and her belief that mankind could conquer such pernicious behavior.

Like other nineteenth-century writers—the Brontes, Dickens, and Bram Stoker—Eliot uses the superstitious belief in blood-sucking ghosts as a metaphor of the ways human beings prey on one another, ruining the happiness and sometimes the lives of their victims. However—whether because of her atheism, her penchant for creating plausible human situations, or for some other reason—Eliot handles the motif somewhat differently from other nineteenth-century writers. As a result, her vampires are plausible human characters rather than romantic figures whose desires are not confined by social mores or legal restrictions.[65] Thus, by eliminating the primal violence and mystery that characterize the vampire in both folklore and in earlier literary works, Eliot moves away from myth and romance and reveals that true vampires are ordinary human beings who can be held responsible for their actions; and the realism with which she presents her vampires makes their destructive behavior at once more understandable and yet more horrifying than the insane blood lust of Bertha Mason. Moreover, Eliot carefully delineates the causes of such predatory behavior and points to the social conditions that reinforce it. Like Dickens, she suggests that if society is to overcome the power and unbridled aggression that characterize the vampiric society, it must emphasize the characteristics that society regards as feminine, such as self-sacrifice, affection, and tolerance.[66]

The first reference to the vampire establishes Eliot's concern with the lives of ordinary human beings. Early in the novel, the narrator briefly sketches the community's reaction to Bulstrode:

There were many crass minds in Middlemarch...and they had a strong suspicion that since Mr. Bulstrode could not enjoy life in their fashion, eating and drinking so little as he did, and worrying himself about everything, he must have a sort of *vampire's feast* in the sense of mastery. (Ch. XVI, my italics)

Later events indicate that these "crass minds" are correct in their suspicions. Bulstrode is a kind of vampire, not because he is openly violent, inhuman, or irrational like the vampire from folklore, but because he is a morally and emotionally incomplete person, a "dead" man who preys on others. He is not literally a bloodsucker, but cheating Ladislaw's mother of her inheritance is both destructive and predatory. He is not a murderer, but he deliberately ignores Lydgate's warning and is, therefore, directly responsible for the death of Raffles. (Eliot underlines the connection in this scene by describing Bulstrode as having "the air of an animated corpse returned to movement without warmth" [Ch. LXX].) Moreover, Eliot uses the fact that Bulstrode represents a relatively new profession—banking—to show how he gains power and control over others:[67]

Mr. Bulstrode's power was not due simply to his being a country banker, who knew the financial secrets of most traders in the town and could touch the springs of their credit; it was fortified by a beneficence that was at once ready and severe—ready to confer obligations and severe in watching the result. He had gathered...a chief share in administering the town charities, and his private charities were both minute and abundant.... In this way a man gathers a domain in his neighbours' hope and fear as well as gratitude; and power...propagates itself, spreading out of all proportion to its external means. It was a principle with Mr. Bulstrode to gain as much power as possible, that he might use it for the glory of God. (Ch. XVI)

Furthermore, while Bulstrode has the power of a relatively new profession, he also—as many professionals and industrialists did in the nineteenth century—knew that he must acquire land. Stoneman observes this fact:

...Bulstrode, who shows the grossest dislocation between ideals and income, buys Stone Court in order to throw 'more conspicuously on the side of Gospel truth the weight of local landed proprietorship'.... In a society where unearned income was the norm for an influential class of people, such dislocation must be endemic.[68]

Although Eliot reveals the ways that Bulstrode gains power over others, she does not stress his demonic or sinister traits as Dickens emphasizes those of Tulkinghorn or Vholes. Therefore her concern with realism ensures that Bulstrode remains a weak and deeply flawed human being— a man whose selfishness produces evil—rather than a mythic and superhuman figure of Evil.

Eliot continues to emphasize the ordinary humanity of her vampiric characters; and when the motif appears for the second time, it is in an equally mundane setting. Disenchanted with her life, Rosamond muses on the man she had married: "The habits of Lydgate's profession, his home preoccupation with scientific subjects, which seemed to her *almost like a morbid vampire's taste*, his peculiar views of things...would have made his presence dull to her" (Ch. LXIV). Rosamond's reverie reveals that she has read the journalistic accounts of the day, for it resembles the arguments of many nineteenth-century thinkers who attempted to explain the belief rationally by attributing vampirism to premature burial, disease, or grave robbing. Similarly, another passage from the novel suggests that other residents of Middlemarch were aware of grave robbing:

If that was not reason, Mrs. Dollop wished to know what was; but there was a prevalent feeling in her audience that her opinion was a bulwark, and that if it were overthrown there would be no limits to the cutting-up of bodies, as had been well seen in Burke and Hare. (Ch. LXV)

William Burke and William Hare murdered a number of people and sold their bodies to a medical school. Burke was hanged in 1829; and Eliot, in her search for historically relevant materials, must have learned about these two real vampires.

Rosamond is less emotional than Mrs. Dollop; and as her thoughts shift from repugnance to boredom, Eliot suggests that such cool scientific explanations destroy both the truth and the horror of the original mythic figure—the fact that people *do* prey on one another. Like the "crass minds" who compared Bulstrode to a vampire, Rosamond is correct in her analysis of Lydgate—but for the wrong reason. Blaming Lydgate's profession—the most noble and philanthropic part of the young physician—for the destruction of her happiness, she fails to understand that Lydgate resembles a vampire not because of his scientific interest in cadavers and other subjects that seem morbid to her, but because his relationships with other people are parasitic and exploitative. These destructive tendencies become most evident in Eliot's careful analysis of the Lydgates' marriage. She reveals that Lydgate marries Rosamond because he believes her beauty and accomplishments will be a pleasant diversion from his rigorous intellectual endeavors. Furthermore, she shows that, from the beginning of his marriage, Lydgate clearly means to be in control, to issue orders as from some regal perogative. That he typically sees women as objects to be manipulated and believes his wife to be "of another and feebler species" (Ch. LXV) goes far to explain his inability to relate to others and his unwillingness to become an active participant in life. Like Grandcourt, his even more exploitative successor, he is cold, detached, sterile. Failing to see Rosamond as a human being with a will of her own, he quickly becomes abusive when he realizes that she will not sacrifice her own wishes to minister to his needs. However, unlike the extreme cruelty and violence of the vampire of folklore or even the sadistic fascination and power that Tulkinghorn exerts over Lady Dedlock or Jasper against Rosa Bud,[69] petty forms of cruelty such as sarcasm and indifference are Lydgate's weapons. Thus, in the shift from physical violence and cruelty to psychological abuse, Eliot transfers the formerly objective world of myth and folklore into the subjective and interpersonal relationships of the realistic novel.

The Finale reveals that Lydgate sees Rosamond as a kind of vampire also, as a parasite who is destroying his happiness and his life: "He once called her his basil plant; and when she asked for an explanation, said that basil was a plant which had flourished wonderfully on a murdered man's brains" (Finale). He had married her because she resembled a beautiful and fragile flower; but he later comes to see the noxious cannibalism of his exotic flower.[70] She is—as one contemporary reviewer described her—"a kind of well-conducted domestic vampire."[71] However—despite T.S. Eliot's confession that she frightens him "far more than Goneril or Regan"[72]—Rosamond bears little resemblance to the hideous and inhuman creature of folklore or even to the insane, semi-human Bertha Mason, for both her cruelty and her violence are psychological, not physical. As Stoneman observes, however, these characteristics are no less deadly:

Rosamond is an unmitigated egoist...an example of the aggressive instinct in spite of her passive behaviour, showing 'that victorious obstinacy which never wastes its energy in impetuous resistance'...and she effectually destroys her husband, who attempts to co-operate and has to end by yielding.[73]

Like Bulstrode and Lydgate, she resembles the vampire of folklore in very subtle ways—for example, in her indifference to the suffering she causes in others, her unremitting egoism, and her emotional and intellectual sterility; and she is like Bulstrode in yet one more way—the fact that she is an economic predator. However, Rosamond's economic predation is sanctioned by social values that prohibit middle-class women from contributing to the family economy or even from understanding economic matters. (Mary Garth and her mother are the only exceptions in *Middlemarch*, and they are pitied by other characters because they have had to work.)

Although Eliot displaces the mythic vampire by making Rosamond an ordinary human woman, she also reminds the reader of the vampire's origins in folklore. Not only is Rosamond an economic bloodsucker, she is also a sexual predator, who ensnares the young physician and ultimately causes his death. (That Lydgate is susceptible to sexually attractive women is also revealed by his past affair with Madame Laure.)

Several mythic allusions draw the reader's attention to Rosamond's potential for cruel and destructive behavior, but Eliot (like Thackeray, who employs the same technique with such success in *Vanity Fair*[74]) uses these allusions ironically to heighten her realism and to focus on Rosamond's ordinary human weaknesses. As a result, her actions are still horrifying, but not in the mysterious and incomprehensible manner of similar characters in Gothic novels. For example, when Farebrother compares her to the sirens, the Homeric monsters whose beautiful singing lured sailors to their deaths, the reader sees Rosamond's singing as the product of Mrs. Lemon's guidance and as an attempt at coy seductiveness rather than as a fearful and overwhelming power. Later, when the narrator compares her to the daughters of Zion, women whose pride and wantonness Isaiah said would be responsible for the fall of Jerusalem, the reader is also able to put Rosamond's pride into its proper perspective. Although aware of her accomplishments and eager for men to desire her, Rosamond is responsible merely for domestic discord and financial embarrassment, not for the crumbling of an entire civilization. Finally, when Lydgate compares her to basil, the vampire plant that feeds on dead men's brains, the reader knows that Lydgate is simply trying to add moral significance to a petty domestic situation, for there is no mythic grandeur or tragic significance to anything the Lydgates do. They are ordinary people, and it is their ordinary traits that make them so horrifying.

By diminishing the vampire's mythic power and concentrating on the kinds of petty cruelty with which her all-too-human characters destroy the lives of others, Eliot focuses the reader's attention on recognizable social evils, particularly on the evils produced by egoism. Throughout her novels, she typically presents egoists as emotionally and mentally incomplete human beings, who are so entirely preoccupied with their own needs that they become responsible for the deaths of those around him (deaths which, although frequently metaphorical rather than literal, are no less real), an obvious analogy to the vampire.[75] According to folklore, the vampire's sole motivation was an insatiable physical need to drink the blood of others, thereby prolonging its own existence; and the egoist is also a monomaniac who manipulates other people to gratify its own desires, a parasite who robs others of their mental and emotional vitality, and a sterile and destructive human being.

Although Eliot generally presents egoism as a crime of individual against individual, she also suggests that the egoism of one individual can have far-reaching consequences that sometimes affect entire groups of people. This is the case with Bulstrode, Vincy, and Brooke, whose positions in the community give them both a great deal of power over their social inferiors and the ability to exploit those social inferiors. (In fact, the reader might identify the three men as representing three of the primary sources of social, economic, and political power in the early nineteenth century, with Bulstrode representing commerce and Evangelical Christianity, Vincy representing industry, and Brooke representing the landowning class. Moreover, the close family relationship between Bulstrode and Vincy—Bulstrode had married Vincy's sister—and the ties between industry and financial backing reveals yet another subtle source of power.) At Peter Featherstone's funeral, Mrs. Cadwallader characterizes Mr. Vincy as a vampire, describing him to Sir James as "one of those who suck the life out of the wretched handloom weavers in Tipton and Freshitt. That is how his family look so fair and sleek" (Ch. XXXVI). A generally comic character, Mrs. Cadwallader is a gossip, a busybody, and a woman who clearly knows the value of money. As a woman with aristocratic connections, she can also be expected to look down on people in manufacturing or trade even when that trade had been established for "three generations, in which there had naturally been much intermarrying with neighbours more or less decidedly genteel" (Ch. XI). Nonetheless she is often perceptive about people; and this time her description of Vincy resembles that of Engels, who also used the vampire motif to condemn the irresponsible behavior of the capitalist class.[76] Thus, Mrs. Cadwallader condemns Vincy both as an individual and as a representative of his class, a judgment that is confirmed by his behavior throughout the novel. As an individual, Vincy is thoughtless and ineffectual rather than deliberately cruel. More concerned with the external trappings of life than he is with its inner complexity, he is a gracious host and a loving (although often insensitive) husband and father. Consequently, the reader who does not analyze his character is likely to see a harmless buffoon rather than a bloodsucker.

However, Eliot also suggests that the traits that make him a likeable individual are more serious when one considers him as a representative of the new industrial class. Like Mr. Brooke, he is a comic character only so long as the reader ignores the social implications of his thoughtless behavior and forgets the real power that Vincy has over the lives of others.

Eliot, who carefully researched the period about which she wrote in *Middlemarch*, presents both an interesting individual portrait and a typical textile manufacturer. As a manufacturer, Vincy is suffering serious financial difficulties (whether caused entirely by Plymdale's inferior dyes or by a change in fashion away from ribbon to lace[77] and lets his daughter know that he cannot lend money to her husband:

'Papa said he had come, with one bad year after another, to trade more and more on borrowed capital, and had had to give up many indulgences: he could not spare a single hundred from the charges of his family.' (Ch. LXVII)

Nonetheless, the Mayor of Middlemarch is shown to be comfortably well off compared to the "wretched hand-loom weavers" that Mrs. Cadwallader mentions, a group that the social historian Asa Briggs describes as the "worst-off section of the working-class population."[78] E.P. Thompson adds, moreover, that the decline of this group took place in two stages:

The first, up to 1830 or 1835 [the industrial revolution in the silk required for Vincy's ribbons preceded that in cotton and wool], in which power was a creeping ancillary cause, although it bulked more largely in psychological terms (and was, in this sense, a lever in reducing wages); the second, in which power actually displaced hand products. It was in the first phase that the major reductions in wages...took place.[79]

Knowing about the history of textile manufacturing allows us to infer that the hand-loom weavers who worked for Vincy would have already suffered a serious decline in real earning power. Furthermore, Vincy, who is revealed to be in serious financial difficulties, is at the point where the typical manufacturer would have had to mechanize his factory or go under. Nonetheless, as Thompson reveals, many manufacturers took stop-gap measures that served to further the decline of the hand-loom weavers:

When markets were sluggish, manufacturers took advantage of the situation by putting out work to weavers desperate for employment at any price, thereby compelling them "to manufacture great quantities of goods at a time, when they are absolutely not wanted." With the return of demand, the goods were then released on the market at cut price; so that each minor recession was succeeded by a period in which the market was glutted with cheap goods thereby holding wages down to their recession level.[80]

With the exception of borrowing money from Bulstrode, Vincy's business strategies are not revealed. Thus, the reader never knows for certain whether Vincy is as exploitative as the manufacturers that Thompson mentions or even whether Vincy plans to install power equipment in his factory. Nonetheless, Vincy the individual is portrayed as being more concerned with his own problems than with those of others. Certainly he reveals no evidence that he is aware of the existence of the men who work for him or of the fact that it is their labor that enables him to play the gracious host. Therefore, the reader suspects that Mrs. Cadwallader may be correct in asserting that Vincy and his family are "fair and sleek" because they never think of the men who work for them, never realize their dependence on them, and treat their laborers as poorly as Brooke treats his tenents.

In *Middlemarch*, four characters are portrayed as vampires and others, because they are self-centered and incomplete human beings, might be classified as vampires as well. What, according to Eliot, causes people to prey on one another? The following passage explains the origin of individual egoism and provides a brief synopsis of the egoist's transformation from predator to contributor:

We are all of us born in moral stupidity, taking the world as an udder to feed our supreme selves: Dorothea had early begun to emerge from that stupidity, but yet it had been easier...to imagine how she could devote herself to Mr. Casaubon, and become wise and strong in his strength and wisdom, than to conceive with that distinctness which is no longer reflection but feeling...that he had an equivalent centre of self, whence the lights and shadows must always fall with a certain difference. (Ch. XXII)

Just as the vampire can be destroyed by a stake through the heart (or by some other act of ritual violence), egoists must experience a kind of death in the recognition that they are small and powerless; and the death of the egoistic self leads to the rebirth of an emotionally, mentally, and morally complete human being. Dorothea experiences this kind of self-recognition when she looks from her bedroom window and realizes that she is a "part of that involuntary, palpitating life" and cannot "look out on it from her luxurious shelter as a mere spectator, nor hide her eyes in selfish complaining" (Ch. LXXX). Furthermore Eliot suggests that all egoists are capable of this kind of rebirth.

Not all egoists experience this rebirth, however; and the reader must understand that certain factors reinforce egoism and prevent characters like Rosamond from experiencing moral and spiritual regeneration. Eliot is justifiably critical of Rosamond's emotional and intellectual vacuity, but she also reveals that Rosamond and others are trained to be egoists and that this training causes them to lack strength of character or sincere interest in others. In fact, the following description shows that

Rosamond's education encouraged narcissism and a kind of vampiric behavior:[81]

She was admitted to be the flower of Mrs Lemon's school, the chief school in the county, where the teaching included all that was demanded in the accomplished female—even to extras, such as the getting in and out of a carriage. Mrs Lemon herself had always held up Miss Vincy as an example: no pupil, she said, exceeded that young lady for mental acquisition and propriety of speech, while her musical execution was quite exceptional. (Ch. XI)

Like Gwendolyn Harleth—whose "lamia beauty" reminds the reader of her vampiric character—Blanche Ingram, and Dickens' Dora Copperfield, Rosamond is clearly a paragon within the society she inhabits. Not only does Mrs. Lemon praise Rosamond's accomplishments and intelligence, but all the men in Middlemarch admire these qualities in her. That these qualities are inadequate preparation for anything but the most sheltered drawing room is something that Gwendolyn eventually discovers and Dora suspects. Rosamond, however, is never enabled to discover her limitations, so she continues blithely destroying the lives of those around her.

While *Middlemarch* shows the dire results of such training on individuals, one of Eliot's early essays suggests that the entire society suffers from women's being trained to be idle parasites:

Men pay a heavy price for their reluctance to encourage self-help and independent resources in women. The precious meridian years of many a man of genius have to be spent in the toil of routing, that an 'establishment' may be kept up for a woman who can understand none of his secret yearnings, who is fit for nothing but to sit in her drawing-room like a doll-Madonna in her shrine. No matter. Anything is more endurable than to run the risk of looking up to our wives instead of looking down on them...and so men say of women, let them be idols, useless absorbents of precious things, provided we are not obliged to admit them to be strictly fellow-beings to be treated, one and all, with justice and sober reverence.[82]

Prevented from contributing to the society in which they live, idle, helpless, and destructive, many women come to resemble vampires, who suck vitality from those around them.

Eliot suggests that women resemble vampires because nineteenth-century education prepares them to be nothing but pampered and protected parasites. In men, the vampiric character originates elsewhere. For example, when readers look at Vincy, Bulstrode, Lydgate, and Grandcourt, they see men who—like Lord Ruthven—have considerable power over others because of their economic and social position and who are willing to exert that power to achieve their desires. In men, the will to power is always present although the specific reason for exerting that power differs from individual to individual.

The difference in men vampires and women vampires continues to exist throughout nineteenth and twentieth-century literature and popular culture. In fact, because of the continued emphasis on physical strength, men vampires remain closer to their bestial origins in folklore. Women vampires in literature are more diversified. Certainly in the nineteenth century, when the roles permitted to women were more narrow, it was comparatively easy to create a threatening image of women. Literally anything that violated the norm could be made frightening.

Eliot's exploration of the vampire motif is especially topical. According to her, many women behave like vampires because—living in a society that does not allow them to provide for themselves—they must become parasites while men behave like vampires when they are granted unlimited power over the lives of others. Thus, in comparing certain men and women to vampires, Eliot comes to grips with the social ideal of "Separate Spheres" so frequently celebrated by Victorian writers. According to proponents of this philosophy, the lives of men and women must be rigidly defined. Men were to concern themselves with the external world of business, politics, and industry and to cultivate the "manly virtues" of assertiveness, intelligence, strength, ambition, and power over others. Women, on the other hand, were to be concerned with the inner domestic world and to develop such "feminine" characteristics as obedience, tenderness and passivity. Regarded as the "weaker sex," they were protected from the harsh realities of the world outside their homes and were to be—in the words of Coventry Patmore—"angels in the house." Although such ideal separation of roles might work in theory, Eliot is a realist who is concerned with things as they were in practice. She reveals that absolute power over others may produce patronizing treatment and exploitation rather than a sincere desire to protect. Furthermore, her portrayal of Rosamond reveals the ugly side of the angelic Victorian woman. Like Dora Copperfield, her comic counterpart, Rosamond knows so little about the world of everyday realities that her only response to impending financial ruin can be helpless tears and the infuriating "What can I do?"[83]

By presenting the Lydgate marriage as a mutually destructive relationship, Eliot exposes the tragedy of "Separate Spheres" and condemns a society that encourages the close personal relationship of two people who can neither understand the hopes nor sympathize with the dreams of each other. In fact, Eliot shows that "Separate Spheres" provide an important source of marital difficulties when the narrator observes, "Poor Lydgate! or shall I say, poor Rosamond! Each lived in a world of which the other knew nothing" (Ch. XVII). Like Vincy and his laborers, Brooke and his tenants, Rosamond and Lydgate might as well inhabit separate worlds, for neither is capable of understanding the other's point of view. His interests are medical and professional, concerns which she cannot understand and which she finds distasteful, even morbid. Lydgate, on the other hand, cannot understand her interest in aristocratic manners or her boredom. The result is that each constantly thwarts the other's desires.

Such narrow training places limitations on human capabilities and creates people who are incomplete, rigid, and ignorant of others. Relationships between such incomplete people—particularly if these people are also egoistic and insensitive to others—are bound to result in failure, frustration, and hatred, for they are unions of people who are attempting to imbibe sustenance from others.

Although Eliot—like Dickens and the Brontes—is concerned with social issues, she generally avoids large political confrontations and concentrates on private experiences (even Mr. Brooke's disastrous try for Parliament focuses largely on the private aspect of his attempt), focusing especially on the institution of marriage; and it is within marriage that the social implications of the vampire motif become eminently clear. A microcosm of the larger society, marriage reveals the relation of vampire and victim, master and slave, more clearly perhaps than a similar rendering of the relationship between master and hand, landlord and tenant.

Unlike so many Victorian novels, which present the marriage of hero and heroine as the culmination of a long and arduous struggle, a reward as it were for fulfilling social obligations, Eliot explores marriage as the "beginning of the home epic" and as a condition that affects most of the people in her world. Within these variations of the "home epic," the Casaubons, the Lydgates, the Chettams, the Vincys, the Garths, and the Bulstrodes become analogues for one another, their similarities emphasized by both imagery and by the novel's structure.[84]

Although the Lydgate's marriage is the most extreme example of a failed marriage, with each partner draining the other of vitality, the Casaubon marriage is also destructive. Dorothea marries the middle-aged scholar because she hopes to devote herself to a great cause and because she wants to escape the "gentlewoman's oppressive freedom." Casaubon, on the other hand, marries Dorothea because he desires someone who will bolster his confidence, act as his secretary, minister to his needs, and enable him to conform to society's expectations. The essence of both marriages is parasitism.

There are, of course, marriages in which neither partner resembles the vampire; and the marriages that Eliot portrays as positive, non-destructive relationships are dominated by neither the masculine nor the feminine partner. Among these happy marriages are the elder Garths, Fred and Mary, the Chettams, and Dorothea and Will. In these marriages, the women, although not economically self-sufficient in the modern sense, are contributors to the marital partnership and share in their husbands' lives outside the home. Furthermore, both Celia and Mrs. Garth are respected by their husbands; their opinions are valued, their advice sought. Thus, instead of being power struggles between opposing forces, these marriages encourage both partners to develop to their full potential. The final chapter, in which Eliot summarizes the future lives of her young characters, draws special attention to the happy relationship of Fred and Mary and establishes them as a kind of model partnership. Without romanticizing them or diminishing the real hardships that they must face and overcome, she portrays a working and loving relationship in which each partner benefits and learns from the other. The reader, therefore, understands that in Eliot's happy marriages (and by analogy in other close human relationships) women are not forced to be idle and useless parasites, condemned to exist always on the periphery of history. Instead, they are esteemed individuals whose intelligence is recognized and who contribute something of value to the world in which they live.

In addition, the reader also observes that the men in these relationships are neither overtly aggressive and domineering nor exploiters of others. In fact, Will, Fred, Caleb, and Sir James have some traits that are generally perceived to be feminine (by the Victorians if not by men and women of our own day) and are characterized by a degree of gentleness, tolerance, and sympathy not found in other male characters. Will is portrayed as childlike and unassuming with a love for children and a tolerance for absurd people and situations, a man who "entered every one's feelings, and could take the pressure of their thought instead of urging his own with iron resistance" (Ch. L). The words are Dorothea's, but the praise seems to be Eliot's as well, for she gives her final paean to Will when she portrays his successful entry into public life. As a legislator, he is one of the people to whom the reader can attribute the "growing good of the world."

In her final novel, Eliot develops the characteristics that had been merely suggested in Will into predominant aspects of Daniel Deronda's character, just as she develops Lydgate's negative and exploitative qualities in the reptilian Grandcourt. She describes Daniel as "moved by an affectionateness such as we are apt to call feminine, disposing him to yield in ordinary details, while he had a certain inflexibility of judgment, an independence of opinion, held to be rightfully masculine."[85] Eliot suggests that, just as in happy and productive marriages, the healthy individual manages to unite rigorous intellectual discipline with affection and devotion; and both *Middlemarch* and *Daniel Deronda* conclude with such complete individuals seeking to make a new history, a history that will not be dependent on the exploitation of others.

Eliot's handling of the question of history has been debated by a number of recent literary critics, including Brian Rosenberg, Sara Moore Putzell, Joy W. Hooton, Bonnie Zimmerman, and Patsy Stoneman.[86] While Putzell observes that Eliot locates value in history, Zimmerman argues that Eliot's celebration of Dorothea and Will is an "unconvincing answer to the questions of historical change":

> The primary movement of history rests not in finely touched spirits, but in the background of *Middlemarch*: in Reform bills and Chartism, the coming of the railroads, the development of modern capital accumulation, Benthamite social welfare schemes, and also those changes in productive, reproductive and sexual forces that severely challenged assumptions about the female role and opened new possibilities and fields of endeavor to the nineteenth-century woman.[87]

To argue in this way is to misread *Middlemarch*, however, for Eliot does not imply that Dorothea and others like her are entirely responsible for meliorating the harsh conditions of the world. In fact, her final praise of Dorothea simply recognizes the contributions of people whom history generally ignores:

> "...the growing good of the world is *partly dependent on unhistoric acts*; and that things are not so ill with you and me...is *half owing* to the number who lived faithfully a hidden life, and rest in unvisited tombs" (Finale, my italics).

Presumably, the other half is due to those larger historical events to which Zimmerman alludes.

Middlemarch is the history of "unhistoric lives," of people whose epic goals are thwarted by circumstances, and of those who never aspire toward those epic goals. It is an exploration of the common, the mundane, and the ordinary. By crediting people like Dorothea and Will with an improvement in the human condition, however, Eliot implies that readers should re-evaluate their notions of history and understand that it is not simply a record of the lives and actions of great men.[88] To encourage the reader to start thinking about the concept of history, Eliot begins the novel with a question: "Who that cares much to know the history of man, and how the mysterious mixture behaves under the varying experiments of Time, has not dwelt, at least briefly, on the life of Saint Theresa...?" (Prelude). The answer to that question should be obvious to any student of history.[89] Dominated by the accomplishments of powerful men, history prior to the twentieth century ignores the very presence of women, overlooks men like Brooke's tenant Dagley and Vincy's factory workers,[90] and celebrates the deeds of men like Cincinnatus, the hero of the younger Garth children; and Eliot suggests that the history of her own time will also record events in a world ruled by men. In such a world, men like Brooke can have authority over the lives of others, can run for political office and conquer empires, but women like Dorothea can live only on the periphery of history and men like Dagley exist only as nameless victims. In its emphasis on ordinary people and events, *Middlemarch* provides the reader with a more expansive version of human history and shows that ordinary people are not without historical importance. This "serious treatment of everyday reality, the rise of more extensive and socially inferior groups to the subject for problematic-existential representation," according to Erich Auerbach, constitutes modern realism[91] just as Eliot's willingness to abandon mythic figures and possibilities distinguishes her from many of her contemporaries.

Middlemarch portrays the rulers of this period as vampiric characters, sucking the blood of others. Acutely aware of the problem, Eliot is clearly dissatisfied with her society's attempts to alleviate it; and her novel conveys her deep distrust of broad political reform programs—indeed her distrust of any program that tries to offer a single solution to a complex problem. Whether the question is Casaubon's search for a key to all mythologies, Dorothea's attempts to recreate pastoral England for her uncle's tenants, or a proposed shift in the national political structure, Eliot portrays these attempts at reform as misleading, duplicitous, harmful—primarily because they obscure the complexity of the problem and the interconnections between human beings. Her distrust of various reform programs, however, does not make her the smug conservative that many of her critics deride, for—like Dickens— she shifts away from the sphere of national politics to the private sphere. Instead of surveying the entire society, she scrutinizes the lives of ordinary people and reveals alternatives to the parasitic and exploitataive relationships that she sees.

The reader soon realizes that Eliot—like Dickens—is working toward a fictional alternative to the world which she portrays as ruled by vampires like Vincy, Bulstrode, and Brooke—men who exert their influence by exploiting and oppressing others and by destroying the happiness and sometimes even the lives of those who oppose them. In this she differs from LeFanu, the Brontes and Stoker, who cannot envision a world devoid of vampire and victim; and she portrays a world in which heart and head, subjectivity and objectivity, masculine and feminine combine to produce a society that is moving toward something radically different from that with which her readers were familiar.

Although Eliot unites masculine and feminine elements in many of her characters, her women characters—as numerous critics have pointed out—are not as strong or as wise as Eliot herself. Furthermore, many of these critics have argued that this failure proves her lack of sympathy with women's endeavors.[92] However, it might also be argued that the same criticism could be leveled against her men characters, for what reader can find in Adam Bede, Felix Holt, Will, or even Daniel Deronda the same fountains of wisdom that one finds in her omniscient narrators?

In fact, to criticize Eliot for not creating characters who are paragons of strength and wisdom is to deny the conventions of the realistic novel and to judge it by standards established in myth or romance. Too committed to a belief in plausible presentation to provide apocalyptic solutions to the problems that confronted her society, she would model neither heroines nor heroes on her own exceptional life. Instead, because she means to write the history of unexceptional men and women, she emphasizes the very ordinary qualities of her characters' lives.

Even with Eliot's predilection for the prosaic, however, her women stand out as characters of immense energy and vitality. While most critics of Eliot belittle or ignore her feminist sentiments, I believe that it is important to conclude this discussion with a look at her relationship to nineteenth-century feminism, and to understand how she differs from the mainstream of feminist thought.

Despite their frequently masculine titles, Eliot's novels focus on the lives of women and the problems that affect them. Furthermore, her letters reveal that she is acutely aware of the oppression and even vicious exploitation of women. Nonetheless her letters—despite her tacit approval of Mill's speech before Parliament, her financial support of Girton College, and her friendship with feminists such as Barbara Smith Bodichon—are generally critical of the feminist movement. For example, she scolds Sophia Hennell for "undertaking to canvass on the Women Suffrage question" and asks her why she burdens herself for an "extremely doubtful good."[93] At another time, she admits to Edith Simcox that she prefers the company of men:

She went on to say, what I also knew, that she cared for the womanly ideal, sympathized with women and liked for them to come to her in their troubles, but while feeling near to them in one way, she felt far off in another; the friendship and intimacy of men was more to her.[94]

Eliot never states her reasons for preferring the company of men although one can well understand why she would have shared very little with Hetty Sorrell, Gwendolyn, Rosamond, or even with Dorothea and Mary Garth. At a time when most women received only a smattering of knowledge, she could count among her friends some of the most intelligent and interesting people of her day, people like Barbara Smith Bodichon, Herbert Spencer, and George Henry Lewes.

In fact, both Eliot's preference for the intellectual companionship of men and her continued praise of the "feminine character" permit us an insight into her criticism of feminism:

And there lies just that kernel of truth in the vulgar alarm of men lest women should be 'unsexed.' We can no more afford to part with that exquisite type of gentleness, tenderness, possible maternity suffusing a woman's being with affectionateness, which makes what we mean by the feminine character, than we can afford to part with the human love, the mutual subjection of soul between a man and a woman—which is also a growth and revelation beginning before all history.[95]

While believing that women should be granted equality with men, Eliot also believes in the positive value of gentleness and affection; and her continued praise of these traits explains her objections to feminism. Although there was no uniform doctrine among nineteenth-century feminists, at least one branch of the feminist movement worked toward equality between the sexes and stressed characteristics that were perceived to be masculine, such as intelligence and ambition. Eliot, on the other hand, is interested in achieving a union of masculine and feminine and in establishing a society that values the traditional feminine virtues of tenderness, affection, gentleness, and tolerance. For that reason, her heroes—as well as her heroines—retain a number of these supposedly feminine characteristics.

Eliot feared that the feminist movement would make women more like men, and *Middlemarch* is much like *Bleak House* in that both present a society ruled by men as a vampiric society in which people oppress, exploit, and victimize one another. Like Dickens in *Bleak House*, Eliot implies in the conclusion to *Middlemarch* that one solution to this condition is to cultivate the feminine virtues of tenderness, gentleness, and sympathy in both men and women. Another, which is also suggested in the novel, is to prepare women to take their rightful place within the larger society. In a letter to Mrs. Nassau John Senior, Eliot explains what must happen before women can achieve equality with men:

...women ought to have the same fund of truth placed within their reach as men have; that their lives (i.e. the lives of men and women) ought to be passed together under the hallowing influence of a common faith as to their duty and its basis. And this unity in their faith can only be produced by their having each the same store of fundamental knowledge. It is not likely that any perfect plan for educating women can soon be found, for we are very far from having found a perfect plan for educating men. But it will not do to wait for perfection.[96]

The same plea for equality of education echoes throughout her writings from her early essays such as "Silly Novels by Lady Novelists," "Margaret Fuller and Mary Wollstonecraft," and "Women in France: Madame de Sable" up through *Middlemarch* and *Daniel Deronda*. (*Felix Holt* provides a variation on this theme in its advocacy of education for the working classes.)

Thus, the future that Eliot envisions is one which, recognizing the traditional virtues of both men and women, will enable both sexes to develop to their full emotional and intellectual potential. Achieving this equality, humanity will conquer the vampires of history, and modern Theresas will be able to discover their epic lives. It is an ideal of human history that is not dependent on the relationship of vampire and victim, exploiter and exploited, master and slave.

Taking the vampire metaphor about as far as it can be taken in realistic fiction, Eliot transforms the Gothic metaphor of an immortal being that sucks the blood of its human victims into a way of presenting certain kinds of human evil—including the egoistic behavior of individuals within marriage as well as the way that both bankers and industrialists exploit others. In so doing, she continues the trend established by the Brontes and by Dickens of using a Gothic motif as a social metaphor.

Novelists were not the only nineteenth-century writers to use the vampire as a social metaphor, however. In much the same way that Eliot uses the vampire to characterize Mr. Vincy, Karl Marx uses the vampire to describe the way industrialists exploit their workers: "Capital is dead labour, that, *vampire-like*, only lives by sucking living labour, and lives the more, the more labour it sucks."[97] Later in the same chapter, he refers to the vampire again:

The prolongation of the working-day beyond the limits of the natural day, into the night, only acts as a palliative. It quenches only in a slight degree the *vampire thirst* for the living blood of labour.[98]

Although Marx was writing a scientific analysis of economic conditions, his familiarity with the Gothic tales of E.T.A. Hoffman and Alexander Dumas gave him a graphic figure of supernatural evil by which he could characterize an ordinary human evil.

However, Marx goes one step beyond Eliot by turning the metaphor into a simile. Therefore, readers of *Capital* are not asked to hold both the social reality and the Gothic belief in mind at once. Instead, they are asked only to see that there is a resemblance between that figure of supernatural evil and the exploitation that they see around them.

Marx's friend Friedrich Engels, who also uses the vampire to characterize the capitalists, is somewhat closer to the literary tradition in that he expects his readers to see both the reality and the superstitious belief. For example, Engels observes that English workers will come to understand that religious beliefs "serve only to weaken the proletariat and to keep them obedient and faithful to the *capitalist vampires*."[99] Because Engels does not explain his reasons for choosing the metaphor, readers who are familiar with the literary tradition are asked to hold both parts of the metaphor in mind simultaneously. Thus they must think of the resemblance between the hideous bloodsucker from both folklore and Gothic literature and the new capitalist class. Later, Engels goes on to condemn the middle classes by calling them vampires who "first suck the wretched workers dry so that afterwards they can...throw a few miserable crumbs of charity at their feet."[100] In both cases, Engels' use of the vampire points to the exploitative relationship between the middle classes and the working classes.

Although most of the writers who use the vampire as a social metaphor do so to illustrate a parasitic economic relationship—whether between wives and husbands, attorneys and their clients, masters and hands—Frayling observes numerous other ways of using the vampire as a social metaphor:

> In 1846, *Knight's Penny Magazine*...lashed out at the 'cheap weekly sheets' which were foisting trashy tales and tired vampire stories on 'the working people, and especially the young'.... But the moralists had to accept defeat, and on the principle 'if you can't beat them join them', various worthy causes decided to harness the obvious commercial potential of the vampire myth. Pamphlets on Temperance (*The Vampire* by 'the wife of a medical man', in which the 'Vampyre Inn' sucks unwary alcoholics to their doom), on the dangers of over-crowding in the vast new metropolitan graveyards (*The Cemetery*...), on the horrors of premature burial (compiled by the procremation lobby), on the evils of gambling...all post-dating the period of Ruthven's greatest success, made their polemicism more accessible to the 'less informed' by using the 'feast of blood' formula.[101]

In these works, the awe and mystery of the original Gothic motif is totally gone.

George Levine observes that this movement from myth to reality is characteristic of nineteenth-century fiction:

> The old myths enter nineteenth-century fiction, but they do so in the mode of realism.... Thus, though it would be absurd to claim Mary Shelley as a direct "influence" on the dominant literary and scientific forms of the century, we can see that in her secularization of the creation myth she invented a metaphor that was irresistible to the culture as a whole.... In writers as central and various as Feuerbach, Comte, Darwin, Marx, Frazer, and Freud we can find Victor Frankenstein's activity: the attempt to discover in matter what we had previously attributed to spirit, the bestowing *on* matter (or history, or society, or nature) the values once given to God.[102]

Levine's analysis is an excellent shorthand description of what happens to the vampire and to other kinds of mythic figures in *nineteenth-century fiction*. However, it does not explain what happens to these mythic figures in twentieth-century literature. That change and the reasons for that change will be covered in detail in the final chapter.

Chapter Six
Making Sense of the Changes

This study of the vampire has focused on the changes the literary character has undergone in the past two hundred years, especially as those changes relate to an evolving sense of self and of one's relationships with others. Despite its necessary interest in the individual (the reading and writing of fiction being intensely individual pursuits—far more so than the writing or hearing of drama or epic), it is closer to the kind of social history practiced by Lawrence Stone (especially *The Family, Sex and Marriage In England 1500-1800*, which I used extensively as background material) and to the psychohistory written by Peter Gay in *The Bourgeois Experience, Victoria to Freud*, which I also consulted extensively,[1] than to the fixed psychological principles expressed by Freud or Ernest Jones.

My choice of orientation has a sound rational basis—including the fact that psychological explanations do not explain either the vampire's popularity at particular historical periods or the changes in the motif— but I should admit openly that focusing on the relationship between literature and the culture that influences writers is also the result of my own interest in recent history, especially as that history has affected the lives of individual men and women. Like Claire Kahane, who makes a similar observation in her study of Gothic literature, I recognize that critical attitudes are often the product of very personal factors:

> Central to that network is my sex, the gender in which I locate myself and am located by others; and which circumscribes how and even what I see. Yet precisely for that reason, I may be sensitive to an aspect of a text either not yet perceived by others, or given a different configuration.[2]

Similar conditions exist in my own study, for what I have seen in the various works is literally determined by who I am and by everything I have experienced. For example, my interest in vampires began in the late 1960s, when a student recommended that I read *Dracula*. At the same time, I was becoming interested in the women's liberation movement, and I initially became interested in women vampires in nineteenth-century literature because of what I perceived as hostility to women in that literature. A greater awareness of historical conditions has made me change my mind—partially—and has enabled me to see that writers like Stoker, Dickens, and Eliot are not necessarily antifeminists or anti-women even though their ideal women are very different from twentieth-century ideals. Understanding the social conditions that influenced such writers has not caused me to wish to adopt a nineteenth-century standard of values—or behavior—however.

In addition, my study has also centered on the vampire in nineteenth-century English literature—primarily because that is the period with which I am most familiar—although I have also tried to provide a sense of the vampire's origins in folklore as well as an overview of some of the literary vampire's offspring in popular culture—from Count Chocula to Jerry Dandridge (in Columbia's *Fright Night*, 1985), from Valan to Faustine in Cornell Woolrich's "Vampire's Honeymoon." Two of these twentieth-century vampires—Count Chocula and Valan—are lighthearted treatments; and even Jerry Dandridge, who ultimately reveals the horrifying truth, is initially presented as a light and debonair figure a la Langella or Hamilton. Faustine, however, has the eerie power associated with the vampire in earlier centuries, when it was taken seriously by nineteenth-century writers and by the primitive peoples that formulated the folklore that preceded. Only in the twentieth century has the vampire become a "camp" figure—often a mere parody of its former self—and even now one runs across highly original formulations—occasionally even figures of power.

Previous chapters have looked at individual works—at twentieth-century popular culture, folklore, Gothic literature, realistic literature, and works that combine realism with Gothic materials. Although the vampire certainly has no "cookie-cutter" uniformity, nineteenth-century vampires appear in roughly three kinds of literary works: those in which living-dead characters suck the blood of victims and in which characters identify "real" vampires within their fictional world; those in which one of the characters suspects another character of being a vampire, and the author neither confirms nor denies this possibility; and those in which one of the characters deliberately uses the term "vampire" as a significant metaphor to focus the attention of another character or the reader on the destructive human being's resemblance to the supernatural figure. Although Chapter One admits that twentieth-century treatments, on the other hand, tend to be much more light and playful than those in the nineteenth century, the tendency of the study as a whole has been to look only at the facts, the "what."

This chapter is much more speculative because it looks primarily at the "whys." For example, why did a primitive superstition suddenly become a popular literary figure at the beginning of the nineteenth century? After all, as most commentators on the subject have observed, the belief in vampires is indigenous to almost all cultures and all periods.

Moreover, why has the vampire evolved so significantly over the past (roughly) two centuries and why has it seemed to change at specific historical times? Finally, why is the vampire in the twentieth century primarily a character in *popular* literature (and in its cinematic equivalents) while its nineteenth-century predecessor attracted the attention of some of that century's most original thinkers—economists and historians as well as imaginative writers—and therefore became an important part of the literary mainstream?

Although there have been numerous variations on the subject of vampires, including vampire plants and people who simply pretend to be vampires, this study does not attempt to come to terms with these one-of-a-kind variations. In fact, all the vampires in this study fit the following definition that was laid out in Chapter One:

The vampire is a reanimated corpse that perpetuates its unnatural existence by feeding on blood, an act of parasitism that drains the victim's life force and can transform the victim into a vampire; it is also an ordinary human being who is characterized as a vampire and who is clearly modeled on vampires with whom writer and reader are familiar.

Despite the apparent uniformity, however, there is a huge difference in the typical twentieth-century vampire and its predecessors. Although identified by three characteristics that were also common to vampires both in folklore and in nineteenth-century literature (bloodsucking, rebellious behavior and eroticism), these characteristics are generally much more positive in the twentieth century. For example, although still requiring blood to survive, the vampire in the twentieth century no longer destroys human beings by sucking their blood. Thus the vampire becomes a more sympathetic figure, a misunderstood outsider rather than a bestial destroyer of human life. Moreover, both the rebelliousness and the erotic behavior tend to be presented in a more favorable light.

The difference can be seen most clearly by contrasting these twentieth-century variations with the vampire from folklore. That the vampire in folklore destroys human beings (often the most innocent or helpless, such as newborn infants or women in labor) by sucking their blood is its main—sometimes its only—characteristic. In fact, most versions tend to emphasize the bestial or inhuman by ignoring any human motivation and by stressing the differences, not the similarities, in vampires and human beings. One of the most extreme examples is the Malaysian Penanggalan, which is little more than a mouth with attached entrails (an image that emphasizes both its oral fixation and habit of destroying its victims by sucking their blood). However extreme the Penanggalan may appear, the majority of folklore examples tend to undermine any possible resemblance between vampire and human.

Furthermore, the vampire in folklore has none of the attractive rebelliousness of the twentieth-century vampire. In fact, the emphasis on rebellion—especially the romantic conflict with a cruel and oppressive world—seems to be a literary invention. There is, however, a latent rebelliousness that writers may have seen and modified. For example, the mere fact that the vampire is a dead body that refuses to stay dead constitutes a subtle form of rebellion even though it was necessary for nineteenth-century writers to add the Faustian elements of grandeur and heroism. Moreover, the connection to certain religious beliefs tends to suggest a kind of latent rebelliousness as well. For example, people might become vrykolakas (a type of Greek vampire) by not being buried according to the rites of the Greek Church, by living an immoral life, or by practicing witchcraft. Similarly, many Roman Catholics believed that the excommunicated became vampires. Thus there was a tendency to believe that those who rebelled against the tenets of the established church—whatever that church might be—were likely to become vampires after death.

If a latent rebelliousness exists in many folklore versions, a subtle eroticism may also exist there as well. Certainly many of the psychological explanations of vampirism focus on the similarities between the vampire's bloodsucking, the "love bite," and infantile incestuous desires. At least there was material for later writers to explore and develop though I am convinced that much of the significance of these characteristics (the rebelliousness and the eroticism though possibly not the fear of violent death, a reality much more common during earlier historical periods) has been attached by twentieth-century commentators.

For example, Montague Summers, the rather unorthodox Anglican clergyman tends to see moral—even religious—significance in many forms of vampire belief. Jones, on the other hand, sees many of the pressures that are characteristic of a nuclear family. However, the kind of love-hate relationship between parents and children that Jones argues is responsible for the belief in vampires is not likely to occur in families before the eighteenth century or in families in most primitive cultures. In fact, Lawrence Stone's description of families in the Early Modern period suggests that the intense emotions so often associated with the modern family could not have existed in families during earlier historical periods (certainly not during the middle ages, where Jones locates the superstitious belief in vampires) or in many of the primitive cultures described by Summers and Masters:

...this combination of delayed marriage, low life expectation and early fostering out of the surviving children resulted in a conjugal family which was very short-lived and unstable in its composition. Few mutual demands were made on its members, so that it was a low-keyed and undemanding institution which could therefore weather this instability with relative ease.[5]

These casual family relationships were unlikely to produce the kinds of intensely emotional responses that Jones associates with the family. That Jones is wrong about family relationships in the middle ages does not keep his analysis from helping us analyze the vampire in the nineteenth and twentieth centuries, a period characterized by a totally different kind of family. Here again, Stone is helpful in providing an overview of the modern nuclear family, one that contrasts with the family in the Early Modern Period:

> The four key features of the modern family—intensified affective bonding of the nuclear core at the expense of neighbours and kin; a strong sense of individual autonomy...; a weakening of the association of sexual pleasure with sin and guilt; and a growing desire for physical privacy—were all well established by 1750.... Further stages in the diffusion of this new family type did not take place until the late nineteenth century during which many of the developments that have been described had gone into reverse.[4]

Thus Stone reinforces the strong emotional bonds between family members that constitute such a strong core for psychoanalysis. Furthermore he observes that evolving notions of both individualism and sexuality may have contributed to the nineteenth-century response to both eroticism and rebellion. That these same traits are seen as positive attributes in twentieth-century literature may stem directly from a changing notion of the self (especially a growing sense of the rights of the individual) and its relationship to other human beings.

Knowing a little about changing patterns of family relationships and notions of the individual may help us to understand one major difference in the typical vampire in folklore and his literary offspring. For example, the literary vampire originated during a period when Romantic literature emphasized the power of the individual. The vampire in folklore, on the other hand, is little more than an animal with a thoughtless appetite for human blood, a creature moreover who happened to attack family members simply because of physical conditions, including the fact that primitive people are likely to live on farms or in villages, where they are also likely to be related to their near neighbors.

Although the vampire as we know it is primarily a creation of nineteenth-century literature, the initial changes in the folklore vampire came during the Enlightenment, when many thinkers became aware of the primitive belief in vampirism; and many of them attempted to explain the phenomenon rationally by speculating about its relationship to disease—especially epidemic disease—and premature burial. Others—including Voltaire—capitalized on the metaphoric possibilities associated with a creature that destroyed others by sucking their blood. These rational explanations continued throughout the nineteenth and twentieth centuries and undoubtedly had much more resonance during the Victorian Era, a period that was literally preoccupied with the idea of death.[5]

Despite these rational explanations, which admittedly helped to keep the vampire before the public eye, the vampire seems to have entered popular consciousness primarily through Romantic literature. Indeed, as many writers have commented, the vampire with which we in the twentieth century are most familiar is a literary creature, not a direct product of folklore. Thus most people would have associated it with awe and mystery rather than with disease or other rational causes (though even a few twentieth-century writers, including Matheson in *I Am Legend*, attribute vampirism to epidemic disease), for the earliest literary versions certainly make little attempt to explain the vampire. Instead, early works of literature—including *Lenore*, "Wake Not the Dead," "The Vampyre" and even the relatively late *Varney the Vampire*—simply accept the fact that such supernatural creatures exist and that they exist primarily to prey on ordinary human beings.

Later, as the nineteenth century progresses, these supernatural beings become incorporated into realistic literature, with writers like the Brontes, George Eliot, and Charles Dickens using the motif more or less metaphorically to emphasize certain characteristics in their ordinary human characters. For example, Charlotte Bronte, who was apparently influenced by German literature, combines the bestial behavior of Tieck's Brunhilda with a violent and irrational eroticism and adds to it the kind of economic dependence that was expected of married women in the nineteenth century. Dickens and Eliot, on the other hand, continue to emphasize economic predation—although not simply the kind mandated for married women—and also suggest that vampiric behavior is connected with aggressive masculinity.

Although the movement in mainstream nineteenth-century literature is from Romanticism to realism, the evolution in the vampire motif is not quite so simple, however, for two of the most Gothic treatments of the vampire—"Carmilla" and *Dracula*—occur late in the century. Even more confusing is the fact that the vampire in the twentieth century has been associated with fantasy rather than with realistic works.

However, if the formal changes in the works that feature the vampire have not been consistent, the thematic changes as the vampire evolves from folklore through mainstream literature to popular culture have been more so. Granted that there are numerous individual exceptions— certainly not surprising for a figure that has been so popular—the vampire has evolved from a merely bestial creature in folklore to an appealing figure in twentieth-century popular culture, becoming literally heroic in Badham's version of *Dracula* and in Martin's *Fevre Dream* (*Live Girls* even suggests this evolution by having the ancient vampire much more cruel than her young "recruits"); and the nineteenth-century literary character occupies a kind of mid-range between the beast and the hero.

This change is perhaps most dramatic when one looks at the vampire as a bloodsucker, the one characteristic that is common to all vampiric figures. While many twentieth-century vampires attempt to alter their unsavory reputations by drinking the blood of animals or minute amounts of human blood and many vampires in folklore drink blood but do not kill their victims, vampires in nineteenth-century literature are almost always responsible for the deaths of those they touch. The exceptions are Varney, who may not be a vampire, and Bertha Mason, who is revealed to be a suffering human being rather than a supernatural figure. In fact, even George Eliot, whose vampiric characters are ordinary human beings rather than supernatural creatures, underlines the utter destructiveness of her vampiric characters by showing that their behavior destroys their victims.

Changing attitudes toward death and dying may be partially responsible for different perceptions of that bringer of death, the vampire. Vampire epidemics and the folklore that accumulated around them were often associated with periods of epidemic disease, including smallpox. Such epidemics continued to plague the Victorians while death continued to strike all ages rather than primarily the old and diseased. Nonetheless the Victorian attitude toward death seems to be more than just a response to these facts. For example, both James Stevens Curl, who wrote the appropriately titled *The Victorian Celebration of Death*, and John Morley, who wrote *Death, Heaven, and the Victorians*, provide the twentieth-century reader with curious illustrations of the Victorian attitude to death, including the fact that Victorian crematoria, which "allowed the mourners to see the coffin disappear into the fire,"[6] made the reality of death much more immediate and the fact that even children were surrounded by reminders of ever-present death in the form of memorial cards and "samplers stitched intricately...with epitaphs for parents and grandparents."[7]

Furthermore Curl contrasts twentieth-century burial customs with nineteenth and thus suggests a significant difference in attitude:

> The romantic nineteenth-century tradition that created Pere-la-Chaise, Kensal Green, Highgate, Mount Auburn, Green-wood, and, to a lesser extent, Arlington National Cemetery, has given way to a new concept. The term 'cemetery' is now in some danger of extinction...for the euphemism 'Memorial-Park' is in vogue. These 'Memorial-Parks'...appear to be superseding the nineteenth-century model cemeteries.... Gentility, euphemism, comfortable suburban death, and banality are replacing the splendours of nineteenth-century cemetery design.[8]

Thus Curl reveals an important fact: the Victorians glorified death while people in the twentieth century attempt to deny its power. Curl attributes this fascination merely to fashion and explains that the modern attitude toward death is simply the result of a changed fashion:

> The post-war generation, and indeed the post-first war generation rejected the dark romantic gloom of Victoriana, and demanded an unmysterious church, a neatly clipped garden of rest, a bright and shining world.... Indeed, the contemporary trend is to look on the Victorian Celebration of Death as something of a joke.[9]

However, such significant cultural changes are rarely the result of fashion. Nancy Hill, who places the Victorian fascination with death within a much larger social and cultural framework—one that differs markedly from its twentieth-century counterpart—offers a more convincing argument:

> Paradoxically we seem to tolerate nearly perpetual warfare, the expectation of atomic annihilation...yet death as an actual occurrence affecting our personal lives has virtually no reality for us. We have to be taught...to deal with death, or else turn the whole unpleasant business over to an antiseptic institution.
>
> In Dickens' age death was still a religious event,...Dickens' contemporaries were still capable of being moved by the medieval Dance of Death...because their religious beliefs still accepted many of the same premises. In Dickens' still Christian era Death serves a summons to appear before the Creator and to answer for one's activities. Death as a conductor between the earthly and the eternal is a far more terrifying figure than Death as a signalman announcing journey's end.[10]

It is likely that all these factors—fashion, religious views, and the very presence of death as well as the Romantic fascination with what was mysterious and awe inspiring—contributed to the nineteenth-century celebration of death and that interest in the vampire, in that century a bringer of death to the young and beautiful rather than to the old and diseased, was part and parcel of that fascination.

Moreover, when we look at the vampire as a destructive creature, a bringer of death, we see one more significant difference between the nineteenth-century vampire and its twentieth-century offspring: Vampires in nineteenth-century literature are generally revealed as being more destructive than their human opponents although—with the exception of Dracula, Bulstrode and Vincy, and the vampires mentioned by social writers—vampires threaten individuals rather than groups of human beings. In fact, it is only in *Dracula,* a kind of turning point for the literary vampire at any rate, that the reader gets a sense of a war between monsters and humans, a war that is explored further in twentieth-century works although often with a surprising difference. In the following passage, Dracula—proud of his warrior heritage—attempts to explain to Jonathan Harker the connection between bloodshed and heroism:

Is it a wonder that we were a conquering race; that we were proud...when, after the battle of Mohacs, we threw off the Hungarian yoke, we of the Dracula blood were amongst their leaders, for our spirit would not brook that we were not free. Ah, young sir, the Szekeleys—and the Dracula as their heart's blood, their brains, and their swords—can boast a record that mushroom growths like the Hapsburgs and the Romanoffs can never reach. The warlike days are over. Blood is too precious a thing in these days of dishonourable peace; and the glories of the great races are as a tale that is told. (Ch. III)

Momentarily impressed by the heroic Dracula, Harker is later terrified when he realizes that the vampire plans to attack everything that Harker holds dear. In addition, although Harker eventually attacks the somnolent Dracula with a sword and Van Helsing and his small band of followers ultimately "declare war" on Dracula, there seems to be no doubt in Stoker's mind that Dracula is the aggressor, his attacks on individuals only an indication of his plan to subdue the entire human species. In fact, Harker sees Dracula's plan to settle in England as nothing less than a declaration of guerrilla warfare:

This was the being I was helping to transfer to London, where, perhaps, for centuries to come he might, amongst its teeming millions, satiate his lust for blood, and create a new and ever-widening circle of semi-demons to batten on the helpless. (Ch. IV)

While Stoker is the only nineteenth-century writer to link the vampire with the mass annihilation of warfare, this connection is made more frequently in twentieth-century works. For example, Sergeant Stanslas in Wellman's "The Horror Undying" and Private Lunkowski in Drake's "Something Had To Be Done" use the horrors of warfare as a cover for their bloodthirsty exploits. However, both Wellman and Drake suggest that their vampires are no more violent than the human beings on whom they prey. Furthermore, Yarbro, in *Hotel Transylvania*, and Chetwynd-Hayes, in *The Monster Club*, indicate that vampires and other supernatural monsters are actually less aggressive and destructive than human beings. Chetwynd-Hayes has one of his monsters, a ghoul, draw the human character's attention to recent history to focus the attention of both fictional character and reader on the horror of *human* aggression:

In the past sixty years the humes [or humans] have exterminated one hundred and fifty million of their own kind.... The humes began with many serious disadvantages, but these they overcame with wonderful ingenuity...they invented guns, tanks, aeroplanes, bombs, poisonous gas, extermination camps, swords, daggers, bayonets, booby-traps, atomic bombs, flying missiles, submarines, warships, aircraft-carriers, and motor-cars.... During their short history they have subjected other humes to death by burning, hanging, decapitation, electrocution, strangulation, shooting, drowning, racking, crushing, disembowelling and other methods too revolting for the delicate stomachs of this assembly.[11]

Certainly far from subtle, this long catalogue is a poignant reminder of why the vampire, a threat only to individuals, is no longer terribly frightening to people in the Post-Hiroshima Age.

As a member of one of the generations born after World War II, I am well aware that warfare today can result in global destruction. However, the social historian Asa Briggs observes that this fear is nothing new, that the horrors of warfare on a global scale and the threat of mass annihilation have been a major part of human consciousness during the entire twentieth century:

> The great European wars of the twentieth century...were very different in scale and character from the 'little wars' of the nineteenth.... The latter had been fought along the lines of many of the wars of the Roman Empire, by small numbers of regular soldiers against hostile forces on distant frontiers...sometimes they were punitive expeditions to enforce law and order, sometimes they were more ambitious campaigns to annexe territory.[12]

Briggs suggests that changes in military strategy as well as technological developments—I hesitate to label these developments advancements—have also altered human attitudes to death and dying. As a result, human beings in the twentieth century have come to fear, not vampires and other threats to the individual self, but vast impersonal forces over which they as individuals have no control.

Moreover, during the twentieth century, the horrors of warfare have become a part of everyone's life, not just part of the lives of professional military men. That warfare has entered the living rooms of ordinary human beings is partially—in recent decades—because modern telecommunications have enabled people continents away to experience the horrors of war and partially because the possibility of being personally affected seems so immediate.[13]

On the other hand, Briggs's discussion of World War I provides a sense that mass awareness of the horrors of war was a reality long before the days of television and nuclear weapons:

> Slaughter was, in fact, appalling.... Death, which was a matter of luck, was not the only human sacrifice to a new Moloch. Injured, gassed, shell-shocked, blinded men staggered back from the wars to a life that would never be the same again.[14]

Compared to the real horrors that people in the twentieth century see around them—either on the battlefield or back at home—dying from a vampire attack appears innocuous—even attractive. Here, at least is an adversary against which one might battle honorably and openly. The vampire is typically a personal threat, not an invisible whiff of poisonous gas, a bomb dropped on an unsuspecting populace, or—most unspeakable of all—what came to be known during the Vietnam War as "friendly fire."

If changing notions of warfare and the possibility of mass annihilation in the twentieth century have been responsible for writers and readers taking a more sympathetic view of the vampire, changing attitudes toward authority and toward rebellion against that authority have also led to a more sympathetic treatment of the vampire, especially when the vampire is shown rejecting a corrupt or vicious society or choosing to live in seclusion. Significant examples of the vampire as an attractive rebel are Badham's Dracula, Yarbro's St. Germain, Saberhagen's Dracula, to name only a few. There are several important exceptions, however, that possibly—it is too soon to tell—signify a changing attitude toward rebellion: *Fright Night* (Columbia Pictures, 1985) and *Last Rites* (1985). *Fright Night*, which was written and directed by Tom Holland, features a truly despicable vampire who feeds on the blood of prostitutes and who turns the young hero's best friend into a vampire also. Dolores, the ancient vampire in *Last Rites* is even more hideous. Wearing the gem-studded cross that had once belonged to the archbishop, one of her former lovers, is an obvious reminder of her contempt for religious authority. It is tempting to draw an analogy between the present social and political climate (especially the renewed strength of fundamentalist religious groups and the fact that once again authority of whatever kind seems to signify right) and the fact that the vampire—always a rebel against authority—is perceived as a threat. However, one movie does not necessarily indicate a trend. (*Fright Night* is complicated by being an artistic attempt to do something new with an old genre. Thus it combines a parody of horror movies with genuinely frightening material.) Furthermore, as Briggs cautions, it is especially difficult for writers to come to terms with their own present:

> The closer the social historian gets to his own times, the more difficult it is for him to be sure that he has grasped what is essential about his period. This is largely a matter of vantage point. Some features of the pattern may not yet even be clearly visible.[15]

Holding Briggs's caution in mind, I will conclude—albeit cautiously—that vampires in the twentieth century have been perceived as more or less attractive rebel figures, ones who *choose* to live outside the society that they, their creators, and their readers (or viewers) regard as problematic—even corrupt. To put it succinctly, vampires have become heroes and heroines in the twentieth century.

Unlike their twentieth-century offspring, writers in the nineteenth century do not choose to make heroes/heroines of their vampires; and the reasons for the change in attitude is partially caused by a changed attitude toward authority. During the nineteenth century the middle classes (which formed the bulk of the reading public) in Great Britain, the United States, and Germany, as Peter Gay observes, were overwhelmingly religious and therefore receptive to both religious authority and to other kinds of authority.[16] Their counterparts one hundred years later, as Briggs observes, are strikingly different:

Even at the beginning of the 1950s...only 10% of the population were regular church goers. Now, in the late 1950s and early 1960s there was a sharp decline, particularly among the Nonconformist sects. The power of the chapel...sharply declined, and many of the great Victorian chapels were pulled down or used for other purposes, even as bingo halls.[17]

Without question, the decline in church attendance suggests that religious authority has diminished significantly since the beginning of the nineteenth century.[18] However, Briggs observes that other factors accompanied the decrease in religious power during the 1950s and further undermined traditional authority: "The real break had come...when, with increased prosperity, educational opportunity and social and physical mobility, society seemed to be more fluid and less willing to accept old ways."[19]

Briggs does not mention the effect that various scandals involving cabinet officials might have had on British respect for political authority although the Hammer films featuring arrogant and sensual vampires had their heyday in the 1960s. Furthermore, vampire films in this country have been most popular during periods of political unrest (for example, during both the Depression and the 1970s, when the lack of faith in political institutions that resulted from both the bungled Vietnam War and Watergate was at an all-time high.) Moreover, greater social and physical mobility had already begun to undermine traditional sources of authority even in the nineteenth century as people immigrated from rural areas to large metropolitan centers and from Europe to the Untied States and other countries. (Gay estimates that 62 million people left Europe between the early 1820s and the early 1920s.[20]) However, in spite of immigration, established institutions, including the church, the government, and even the public house, managed to retain their authority over the individual until mid-twentieth century. At that point, greater suspicion—even contempt—of established authority created more interest in and respect for individuals who rebelled against established authority.

Even though they are not presented as attractive figures who offer positive alternatives to the status quo, many vampires in the nineteenth century are presented as rebels, the most prominent being Lucy Westenra, Dracula, Catherine Earnshaw, Heathcliff, and Bertha Mason. Lucy, who is modeled on the New Woman of the 1890s, rebels subconsciously against the constraints (especially the sexual constraints) placed on women even before she meets Dracula; and she becomes openly rebellious after her "initiation." Dracula himself also rejects English authority though he is usually careful to be circumspect about that rejection. In fact, he invites Jonathan Harker to Transylvania to learn more about English law and customs. Furthermore, Dracula is especially frightening to Stoker's middle class narrators (and probably to his middle class readers as well) because he flaunts his freedom from everything that restricts them. Catherine, Heathcliff, and Bertha Mason simply long for the evasive freedom that Dracula possesses. Unable to find the freedom that they seek within their society—freedom to marry whomever they choose, for example, or to adopt a more congenial social role—Catherine and Heathcliff rebel against that society; and Emily Bronte, who lived during a time when both women and propertyless orphans like Heathcliff had very few social options, suggests that they can find the freedom they seek only in death. Her sister Charlotte also uses the vampire to reveal the circumstances that were likely to cause women to rebel; and her vampire, Bertha Mason, is literally imprisoned (appropriately in the attic of her husband's ancestral home) by a society that regards openly sexual behavior—indeed any kind of assertive behavior—in women as inappropriate. Bronte shows that Jane is also tempted to rebel against the society that attempts to imprison her, but she also provides acceptable ways for Jane to rebel against the constraints of her society even if that rebellion ultimately falls short of the mark for most twentieth-century feminists.

Lucy Westenra, Dracula, Catherine Earnshaw, Heathcliff, and Bertha Mason are perhaps the most rebellious vampires in nineteenth-century literature. Nonetheless, a kind of latent rebellion exists in *all* vampires— even in those like Lord Ruthven, Carmilla, Vholes, Bulstrode, and Vincy whose exploitative behavior is used by their creators to mirror the corruption that exists in an exploitative society. That rebellion consists of a refusal to live by the rules of their society and even—in the case of the supernatural vampires—the natural laws that govern the human species.

Though bloodsucking and rebellion are common traits of the literary vampire in the nineteenth century, the single most prominent trait is their eroticism. In fact, like the vampires in twentieth century popular culture that were discussed in Chapter One, the exceptions prove the rule. Vholes and Tulkinghorn, Bulstrode and Vincy are the *only* nineteenth-century vampires who are not defined by their erotic behavior; and Eliot even hints at a degree of sensuality in Bulstrode's past character when she refers to his power over his wives.

There is, however, one critical difference in the ways this eroticism is depicted. While twentieth-century writers treat the eroticism of their vampires as a positive trait, their nineteenth-century counterparts definitely do not.[21] To see the difference clearly, one need only contrast Mr. Varri's gentle seduction of Anna in "Softly While You're Sleeping" with Varney's brutal attack on the sleeping Flora Bannerworth or with Lord Ruthven's even more bestial attack on Ianthe. Furthermore, one might also contrast Yarbro's scholarly St. Germain, Daniel's Don Sebastian, Herzog's Nosferatu and the interpretations of Dracula by Frank Langella or George Hamilton with Lord Ruthven, Vholes, or Dracula. The comparison reveals that men vampires in the twentieth century— except when they merely imitate Stoker's character—are courtly and gentle, often as vulnerable as their human victims. Men vampires in the nineteenth century, on the other hand, use great physical and political power to attack sleeping or otherwise defenseless victims, giving them no opportunity to protect themselves or even to understand what is happening to them. In this sense, even Lydgate reveals his origins in the eighteenth-century rake and Gothic villain, for he uses his aristocratic family and cosmopolitan background to overwhelm—albeit unconsciously in his case—the provincial Rosamond. Eliot's use of literary source material is much more subtle than Polidori's, however, so Lydgate is a realistic character in his own right as well as an inheritor of a popular eighteenth-century literary tradition that emphasized diabolical masculine power.

An even more striking change takes place in women vampires, who are more interesting because they are somewhat less dependent on a popular literary tradition and are, therefore, the products of their creator's individual imaginations. Understanding the social conditions that influenced their creators enables us to see that the vampire motif enabled writers to explore changes in women's lives and especially to focus on questions of power and powerlessness. In the twentieth century, women vampires—including Miriam, Sterling, Valan, Madelaine, and Vampirella—are both overwhelmingly sensual and appealing, but their nineteenth-century counterparts are considerably less attractive. Like Varney and Lord Ruthven, Carmilla and Bertha Mason are characterized by their brutal attacks on sleeping victims; Lucy Westenra and the women in Dracula's castle are murderers of children as well as violently sexual beings, who both seduce and terrify their male victims; and even Catherine Earnshaw—perhaps the most sympathetic vampire in nineteenth-century literature—is terrifying when she first appears outside Lockwood's window.

Thus, one can begin to see a trend. Not only are vampires in twentieth-century popular culture more attractive than their forerunners in nineteenth-century literature, but they seem to be more appealing *and* less destructive precisely because of the same characteristics.

Before going on to discuss the reasons for these changes in the vampire motif, however, one more related trend should be noted—the fact that women vampires, as I observed in Chapter Four, tend to replace men vampires in the middle of the nineteenth century. Frayling explains:

In general, the Satanic Lord was fashionable...up to 1847, when he gorged himself to death in *Varney the Vampire*. The Fatal Woman made tentative appearances in Germany and France during the early period of Romanticism, but came into her own during 1840-80.[22]

Part of the reason is undoubtedly literary influence just as the numerous versions of Dracula in the twentieth century are a tribute to the immense popularity of Stoker's novel. However, both Frayling and Mario Praz (who erroneously attributes the interest in vampires entirely to the fascination with Lord Byron[23]) seem to oversimplify the paradigm while Judith Newton, who analyses both fiction written by women and household manuals addressed to middle class women, suggests that the growing nineteenth-century interest in powerful women characters may have stemmed from its concern—even obsession—with women's actual power, an obsession that increased as the century progressed:

This same tension and counterinsistence in relation to women's power leave traces on periodical literature addressed to the "woman question." In 1810, for example, an author for the *Edinburgh Review* makes only one reference to women's influence, giving far more emphasis to the dignity, the delightfulness, and the ornamental quality of women's character and to the importance of their personal happiness. But by 1831, in literature of the same kind, power and influence are frequent subjects of concern and references to both are accompanied by a sharpening distinction between what is appropriate to women and what to men.[24]

This particular passage concerns non-fiction prose rather than fiction, but it reveals the same trend that we have observed in popular fiction. In fact, the growing awareness of women's power and influence may explain the increasing popularity of fatal women (of which the woman vampire is merely one important sub-type) during the second half of the nineteenth century when women gained power and influence and feminists began to petition for additional rights for women. Concerned with women's power and influence, writers in the nineteenth century often responded by creating powerful women characters, the vampire being one of the most powerful negative images.

Though the observations of Praz, Carter, and Frayling focus on literary influence, Newton and Gay, who look at the relationship between literature and the society that influences its creators, offer a more complete analysis of a complex phenomenon. Gay, who observes that "no century depicted woman as vampire, as castrater, as killer so consistently...as the nineteenth,"[25] connects "the vengeful female, the murderous courtesan, the immortal vampire...the castrating sisterhood: Salome beheading John the Baptist, Judith punishing Holofernes"[26] with social concerns, especially with the increase in feminist activity. Looking back over this study reveals that the bulk of the vampires in the nineteenth century were women—Catherine Earnshaw, Bertha Mason, Carmilla, Rosamond Vincy, Lucy Westenra and the three vampires in Dracula's castle—and that even Dracula and Heathcliff share characteristics with their women companions. (Varney and Ruthven are more specifically Byronic in origin.) Furthermore, as Gay correctly observes, this dialectical relationship between the evolving position of women (and feminists' demands for increased social, economic, and political power) and negative responses to powerful women or even to potentially powerful women seems to have originated during a period when many people were exploring the position of women within their society. For a variety of reasons, the hostile responses to powerful women diminish greatly during the twentieth century as the remainder of this chapter will reveal. The result is a vastly different response to women in general and an increasingly attractive portrayal of women vampires in twentieth-century popular culture.

Nonetheless, despite the fact that hostility toward powerful women continues throughout the nineteenth century, it would be a mistake to assume that the actual condition of women did not evolve during that period or that the focus for hostility and fear did not change accordingly. Sheila Rothman, in fact, cautions against looking for "a unitary, static, and invariably subservient role for women."[27] Nonetheless, both Rothman, who studies the changing roles for American women in *Woman's Proper Place: A History of Changing Ideals and Practices, 1870 to the Present*, and Jane Lewis, who evaluates English women during roughly the same period in *Women in England 1870-1950: Sexual Divisions and Social Change*, discover that women's roles have changed according to certain stages though both recognize "links before and survivals afterward."[28] Rothman, Lewis and other students of women's history identify roughly five major stages for middle-class women since the 1870s and acknowledge that working class women typically had lives outside their homes that made their existence less restricted through undoubtedly more physically arduous:

1. During the first three-quarters of the nineteenth century, the virtuous woman as wife and mother was expected to isolate herself within the home. As a result, women had a certain degree of influence within their "proper sphere." However, single women during the period, even those who were forced to support themselves financially, had few economic opportunities.

2. During the latter decades of the nineteenth century and the beginning decades of the twentieth, feminists attempted to introduce the virtues of women's sphere into the wider public arena. Single women gained economic and educational opportunities, but married women (especially those with children) were still expected to devote themselves to their families. In fact, the cult of educated motherhood made that

particular part of woman's role more important (and possibly more restrictive) than ever before.

3. World War I temporarily changed the lives of women as more of them were given the opportunities to work outside the home. However, after the war, women were expected to return to the home. The biggest change was that wives were now encouraged to be sexual companions to their husbands, in fact to be more interested in their husbands than in their children.

4. World War II gave women even more opportunities for advancement. However, the biggest change came in the post-war years when many women chose not to return to their homes. Furthermore, those who did return home grew increasingly disenchanted with the restricted roles permitted to them.

5. The end result of women's disenchantment with their roles as housewives and mothers came during the 1960s, when the women's liberation movement began to demand equality (both professional and sexual) with men. At the same time advances in birth control technology made sexual equality possible for the first time in human history.

As we can readily infer, these stages have had a profound impact on the lives of women during the past hundred years. Moreover, the increasing acceptability of women's sexuality (first within monogamous marriage and gradually outside marriage as well) and the rising sense that men and women are more equal than different (at least in terms of their educational and economic needs) has had a profound effect on men as well, not to mention the subject of this particular study, the vampire.

However, this study of the vampire opens at the beginning of the nineteenth century, long before the 1870s, the period chosen as a starting place by both Rothman and Lewis. Therefore, because of the perimeters surrounding the vampire, this discussion of evolving attitudes toward women properly begins in the eighteenth century. A period that was much more open about sexual matters than the nineteenth, the eighteenth century had also permitted women to join men in the salons as intellectual equals although there can be no discussion of actual equality until improved methods of contraception protected married women from the dangers of almost constant childbearing and until improved sanitation eliminated the risks of dying in childbirth, improvements in medicine reduced the chances of being permanently maimed by incompetent physicians,[29] and women had the same opportunities for economic and educational advancement as men. This was not the case. In fact, even during a period when women had greater rights and opportunities in so many areas, Lewis observes that middle-class women were losing ground, especially in the economic sphere:

As the workplace became separated from the home, so a private, domestic sphere was created for women, divorced from the public world of work, office and citizenship. Moreover, during the early period of industrialization this separation of spheres between the public and the private was given legal sanction: married women were not permitted to own property or make contracts in their own names. They were thus shut out from the world of business. Furthermore, the 1832 Reform Bill made their exclusion from political citizenship explicit for the first time.[30]

The erosion of economic opportunities and legal rights continued during the early decades of the nineteenth century and was not reversed until the late nineteenth and early twentieth centuries when the Married Women's Property Acts and the franchise provided women with the economic and political rights they had lost.

Lewis argues that changes in women's material conditions— especially the separation of the home and the workplace—were largely responsible for all the other changes that narrowed women's sphere of influence and made her a virtual prisoner (albeit a prisoner who sometimes had a great deal of influence) within her own home. Warning readers about oversimplifying this process because a number of goods, including "sweets, cutlery, chains and clothing were still produced in household kitchens and backyard workshops," she nonetheless argues that removing "paid employment from the home (including retail businesses which in the early nineteenth century employed wives and daughters)" was largely responsible for the unique condition of women in the nineteenth century.

Equally important to the evolving condition of women was the fact that the sexually permissive eighteenth century gave way to the sexually repressive nineteenth century. This is *not* to argue that everyone was equally repressed. Prostitution, for example, flourished during both centuries though the eighteenth was certainly more open about its existence;[31] moreover, historians now use letters, diaries, marriage manuals, and even one survey of sexual attitudes to argue that the Victorians were in fact far less restrained than has usually been supposed. The historian Carl Degler is most eloquent in asserting the error of accepting the "prescriptive or normative literature" of Acton, Kellogg, and others "as revealing very much about sexual behavior in the Victorian era." Although one can "derive a sexual ideology from such writers," it is erroneous to assume that the ideology characterizes the society or reveals behavior. Degler in fact argues precisely the opposite, that "the attitudes and behavior of middle-class women were only peripherally affected by that ideology," and he cites as evidence both the testimony of women themselves and the fact that many medical writers advised women that sexual repression was bad for their health and for their husbands' health.[32]

While there seems to be some question about the degree and kind of sexuality recommended for married men and women, the sexuality so often associated with the vampire—the crude excesses of Bertha Mason, the lesbianism of Carmilla, the violent and exploitative behavior of Ruthven and Varney, and the promiscuity of Lucy Westenra and Dracula's three companions—fall outside what was recommended behavior. Besides being violent and excessive it also fell outside monogamous marriage. Thus this behavior was regarded as threatening both to individual health and to the social order.

Aside from reasons of health, however, one of the reasons that physicians and other thinkers encouraged the sexuality of married couples was the immense value placed on motherhood; and Gay argues that "the bourgeois conscience, whether religious or secular," during most of the nineteenth century assumed that motherhood was a woman's highest duty.[33] Moreover, Lewis suggests yet another reason that the wife and mother at home became an important moral force especially after mid-century—the fact that "evolutionary ideas had shaken the religious faith of so many. The hearth itself became sacred, and the chief prop of a moral order no longer buttressed by belief."[34]

During the last few decades of the nineteenth century and the first few decades of the twentieth, motherhood became even more important, partially because the new schools for women emphasized women's responsibility to bring up healthy, well-adjusted children. Lewis adds yet one more reason for the increasingly positive view of motherhood, "eugenic concern about the quality of the race."[35] Certainly this emphasis on maternal virtues suggests one reason that the woman vampire changes from the sexual temptresses presented by Gautier at the beginning of the century and even by Emily Bronte at mid-century to the bad mothers created by LeFanu, Eliot, and Stoker later in the century. While the ideal woman at the end of the century was characterized by her desire to nurture and protect children, Carmilla, Lucy, and Dracula's three companions are characterized by their predatory relationships to children. Carmilla, for example, though revealed primarily as a threat to young women, first appears to Laura when Laura is a child of six. Stoker's women vampires, although they are also threats to other adults, seem to practice their vampire skills on children; and Harker is horrified when Dracula presents his hungry companions with a bag containing a "half-smothered child." Lucy tempts young children as the "bloofer lady" before she drinks their blood. Even Rosamond, who miscarries when she defies her husband's warning against horseback riding, can be viewed as a bad mother, certainly in this case as the destroyer of her unborn child. Thus, women vampires in the second half of the nineteenth century, though still presented as erotic threats to the men around them, are also shown to be bad mothers who, instead of nurturing and protecting children, destroy them. Despite the change in the woman vampire, however, the continuing interest in powerful women characters suggests that people continued to be concerned with the evolving role of women within their society.

Although women's role as mother initially confined them to the home, it was ironically their experience as nurturers and protectors that helped them to extend their limited sphere of influence beyond the home. Nineteenth-century feminists, instead of insisting on women's equality with men, argued that women should carry their maternal virtues outside the home to the wider public sphere. The result was that women made progress in certain fields and even professions associated with morality, nurturance, and protection: education, nursing, and philanthropy. Furthermore, growing numbers of young women entered institutions of higher education because feminists often argued that better educated women were better mothers.

The result of the cult of scientific motherhood after the turn of the century was that more and more young women entered colleges and universities and that many of these same young women worked outside the home after graduation and before marriage. This trend continued until World War I when the need for women to replace men in various jobs temporarily placed women—occasionally even married women with children—in positions of equality. Although their economic equality rapidly disappeared after the war, one change remained, however, as Lewis observes; and that was greater sexual equality for married couples:

The alliance between social purity campaigners and feminists weakened significantly during the inter-war years. Above all, feminists changed their views on non-reproductive sex, campaigning for greater access to birth control and becoming increasingly attracted to the possibility of a greater marital equality whereby sexual pleasure, as well as employment opportunities and interests outside the home, might be more equally distributed.[36]

The result of this shift in attitude was that sexuality *per se* was no longer especially threatening even though a sexual double standard regarding premarital or extramarital sexuality continues to exist in more conservative areas.

World War II provided women with additional opportunities—both economic and personal. However, because fewer married women returned to the home after the end of World War II, the composition of the labor force began to show a significant change, a trend that has continued and intensified especially with the decades following the 1960s.

This economic trend is undoubtedly important because it provided yet another argument for the new wave of feminism that began during the 1960s, a movement that differed significantly from its forerunner in the nineteenth and early twentieth centuries. Rothman observes that the new group of feminists took a radically different approach to the problems that affected women, arguing for equality between men and women rather than for essentially different treatment:

Woman was not to be defined by her household role, by her responsibilities as wife or mother; she was in no way to be limited by any special gender characteristics. This new definition of womanhood emphasized the similarities between the sexes, not the differences. It rendered the notion of special protection outmoded and irrelevant. In brief, woman as person was fully capable of defining and acting in her own best interest.[37]

This emphasis on equality between the sexes had important ramifications for women's identity. Moreover, the clinical research done by Masters and Johnson, which proved that women were men's sexual equals, had especially important ramifications for women's sexual identity. For example, Rothman observes that Masters and Johnson presented a "new image of female sexuality.... There was no difference between vaginal and clitoral orgasm; female sexual responses were at least as intense as the male's, perhaps even more."[38] Because of these findings, it became increasingly difficult to argue in favor of women's essential passivity— sexual or otherwise. Furthermore, this new ideology of womanhood came at a time when new birth control technology—the oral contraceptive pill, the IUD, and legal abortion to name just a few—gave women more genuine choices about their sexuality. As a result, women now had the same opportunities for sexual experimentation before marriage and outside marriage as men. They could choose not to marry or to marry later in life. Perhaps even more important in terms of their growing independence, they could choose to limit the size of their families—even choose not to have children at all.

The past centuries have involved great social flux; and it is during the periods of greatest social flux that the vampire—especially the woman vampire—seems to thrive. Our study suggests that men vampires seem to be products of literary influence—including such popular types as the rake, the Gothic villain, and the Byronic hero—although they too are likely to appear during periods when human beings feel most threatened by the forces that surround them. However, women vampires have appeared during periods of intense interest in individual identity, periods during the past two centuries that have focused directly on the changing social condition of women and indirectly on the social condition of men.

Because of these changing attitudes to individual identity and because of the changing attitudes toward rebellion, death, and warfare, the man vampire has also evolved to become more attractive and less threatening in the twentieth century. One need only compare the Count on Sesame Street or more serious literary versions—Anne Rice's Lestat, Saberhagen's

Dracula, or Martin's Joshua York—to their nineteenth-century counterparts—especially Ruthven and Dracula—to see that the vampire is no longer a serious threat to the human race.

However, the evolving nature of the woman vampire is much more significant and interesting because it is directly linked to changing social and personal ideals for women, ideals that have contributed to the popularity of the woman vampire during the past two hundred years.

As a direct response to the sexually indulgent eighteenth century, both men and women vampires in the early years of the nineteenth century are characterized as sexually voracious creatures. In fact, Varney is often described as an eighteenth-century gentleman though the distinction is sometimes blurred by the writer's frequent anachronisms. However, during a period that demanded female purity, the sexually aggressive woman vampire is doubly condemned in French, German, and English literature. Gautier's beautiful courtesan, Hoffman's returning wife, LeFanu's Carmilla, and Bronte's Bertha Mason all reveal their authors' loathing of overt expressions of women's sexuality; and even the character of Catherine Earnshaw, who seems to prefer freedom to her wifely responsibilities and motherhood, is influenced by this attitude.

Although Catherine Earnshaw dies in childbirth and never gets an opportunity to prove herself a bad mother, women vampires after the mid-nineteenth century often directly contradict the view—held even by feminists—that women's chief responsibility was to be good mothers. In fact, Carmilla, who is perceived as a sexual threat, is also a bad mother who seeks out motherless adolescent girls to seduce. Rosamond Vincy is directly responsible for the miscarriage of her first child, but she presumably settles down to provide for the training of her four daughters, daughters who one imagines will be carbon copies of her. Presented even less ambivalently are Lucy Westenra and the three women in Dracula's castle, who openly prey on children, and Catherine, the formerly doting mother in Bierce's "The Death of Halpin Frasier," who turns on her son and destroys him.

Sexually aggressive, rebellious, or bad mothers, women vampires in nineteenth-century literature invariably destroy the human beings around them. Thus, they become a negative version of what nineteenth-century women were expected to do and be; and the major emphasis changes as the corresponding ideals for women change.

Although vampires of both sexes figure prominently in literature and drama during the last decades of the nineteenth century, the first half of the twentieth century represents a relative low point for the vampire.[39] In fact, many vampires—including Tod Browning's *Dracula* and Murneau's *Nosferatu* (Germany, 1922)—merely rehash earlier versions of the vampire myth. (Murneau's version was, in fact, so close to Stoker's *Dracula* that Stoker's widow filed suit.) Notable exceptions are Stoker's *The Lady of the Shroud*, in which the belief in vampires is used to provide a cover for a political refugee and *Dracula's Daughter* (Lambert Hillyer, USA, 1936), in which Gloria Holden plays a reluctant vampire, almost in the spirit of vampires in the 1960s, 70s, and 80s. However, unlike these later vampires, the Countess Marya Zaleska is unable to control her blood lust despite her attraction to a young human physician.

The genre remained viable during the 1940s and 50s, mostly through a variety of parody versions, including *Abbott and Costello Meet Frankenstein* (Charles T. Baron, USA, 1948). However, as many commentators, including Stephen King and Raymond T. McNally note, few "serious" vampire films were released between 1940 and 1965. McNally observes:

Pearl Harbor on December 7, 1941, delivered the *coup de grace* to the horror movies and to horror fiction. When faced with *real* horrors, the straightforward horror movie found no audience.[40]

Thus McNally concurs with the idea that changing attitudes to warfare and death are responsible for the evolution of the vampire motif.

Genuine fears about mass annihilation, however, do not explain the increasing interest in the vampire—especially in the woman vampire—during the 1960s, 70s, and 80s; and it was my questions about what caused this change that led me to explore the vampire motif to begin with. Indeed the change in the vampire motif seems more directly linked to changing attitudes toward sexuality than to increased fears about death. Certainly the numerous Hammer films, beginning with *Horror of Dracula* (England, 1958), feature Christopher Lee as a vampire whose sensuality delights his equally sensual women victims. Michael Carreras, of Hammer Films, agrees:

The greatest difference between our Dracula and anybody else's was the sexual connotations. There was no real horror in it, the women were eager to be nipped by Dracula and I think that gave it a fresh look.[41]

More significant changes occur later, however, with appealing women vampires, such as Miriam, Sterling, Valan, and Madelaine, and with human women who openly choose to seduce their vampire lovers rather than wait to be seduced. In fact, both Lucy (played by Kate Nelligan in John Badham's 1979 version of *Dracula*) and the neurotic model (played by Susan St. James in Stan Dragoti's 1979 *Love at First Bite*) are appealing precisely because they recognize their full human potential as individuals, a potential that includes the right to choose a fulfilling sexual relationship. Like the buxom cartoon character Vampirella, these new women vampires openly acknowledge that sexuality is a healthy and normal response, not a threat to the individual or the society. In fact, in most recent versions, the vampire often appears as more positive than his or her human counterparts.

During the past three decades, writers who have featured the vampire have focused on the individual's right to choose a different kind of existence, especially when that alternative does not cause harm to other individuals. Thus there has been increasing emphasis on the positive aspects of the vampire's eroticism and on his or her right to rebel against the stultifying constraints of society and a decreasing emphasis on the vampire's quarrel with traditional religious beliefs. In fact, recent writers have emphasized their vampires' desires for peaceful coexistence with human beings.

As a result of this more positive attitude, most twentieth-century interpretations of the vampire have been more light and playful than either their counterparts in nineteenth-century literature or even earlier folklore. This greater tolerance is undoubtedly the result of our growing acceptance of variations—even extreme variations—in individual behavior, an acceptance revealed partially by the number of films featuring lesbian vampires during the 1970s.[42] In fact, Margaret L. Carter comments specifically on this growing toleration when she observes that the vampire is no longer "the universally feared and hated villain of nightmare tradition":

Increase in knowledge of psychology and sociology no doubt contributes to the change in attitude. Today we no longer feel qualified to judge any man...as a monster. Current emphasis on minority problems may even cause a monster to be an appealing character, because he suffers for being "different." Furthermore, moral ambiguity is more acceptable in this century than the last; we are less apt than Stoker to consign any creature to irrevocable damnation. There is also the simple artistic problem of an overworked plot motif. Too many imitations of the "Dracula" pattern must inevitably pall on the reader.[43]

Although Carter persists in referring to the vampire as a male figure, she is undoubtedly correct about the reasons for this increasing toleration, not to mention simple boredom with a literary motif that has become a cliche. Formerly monsters to be feared, both because of their sexual preferences and their bloodthirsty habits, vampires in twentieth-century popular culture are often presented as appealing figures rather than as threats; and the rare exceptions to this trend—*Fright Night* and *Last Rites*—suggest that the pendulum may be swinging away from this acceptance of human differences. However, it is simply too soon to make that judgment.

The character of the vampire continues to evolve, but one thing remains certain: The vampire in the twentieth-century has returned to being a kind of folk figure, a character in paperback novels—especially in science fiction, fantasy, and children's literature—in popular films and television, even in advertising. Originating in that most popular of literary forms—folklore—the vampire in the eighteenth-and nineteenth-centuries entered the cultural mainstream, when it attracted the attention of serious artists, writers, and thinkers. Today, despite the tremendous evolution in the vampiric character, the vampire itself seems to have returned to its rightful place as a subject of folk interest. Laughing uneasily about the obvious Freudian references or even aroused by the openly sensual nature of the twentieth-century vampire, the modern reader or viewer grasps intuitively a fact that his more avant garde eighteenth and nineteenth century counterparts often attempted to present through various artistic media: The haunting face of the vampire is simply a darker version of our own.

Notes

Chapter One

[1]Jody Scott, *I, Vampire* (New York: Ace Science Fiction Books, 1984), p. 13.

[2]Charles Beaumont, "Blood Brother," in *The Rivals of Dracula: A Century of Vampire Fiction*, ed. Michel Parry (London: Corgi Books, 1977), p. 165.

[3]Beaumont, p. 165.

[4]Robert Bloch, "The Bat is My Brother," in *The Rivals of Dracula*, p. 162.

[5]Whoever developed the Count figure for Sesame Street must have known of one of the more strange characteristics associated with vampires in Rumania—the fact that they were compulsive counters. In fact, human beings could protect themselves from vampire attack by scattering millet over the grave of a suspected vampire. The vampire, who could not leave the grave until every grain was counted, was therefore trapped in the grave and prevented from preying on the populace.

[6]Clive Leatherdale, *Dracula: The Novel and the Legend* (Wellingborough, Northamptonshire: The Aquarian Press, 1985), p. 224.

[7]A number of critical studies have focused on the sexuality of the vampire. The most comprehensive of these are Ernest Jones, *On the Nightmare* (1951; rpt. New York: Liveright, 1971), a book-length study prepared by one of Freud's pupils; David Pirie's *The Vampire Cinema* (London: Hamlyn, 1977), which argues that "the function of the vampire movie is precisely to incarnate the most hostile aspects of sexuality in a concrete form" (p. 100); and James B. Twitchell's *Dreadful Pleasures: An Anatomy of Modern Horror* (New York: Oxford University Press, 1985), which asserts that "modern horror myths prepare the teenager for the anxieties of reproduction" (p. 7). There are others, of course, including C.F. Bentley, "The Monster in the Bedroom," *Literature and Psychology* 22 (1972), 27-34; Joseph S. Bierman, "*Dracula*: Prolonged Childhood Illness, and the Oral Triad," *American Imago* 29 (1972), 186-98; Royce MacGillivray, "*Dracula*: Bram Stoker's Spoiled Masterpiece," *Queens Quarterly* 79 (1972), 518-27; and Maurice Richardson, "The Psychoanalysis of Ghost Stories," *The Twentieth Century* 166 (1959), 419-31.

[8]Most actors who have played vampiric roles have been aware of this erotic appeal. Lugosi, for example, received hundreds of pieces of fan mail weekly, most of it from women; and Lee, during an interview with Leonard Wolf (*A Dream of Dracula: In Search of the Living Dead* [Boston: Little, Brown and Company, 1972]), makes the following observations about the vampire:

> He had also to have an erotic element about him (and not because he sank his teeth into women)....That erotic appeal has to be projected....It's a mysterious matter and has something to do with the physical appeal of the person who's draining your life. It's like being a sexual blood donor....Women are attracted to men for any of hundreds of reasons. One of them is a response to the demand to give oneself, and what greater evidence of giving is there than your blood flowing literally from your own bloodstream. It's the complete abandonment of a woman to the power of a man. (p. 178)

One might question Lee's analysis (especially his sense of women as masochists), but not the eroticism of his portrayal of the vampire.

[9]A more consciously artistic version is Herzog's *Nosferatu the Vampyre* (1979). Gregory A. Waller notes that Herzog points to his creation's humanity: " 'He is so suffering, so human, so sad, so desperately longing for love that you don't see the claws and fangs any more.' " (*The Living and the Undead: From Stoker's Dracula to Romero's Dawn of the Dead* [Urbana: University of Illinois Press, 1986], p. 206). One need only contrast Herzog's version with Murnau's *Nosferatu* (1922) to see how the vampire has evolved in the twentieth century.

[10]David Drake, "Something Had To Be Done," in *The Rivals of Dracula*, p. 169.

[11]Ronald Chetwynd-Hayes, *The Monster Club* (London: New English Library, 1975), pp. 45-46.

[12]Suzy McKee Charnas, *The Vampire Tapestry* (New York: Simon and Schuster, 1980), p. 284.

[13]Evelyn E. Smith, "Softly While You're Sleeping," in *The Curse of the Undead: Classic Tales of Vampires and Their Victims* (Greenwich, Ct: Fawcett, 1970), p. 189.

[14]Kathryn Ptacek, *Blood Autumn* (New York: Tom Doherty Associates, 1985), p. 128.

[15]Chelsea Quinn Yarbro, *Hotel Transylvania* (New York: Signet, 1978), p. 278.

[16]*I, Vampire*, p. 130.

[17]Although Chapter Three looks at some of the inconsistencies in Stoker's point of view, the most thorough analysis of the problem can be found in an earlier article: Carol A. Senf, "*Dracula*: The Unseen Face in the Mirror," *The Journal of Narrative Technique*, 9 (1979), 160-171.

[18]Fred Saberhagen, *The Dracula Tape* (New York: Warner, 1975), p. 7.

[19]Fritz Leiber, "The Girl with the Hungry Eyes," in *The Midnight People*, ed. Peter Haining (New York: Popular Library, 1968), p. 205.

[20]Everil Worrell, "The Canal," in *The Undead*, ed. James Dickie (New York: Pocket Books, 1976), p. 199.

[21]Steven Utley, "Night Life," in *The Rivals of Dracula*, p. 177.

[22]Les Daniels, *Citizen Vampire* (New York: Ace Fantasy Books, 1981), p. 58.

[23]Beaumont, p. 165.

[24]Raymond T. McNally, *Dracula Was A Woman: In Search of the Blood Countess of Transylvania* (New York: McGraw-Hill, 1983), pp. 215-244.

[25]King admits that he was consciously reworking *Dracula*, as Douglas E. Winter explains in *Stephen King: The Art of Darkness* (New York: New American Library, 1984):

> 'Salem's Lot' was written in 1973; the idea resulted from a dinner conversation in which King, his wife, and his long-time friend Chris Chesley discussed what might happen if Dracula returned in modern times, not to London, but to rural America. When King jokingly said that the FBI would quickly put him to rest, a victim of wiretaps and covert surveillance, his companions noted that almost anything could occur unnoticed in the small towns of Maine. (pp. 36-37)

There are, however, major differences. Waller notes:

> King is much less optimistic than Stoker about man's ability to unite in a moral community that will triumph once and for all over the undead

and so become the basis for a regenerated existence in the twentieth century. (p. 249)

Robert Lidston (*Dracula* and *'Salem's Lot*: Why the Monsters Won't Die," *West Virginia University Philological Papers*, 28 [1982]) observes that Barlow is much weaker than Dracula:

> King dilutes Barlow as the center of all evil by mixing him up with the much more petty evils of bootlegger Hubie Marston. Through this connection King attempts to identify evil with Marston's house and with the town as a whole. At the novel's end, Barlow has been dispatched and a multitude of quite ordinary citizens turned vampires are about to be destroyed by a brush fire. This diffusion of evil may . . . be a good device, but Barlow is proportionately reduced. (pp. 76-77)

[26]James B. Twitchell, *The Living Dead: A Study of the Vampire in Romantic Literature* (Durham, NC: Duke University Press, 1981), ix. In *Dreadful Pleasures*, Twitchell explains why horror appeals to the adolescent audience, observing that "horror sequences are really formulaic rituals coded with precise social information needed by the adolescent audience" (p. 7). However, there are far too many variations on this theme to be quite so reductive. Certainly, horror in the nineteenth century attracted the attention of major writers and thinkers.

[27]Ernest Jones, p. 130. Twitchell also attributes much of our fascination with horrifying images to a concern with incest:

> I believe they [the vampire, the werewolf, the manmade, no-name creature] enjoy a long life because, within the horror that surrounds these monsters, there is a sexual truth preserved by our culture: a truth about incest so important that we feel uneasy explaining it, let alone even dreaming it. (*Dreadful Pleasures*, p. 93)

[28]Arthur Nethercot's classic study, *The Road to Tryermaine* (1939; rpt. New York: Russell and Russell, 1962), argues that Coleridge was working with both the Greek myth of the lamia and the East European superstition of the vampire when he wrote *Christabel*; and Twitchell makes a good case for the fact that Keats, James, and Shelley were all familiar with the vampire.

[29]Cited in a review of two translations of Burger's *Lenore*, *The Monthly Review*, 20 (July 1796), p. 322.

[30]Montague Summers, *The Vampire: His Kith and Kin* (1928; rpt. New Hyde Park, NY: University Books, 1960), p. 271.

[31]Margaret L. Carter, *Shadow of a Shade: A Survey of Vampirism in Literature* (New York: Gordon Press, 1975), p. 3.

[32]An essay in *Colburn's New Monthly Magazine*, 7 (1823) defines the vampire as "a corporeal creature of blood and unquenchable blood-thirst—a ravenous corpse, who rises in body and soul from his grave for the sole purpose of glutting his sanguinary appetite with the life-blood of those whose blood stagnates in his own veins" (p. 141). Likewise an essay in *Chamber's Journal*, 73 (1896) defines a vampire as a "man or woman, who, after death, returned to the scene of his or her past life, and sucked the blood of living people" (p. 731). An essay in *The Open Court*, 7 (1893) cites "an old eighteenth century authority, Horst," who defines a vampire as a "dead body which continues to live in the grave, which it leaves, however, by night for the purpose of sucking the blood of the living, whereby it is nourished and preserved in good condition, instead of becoming decomposed like other dead bodies" (p. 3607). Thus the nineteenth-century definitions agree with Carter's in focusing on the vampire

as a dead body that maintains its unnatural existence by drinking the blood of human beings.

³³*The Vampire: Lord Ruthven to Count Dracula*, ed. Christopher Frayling (London: Victor Gollancz Ltd., 1978), p. 64.

³⁴Frayling, p. 64.

Chapter Two

¹Anne Rice, *The Vampire Lestat* (New York: Alfred A. Knopf. 1985), p. 200.

²Montague Summers, *The Vampire: His Kith and Kin* and *The Vampire in Europe* (1929; rpt; New Hyde Park, NY: University Books, 1968); Anthony Masters, *The Natural History of the Vampire* (New York: G.P. Putnam's Sons, 1972).

³Masters catalogues the belief in vampires according to country of origin in *The Natural History of the Vampire*, pp. 43-150.

⁴*The Vampire: His Kith and Kin*, p. 179.

⁵Nicholas K. Kiessling, "Demonic Dread: The Incubus Figure in British Literature," in *The Gothic Imagination: Essays in Dark Romanticism*, ed. G.R. Thompson (Pullman, Wash: Washington State University Press, 1974), p. 30.

⁶Leatherdale provides an interesting gloss on Irish folklore, however, one that reminds us that Stoker and LeFanu are Irish while the Brontes' ancestry was Irish also:

> The Dearg-due (the red bloodsucker) of ancient Ireland was reputed to use her beauty to tempt passing men and then suck their blood. Similarly, the Leanhaun Shee (the fairy mistress) was supposedly an eye-catching fairy whose charms were irresistible to men. Energy would be drawn from the ensnared male until he eventually wasted away, or else procured an alternative victim to take his place. (p. 77)

Leatherdale adds:

> One specific instance of Irish lore discernible in *Dracula* concerns the climax of the novel. The Count is destroyed on 6 November. In Ireland the feast of St. Martin is celebrated on the 11th of that month, and it is the custom for blood to be shed either on St Martin's Eve or earlier—during the nine-day interval following Hallowe'en. If St Martin fails to receive his blood sacrifice in that timespan the neglectful family can expect ill luck in the year ahead. Dracula's destruction, occurring when it does, thereby fulfills the hunters' obligation to St Martin. (p. 78)

⁷Frayling, p. 27.

⁸Gabriel Ronay, *The Truth About Dracula* (New York: Stein and Day, 1972), p. 16.

⁹Ronay, p. 21.

¹⁰Leatherdale observes that the moral element was not part of the original folklore:

> The pre-medieval heritage...did not distinguish between the innocent and the guilty when recruiting for the undead. People would invariably be cast as vampires through no fault of their own, such as by being stillborn or drowning, or by meeting their deaths violently. The vampire taint could be hereditary. (p. 27)

¹¹Frayling, p. 31.

¹²Ann B. Tracy, in *The Gothic Novel 1790-1830: Plot Summaries and Index to Motifs* (Lexington: The University Press of Kentucky, 1981), provides 208 plot summaries. Of these, six novels feature examples of blood drinking. Charlotte Smith's *Marchmont. A Novel* (London: Sampson Low, 1796) also features an "unusually

loathsome attorney named Vampyre" (p. 169). However, there is no indication that Vampyre is supernatural.

[13]Cited by Frayling, p. 33.

[14]One nineteenth-century writer argues that superstition still holds sway over the minds of ignorant people. Charles Mackay, *Extraordinary Popular Delusions and the Madness of Crowds* (1852; rpt. New York: Farrar, Straus and Giroux, Inc., 1974):

> Many houses are still to be found in England with the horseshoe (the grand preservative against witchcraft) nailed against the threshold. If any over-wise philosopher should attempt to remove them, the chances are that he should have more broken bones than thanks for his interference. Let any man walk into Cross Street, Hatton Garden, and from thence into Bleeding-Heart Yard, and learn the tales still told and believed of one house in that neighbourhood, and he will ask himself in astonishment if such things can be in the nineteenth century. (p. 558)

[15]Jeffrey B. Russell, *A History of Witchcraft: Sorcerors, Heretics, and Pagans* (New York: Thames and Hudson, 1980), p. 128.

[16]Twitchell, p. 16. Summers, in *The Vampire: His Kith and Kin* (pp. 135-36), discusses this blood-sucking creature that inhabits South and Central America:

> Their attacks on men and other warm-blooded animals were noticed by very early writers. Thus Peter Martyr (Anghiera) who wrote soon after the conquest of South America, says that in the Isthmus of Darien there were bats which sucked the blood of men and cattle when asleep to such a degree as even to kill them. Condamine in the eighteenth century remarks that at Borja, Ecuador, and in other districts they had wholly destroyed the cattle introduced by the missionaries.

Stoker also alludes to the vampire bat, when he has the American adventurer Quincy Morris refer to his experiences in South America.

[17]Mackay, p. 464.

[18]"Letters on the Truths Contained in Popular Superstitions," *Blackwoods* 61 (March 1847), 439.

[19]"Vampires," *Household Words* 11 (1855), 42; "Concerning Vampires," *Chamber's Journal* 73 (1896), 733.

[20]Frayling, p. 31.

[21]M.M. Carlson, "What Stoker Saw: An Introduction to the Literary Vampire," *Folklore Forum* 10 (1977), 26. Leatherdale agrees, observing that the "notion of tall, handsome aristocrats inhabiting inaccessible, run-down castles is the product of the literary imagination, not traditional folklore" (p. 31).

[22]Carlson, p. 30.

[23]Leatherdale, p. 54.

[24]Northrop Frye, *The Secular Scripture: A Study of the Structure of Romance* (Cambridge, Mass: Harvard Univ. Press, 1976).

[25]Edith Birkhead, *The Tale of Terror: A Study of the Gothic Romance* (London: Constable & Co., 1921), p. 79.

[26]Judith Wilt, *Ghosts of the Gothic: Austen, Eliot, and Lawrence* (Princeton: Princeton University Press, 1980), ix.

[27]Devendra P. Varma, *The Gothic Flame* (London: Arthur Barker Ltd., 1957), p. 199.

[28]Wilt, p. 118.

[29]*Vanity Fair*, ed. Joseph Warren Beach (New York: Vintage Books, 1950), pp. 671-72.

[30]Cited by Wilt, p. 20.

[31]G.R. Thompson, "Introduction," *The Gothic Imagination*, p. 6.

[32]George Eliot, *Adam Bede* (1859; rpt. Boston: Houghton Mifflin, 1968), p. 89.

Chapter Three

[1]M.L. Carter, pp. 60-61.

[2]*The Vampyre: A Tale* (London: Sherwood, Neely, and Jones, 1819), xix.

[3]Twitchell, p. 111.

[4]Carrol L. Fry, "Fictional Conventions and Sexuality in *Dracula*," *Victorian Newsletter*, 42 (Fall 1972), p. 21.

[5]Carter, p. 26.

[6]James Rieger cites Polidori's *Ernestus Berchtold* (vii-viii) in "Dr. Polidori and the Genesis of *Frankenstein*," *Studies in English Literature* 3 (Autumn 1963), 470-71.

[7]*The Diary of Dr. John William Polidori*, ed. William Michael Rossetti (London: Elkin Mathews, 1911), 4.

[8]Rossetti, pp. 215-16.

[9]Frayling, p. 17. Mario Praz, *The Romantic Agony*, trans. Angus Davidson (New York: Oxford University Press, 1970).

[10]Twitchell, p. 5n.

[11]Montague Summers, *The Vampire: His Kith and Kin* (1928; rpt. New Hyde Park, NY: University Books, 1960), p. 303. The same point is made by a writer in *Colburn's New Monthly Magazine*, 7 (1823), p. 140:

> But at Paris he [the vampire] has been received with rapturous applause at almost all the spectacles, from the Odeon to the Porte St. Martin.... Where are the descendants of the Encyclopedists and the worshippers of the goddess Reason, when Parisian readers and audiences are running mad after *"loups-garoux"* and *"apparitions nocturnes," "cadavres mobiles,"* &c., all *"puisees dans les sources reeles"*? Thirty years ago, what book-seller in the Palais Royal would have risked the conflagration of his whole stock by exposing for sale any of these superstitious treasures drawn from sacred legends and monkish impositions?

[12]Donald F. Glut, *The Frankenstein Legend: A Tribute to Mary Shelley and Boris Karloff* (Metuchen. NJ: The Scarecrow Press, 1973), p. 38.

[13]*The Hour of One: Six Gothic Melodramas*, ed. and introduced by Stephen Weschhusen (London: Gordon Fraser, 1975), pp. 9-10.

[14]James Robinson Planche, *Recollections and Reflections: A Professional Autobiography*, Rev. Ed. (London: Sampson Low, Marston and Company, Ltd. 1901), pp. 26-27.

[15]Planche, p. 104.

[16]*The Hour of One*, p. 85—a facsimile of the original playbill.

[17]The publishing history of *Varney the Vampyre* is obscure. E.F. Bleiler's introduction to the Dover edition (New York, 1972) explains that it "has been printed twice—the original parts by Lloyd in the early 1840's, and then a reissue, also by Lloyd, in the later 1840's" (viii). However, Summers observes in *The Vampire* that *Varney* was "reprinted in 1853 in penny parts" (p. 333). Authorship is also in doubt. The usual answer is given as Thomas Peckett Prest, but Bleiler's stylistic analysis suggests that J.M. Rymer is the more likely author (xvii-xviii).

A thorough study of the social and cultural milieu that surrounded *Varney the Vampire* appears in Louis James, *Fiction for the Working Man, 1830-1850: A Study of Literature Produced for the Working Classes in Early Victorian England* (New York: Oxford University Press, 1963).

[18]*Varney the Vampyre*, Ch. CLXVI (1840s; rpt., New York: Dover, 1972); future references will be to this edition and will be included in the text.

[19]Frayling, p. 42.

[20]Carter, p. 48.

[21]Bleiler, xv.

[22]Twitchell, p. 122.

[23]Twitchell, p. 210. Weddings were less important in the nineteenth century than they are in the twentieth, especially for members of the working class. In fact, families might not even take off work to attend the wedding of a son or daughter. Thus Twitchell's observation about the embarrassment of the woman who was "stood up" may be anachronistic.

[24]Twitchell, p. 211.

[25]Bleiler explains the abrupt conclusion to *Varney*:

The ending of Rymer's novel seems to have been dictated by external necessity. We can guess that Lloyd left a message for Rymer: "Mr. Rymer, be pleased to end *Varney* immediately." Mr. Rymer, in all probability, had written an ending far in advance, and simply submitted it. (xv)

[26]Arthur H. Nethercot, *The Road to Tryermaine: A Study of the History, Background, and Purposes of Coleridge's "Christabel"* (1939; rpt. New York: Russell and Russell, 1962).

[27]"Carmilla," Ch. III; in *A Clutch of Vampires*, ed. Raymond T. McNally (Greenwich, CT: New York Graphic Society, 1974); future references will be to this edition and will be included in the text.

[28]Joseph Sheridan LeFanu, *Uncle Silas* (1864; rpt. New York: Dover, 1966), xvii.

[29]Marx, Engels, and George Eliot make a similar connection.

[30]William Veeder makes the same point in *"Carmilla*: The Arts of Repression," *Texas Studies in Literature and Language*, 22 (1980), when he observes that "Laura is unnamed for forty pages, is never given a last name, and is not located specifically in time because she is everyperson—all men and women in every era who overdevelop the conscious" (p. 199). However, the extremely feminine Laura is an everywoman, not an everyperson; and her father's careful protection of her, her secluded life, and her innocence of the world are all more characteristic of women during the nineteenth century than of men.

[31]Waller observes that "Carmilla" reveals a "father's fantasy of unchallenged possession, affection, and stasis":

a juvenile, doting, nineteen-year-old daughter with no mother or suitors and few friends, living with her elderly father in a world of his making that seeks to exclude sexuality and maturity. (p. 52)

[32]Waller, p. 53.

[33]In *The Rape of Clarissa: Writing, Sexuality and Class Struggle in Samuel Richardson* (Minneapolis: University of Minnesota Press, 1982), Terry Eagleton focuses on writing as a manifestation of female powerlessness:

The letter in *Clarissa*, then, is the site of a constant power struggle. For Clarissa herself, writing, like sexuality, is a private, always violable space, a secret enterprise fraught with deadly risk. In an oppressive society, writing is the sole free self-disclosure available to women, but it is precisely this which threatens to surrender them into that society's power. The Harlowes wrest writing materials from Clarissa in what she explicitly terms an 'act of violence'...(p. 45)

However, writing can also be an act of power, of conveying knowledge that will help another. In "Carmilla," for example, Laura shares her experience with another woman and provides that woman with the power that may enable her to avoid Laura's mistakes.

[34]Among the studies that focus on perverse love in "Carmilla" are Veeder, Twitchell, and Michael Begnal, *Joseph Sheridan LeFanu* (Lewisburgh, PA: Bucknell University Press, 1971). For example, Twitchell compares "Carmilla" and *Christabel*, calling both stories of "a lesbian entanglement, a story of the sterile love of homosexuality expressed through the analogy of vampirism" (p. 129). Begnal argues:

LeFanu's purpose is not to attack...homosexuality, but rather to comment on the self-destruction of a total submission to sexuality. Just as Carmilla will drain the life's blood from her prey, so too will lust destroy the moral and physical lives of its victims. (p. 44)

[35]Nina Auerbach, *Woman and the Demon: The Life of a Victorian Myth* (Cambridge, Mass: Harvard Univ. Press, 1982), pp. 106-107.

[36]Lewis observes that the people who read the penny novels were rarely the same people who read the works of middle-class novelists like Dickens. Thus it seems unlikely that Stoker could have been influenced by *Varney*, a work that was rarely preserved in its entirety.

[37]Bram Stoker, "Dracula's Guest," in *The Bram Stoker Bedside Companion*, ed. Charles Osborne (New York: Taplinger Publishing Co., 1973), pp. 29-41.

[38]Daniel Farson, *The Man Who Wrote Dracula: A biography of Bram Stoker* (London: Michael Joseph, 1975), p. 144; Harry Ludlam, *A Biography of Dracula: The Life Story of Bram Stoker* (New York: W. Foulsham and Co., 1962), p. 115.

[39]Fry, pp. 20-21.

[40]Wolf comments on this characteristic in the preface to *The Annotated Dracula:*

Here, then, is the figure that Bram Stoker created—a figure who confronts us with primordial mysteries: death, blood, and love, and how they are bound together. Finally, Stoker's achievement is this: he makes us understand in our own experience why the vampire is said to be invisible in the mirror. He is there, but we fail to recognize him since our own faces get in the way.

The Annotated Dracula, ed. Leonard Wolf (New York: Clarkson N. Potter, 1975). Future references to *Dracula* will be to this edition and will be included in the text.

[41]Burton Hatlen, "The Return of the Repressed/Oppressed in Bram Stoker's Dracula," *Minnesota Review*, 15 (1980), 80-97.

[42]Christopher Craft ("'Kiss Me with Those Red Lips': Gender and Inversion in Bram Stoker's *Dracula*," *Representations*, 8 [1984] provides a brilliant reading of sexuality in *Dracula* and the fact that Stoker and his audience were horrified by the sexual mobility in *Dracula*. He argues that "the vampiric kiss excites a sexuality so mobile, so insistent, that it threatens to overwhelm the distinctions of gender," (p. 117) distinctions of utmost importance to Stoker's readers. Craft's analysis of the vampire's mouth focuses on this blurring of Victorian gender distinctions:

As the primary site of erotic experience in *Dracula*, this mouth equivocates, giving the lie to the easy separation of the masculine and the feminine. Luring at first with an inviting orifice...but delivering instead a piercing bone, the vampire mouth fuses and confuses...the gender-based categories of the penetrating and the receptive, or...the complementary categories of "brave men" and "good women." With its soft flesh barred by hard bone, its red crossed by white, this mouth compels opposites and contrasts into a frightening unity, and it asks some disturbing questions. Are we male or are we female? Do we have penetrators or orifices? And if both, what does that mean? And what about our bodily fluids, the red and the white? What are the relations between blood and semen, milk and blood? Furthermore, this mouth, bespeaking the subversion of the stable and lucid distinctions of gender, is the mouth of all vampires, male and female. (p. 109)

[43]Craft, p. 111.

[44]Auerbach, pp. 22-23.

[45]Stephanie Demetrakopoulos, "Feminism, Sex Role Exchanges, and Other Subliminal Fantasies in Bram Stoker's *Dracula*," *Frontiers: a journal of women studies*, 2 (Fall 1977), 105.

[46]Judith Roth, "Suddenly Sexual Women in Bram Stoker's *Dracula*," *Literature and Psychology*, 27 (1977), 105. Roth continues this line of thinking in her full-length study, *Bram Stoker* (Boston: Twayne Publishers, 1982).

[47]Judith Weissman, "Women and Vampires: *Dracula* as a Victorian Novel," *Midwest Quarterly*, 18 (July 1977), 405.

[48]Gail B. Griffin, " 'Your Girls That You All Love Are Mine': *Dracula* and the Victorian Male Sexual Imagination," *International Journal of Women's Studies* 3 (1980), 458.

[49]Weissman, p. 403.

[50]Weissman is more cynical. She argues that Mina "wants to defend women from the dangers of feminism, but admits that she has an appetite that not even what she imagines nineteenth-century feminism would be able to accept" (p. 400).

[51]Gail Cunningham, *The New Woman and the Victorian Novel* (New York: Barnes and Noble, 1978), p. 2.

[52]Cunningham, p. 2.

[53]Lloyd Fernando, *"New Women" in the Late Victorian Novel* (University Park: Pennsylvania State University Press, 1971), p. 129.

[54]Sarah Grand, *The Heavenly Twins* (London: William Heinemann, 1893), III, 26.

[55]Linda Dowling, "The Decadent and the New Woman in the 1890's," *NCF*, 33 (1979), 435.

[56]A.R. Cunningham, "The 'New Woman Fiction' of the 1890's," *Victorian Studies*, 17 (1973), 178.

[57]*Mrs. Lynn Linton: Her Life, Letters, and Opinions*, ed. G.S. Layard (London: Methuen, 1901), p. 292. Cited in Elaine Showalter, *A Literature of Their Own: British Women Novelists from Bronte to Lessing* (Princeton: Princeton University Press, 1977), p. 205.

[58]Dowling, pp. 440-41.

[59]Farson, p. 13.

[60]Ludlam, p. 13.

[61]Ludlam, p. 14.

[62]Farson, p. 214.

[63]Farson, p. 234.

[64]Craft also observes this discomfort at sex role reversal:

Harker awaits an erotic fulfillment that entails both the dissolution of the boundaries of the self and the thorough subversion of conventional Victorian gender codes, which constrained the mobility of sexual desire and varieties of genital behavior by according to the more active male the right and responsibility of vigorous appetite, while requiring the more passive female to "suffer and be still" (p. 108).

[65]Showalter, p. 188.

[66]Craft, p. 128.

[67]Roth, "Suddenly Sexual Women," p. 117.

[68]Griffin, p. 460.

[69]Wolf, p. 206.

[70]Leatherdale, p. 204.

[71]Craft, p. 130.

[72]For a thorough discussion of the way Stoker perceives the group, see Waller's *The Living and the Undead:*

> Stoker in *Dracula* contrasts the newly formed community of courageous, mutually dependent vampire hunters with the selfishness and skepticism of late-Victorian society as well as with Count Dracula and his vampiric brides. (p. 15)

In fact, one of the focal points of Waller's book is the way stories about the undead reveal an individual writer's perception of the status quo.

[73]*The Jewel of Seven Stars* (1912; rpt, New York: Kensington Publishing Corp., 1978), p. 31.

[74]*The Man* (London: William Heinemann, 1905), p. 83.

[75]Fernando, p. 145.

[76]Hatlen, for example, discusses the political ramifications of *Dracula*, including the fact that Victorians may have seen the Transylvanian Count as an imperialistic threat. Richard Wasson also makes the connection between Dracula's plan to conquer England and British imperialism in "The Politics of Dracula," *English Literature in Transition*, 9 (1966), 24-27. Others, including Wolf in *The Annotated Dracula*, have commented on Stoker's awareness of scientific developments and the way he integrates these developments into his story.

Leatherdale provides a succinct overview of the numerous ways *Dracula* has been read:

> *Dracula* can be read as an instrument of sexual repression; it readily yields to Freudian psychoanalysis; it is a testament to the perceived arbitrariness and tangible power of Christ; it pays homage to occult and literary myths in the shape of the Tarot and the Holy Grail; and it opens a window on to the social and political tensions operating in late Victorian Britain. (p. 13)

Chapter Four

[1]Bram Stoker, *The Lady of the Shroud* (1909; rpt. London: Arrow Books, Ltd., 1962), Book V. Future references will be to this edition and will be included in the text.

[2]Emily Bronte, *Wuthering Heights*, ed. William M. Sale, Jr. (New York: Norton, 1963), Ch. XXXIV. Future references will be to this edition and will be included in the text.

[3]An article by Bernard J. Paris—" 'Hush, hush! He's a human being' ": A Psychological Approach to Heathcliff," *Women and Literature*, 2 (1982), 101-117—focuses on Heathcliff as a plausible human being whose apparently extreme behavior can be explained by the psychological theories of Karen Horney. Furthermore Paris believes, as I do, that *Wuthering Heights* is as realistic as most other mainstream Victorian novels:

Except for the possible presence of ghosts...*Wuthering Heights* is as realistic as most other Victorian novels. Heathcliff, Cathy, the Lintons, Lockwood, and Nelly are all mimetic characters whose behavior is intelligible in terms of their psychological traits.... What often happens in Victorian fiction is that the abused characters develop self-effacing trends which are then glorified by the authors.... Emily Bronte understands better than most of her contemporaries that bad treatment is harmful to people, and she portrays very vividly its destructive consequences. Heathcliff is such a memorable character not because he is a demon, symbol, or principle, but because he acts out in an extreme way responses that we have all had to loneliness and rejection. (p. 116)

[4]In his introduction to *Famous Imposters*, Stoker points to the ubiquitous nature of imposture and also suggests his own profound interest in the subject: "The subject of imposture is always an interesting one, and imposters in one shape or another are likely to flourish as long as human nature remains what it is, and society shows itself ready to be gulled." (*Famous Imposters* [New York: Sturgis and Walton Company, 1910], V.)

[5]Examples of the gothic in Victorian fiction are too numerous to cite. However, a few examples should convince the reader that gothic materials often appear in novels which we regard as realistic. For example, Nina Auerbach first drew my attention to witch imagery in *The Mill on the Floss* in "The Power of Hunger: Demonism and Maggie Tulliver," *Nineteenth-Century Fiction*, 30 (1975), 150-71. Thackeray, in *Vanity Fair*, compares Becky to the sirens from Greek mythology while Eliot uses the same image to characterize Rosamond in *Middlemarch*; Dickens uses the vampire in *Bleak House* to describe both Krook and Vholes; and Charlotte Bronte uses the vampire to characterize Bertha Rochester in *Jane Eyre* and the ghost in *Villette* as an objective manifestation of Lucy's fears. In all these novels, the suspected supernatural figures are finally revealed as human beings. However, that revelation does not negate their metaphoric power.

Moreover, a number of critics have looked at Emily Bronte's use of gothic material. Among these are Syndy McMillen Conger, "The Reconstruction of the Gothic Feminine Ideal in Emily Bronte's *Wuthering Heights*," *The Female Gothic*, ed. Juliann E. Fleenor (Montreal: Eden Press 1983), 91-106, and Cynthia Griffin Wolff, "The Radcliffean Gothic Model: A Form for Feminine Sexuality," *The Female Gothic*, 207-223.

[6]Wolff, for example, discusses the Gothic use of place:

Radcliffe's novels are all set in some undefinable location, deliberately distanced from real-world, eighteenth-century England—in Scotland during "the dark ages" or to the south "in Italy." Modern Gothics follow in the tradition of Radcliffe's work.... Clearly the ritualized story is *meant* to be placed in a never-never land, existing beyond the reach of spatial or temporal constraints. (p. 211)

Equally relevant to this discussion is the fact that Anne Bronte's *The Tenant of Wildfell Hall*, which was written at approximately the same time as *Wuthering Heights*, uses the same narrative strategy, for Anne roots her novel solidly in time and place. For example, the first sentence asks the reader to go back "to the autumn of 1827." *The Tenant of Wildfell Hall* (1848; rpt. New York: Penguin Books, 1980), p. 35. The last words refer to both a date and a place: "Staningley, June 10th, 1847" (p. 490).

[7]Judith Newton, *Women, Power, and Subversion: Social Strategies in British Fiction, 1778-1860* (Athens: University of Georgia Press, 1981), p. 2.

Nina da Vinci Nichols—"Place and Eros in Radcliffe, Lewis, and Bronte," *The Female Gothic*, 187-206—makes a similar observation:

> Female powerlessness was built into eighteenth—and nineteenth-century social institutions of which marriage was the cornerstone. Single women outside of marriage were social non-entities.... By the nineteenth century, nevertheless, cultural images favor the Virgin Mother over Virgin Mary and acknowledge motherhood as the source of women's greatest power. The Gothic heroine comes into her own with a formidable combination of strengths and weaknesses as a governess: that is, an emotional child, a chronological adolescent, and a surrogate mother.... As governess she gains financial security as well as privileged position in the house she inherits at the book's end. (p. 194)

[8]A number of critics have commented on the two men in Catherine's life. One of the most interesting is Joy Ellis McLemore—"Edgar Linton: Master of Thrushcross Grange," *RE: Artes Liberales*, 8 (1981), 13-26. McLemore takes a unique approach to Edgar Linton, calling him "a symbol of quieter power than the main characters either possess or understand. His personal force contributes significantly to the strength of *Wuthering Heights*." (p. 23) Most other critics have focused on the awesome—though not necessarily sanctioned—power of Heathcliff.

[9]James B. Twitchell, p. 122.

[10]Louis James focuses on the popularity of German literature at the end of the eighteenth century:

> German fiction and drama enjoyed an immense vogue in England towards the end of the eighteenth century, and took a leading part in the Gothic tradition; two of the 'horrid novels' in Jane Austen's *Northanger Abbey*, *Horrid Mysteries*, and *The Necromancer* are German.... Some of the most popular German tales of terror were short folk tales, brought out in volumes like the frequently reprinted *Popular Tales of the German* (1791) by J.C.A. Musaeus, and *Grimm's Marchen* (1823).... One of the most popular was Burger's *Lenore*, translated by Walter Scott as 'The Chase' in 1796. Like the latter work, most of these stories illustrated the terrible results of wishing the dead to return. (p. 80)

Bronte could have read these stories on her own or during her stay at the Pensionnat Heger.

[11]The essays by both Conger and Wolff focus on Catherine as a new kind of Gothic heroine.

[12]Gerda Lerner, "New Approaches to the Study of Women in American History," in *Liberating Women's History*, ed. Bernice A. Carroll (Urbana: University of Illinois Press, 1976), p. 351.

[13]Winifred Gerin, *Emily Bronte: A Biography* (Oxford: Clarendon Press, 1971), pp. 22-23.

[14]Sanger's essay, which was originally read to the Heretics, a society at Cambridge, is included in the "Essays in Criticism" section of the Norton Critical Edition of *Wuthering Heights*, ed. William M. Sale, Jr. (New York: Norton, 1972), pp. 286-98. Other evidence of Bronte's familiarity with English law is revealed by Twitchell and by Barbara Gates, "Suicide and *Wuthering Heights*," *The Victorian Newsletter*, 50 (1976), 15-19.

[15]Margaret Homans, "Dreaming of Children: Literalization in *Jane Eyre* and *Wuthering Heights*," *The Female Gothic*, p. 274.

[16]Homans, p. 278.

[17]Newton, p. 3.

[18]Sandra M. Gilbert and Susan Gubar, *The Madwoman in the Attic: The Woman Writer and the Nineteenth-Century Literary Imagination* (New Haven: Yale University Press), p. 261.

[19]*Madwoman*, p. 288.

[20]James observes that the same trend occurs in popular literature:

> *Varney the Vampyre*...shows the author in the actual process of shifting his styles and attitudes as he tries to find a more congenial type of fiction.... In the first half, Varney is presented early on as an embittered character with sardonic detachment like that of Schedoni.... He then becomes more humane. He begins to take considerable trouble not to cause undue suffering.... Rymer is showing himself ill at ease with the traditional Gothic attitudes, and is turning to a more human type of character. (pp. 85-86)

Of course, as James observes, Rymer wanted to write for middle-class audiences. Thus, he may have been more influenced by mainstream fiction than some of his contemporaries.

Chapter Five

[1]Catherine Gallagher, in *The Industrial Reformation of English Fiction: Social Discourse and Narrative Form 1832-1867* (University of Chicago Press, 1985) reminds us that "the point of a metaphor is to find likeness in difference" and adds that "its terms normally replace one another" (p. 152). Thus we can see clearly how the metaphor of the vampire brings the whole Gothic world into the middle of the realistic novel.

[2]For example, Ann B. Tracy, whose book on the Gothic novel alludes to numerous bigamous marriages, provides a summary of a plot that is remarkably similar to the plot of *Jane Eyre* (Sophia Reeve, *The Mysterious Wanderer* 3 vols [London: C. Spilsbury, 1807]):

> Captain Howard as a young man flirted with an ugly spinster named Deborah Fangress, who subsequently proposed to him. His father and brother pressed him into an intolerable marriage with her. Later he left her and met, loved, and bigamously married Ellenor. When Deborah pursued him to his new home, Ellenor, pregnant, ran away, telling the Captain to look her up after Deborah's death but not before.

The Gothic Novel 1790-1830: Plot Summaries and Index to Motifs (Lexington: The University Press of Kentucky, 1981), p. 142.

Of course, Bronte might also have been inspired by Radcliffe's *Mysteries of Udolpho* or *Sicilian Romance*. For example, Emily (in *Mysteries of Udolpho*) follows a trail of blood to a turret, where she finds her aunt, who has been imprisoned by her husband. In addition, she finds the former mistress of Udolpho, a nun who was driven mad by licentiousness. Similarly, Radcliffe's *Sicilian Romance* includes a former wife, who is concealed in an uninhabited wing of the abbey and whose presence leads to rumors of the supernatural.

Peter Penzoldt cites another possible source, Joseph Sheridan Le Fanu, in *The Supernatural in Fiction* (London: Peter Nevill, 1952):

> There is, indeed, a marked resemblance between the tenth narrative of the *Purcell Papers*, 'A Chapter in the History of a Tyrone Family,' a tale of 'actual and intended bigamy', and *Jane Eyre* (1847). LeFanu's story is about a certain Lord Glenfallen, who keeps his blind wife in a secret part of his castle. He subsequently marries the girl Fanny Richardson. But the wife nightly escapes from her apartments, and informs the unfortunate girl that she is the real Lady Glenfallen.

> Finally there is a murderous attack on Fanny in her bedroom.... The end
> of the story is, however, more tragic than that of *Jane Eyre*. Lord Glenfallen
> cuts his throat, his wife is hanged, and Fanny retreats to a convent. (pp. 72-
> 73)

Finally, Bronte might have even been inspired by vampire stories in German Romantic
literature. For example, Bronte's Bertha Mason resembles the title character in
Hoffman's "Aurelia": "As soon as those words had passed his lips, the Countess
flew at him, uttering a sound between a snarl and a howl, and bit him on the breast
with the fury of a hyena" (Cited by Frayling, p. 210).

³Karen F. Stein ("Monsters and Madwomen: Changing Female Gothic" in *The
Female Gothic*) argues that the image of the monster is often found in Gothic novels
by women:

> In the Gothic mirror, the self is reflected in the extreme poses of rebel, outcast,
> obsessive seeker of forbidden knowledge, monster. Monsters are particularly
> prominent in the work of women writers, because for women the roles of rebel,
> outcast, seeker of truth, are monstrous in themselves. For a man to rebel, to
> leave a comfortable home and to search for truth are noble acts.... For women,
> however, such assertions of questing self-hood have been deemed bizarre and
> crazy; consequently the Gothic mode—and in particular the concept of self
> as monster—is associated with narratives of female experience. (p. 123)

⁴Edith Birkhead, pp. 224-25.

⁵Letter to William Smith Williams, January 4, 1848, *The Shakespeare Head
Bronte: The Life and Letters,* ed. Thomas J. Wise and J. Alexander Symington (Oxford:
The Shakespeare Head Press, 1932) II, 173-74. Future references to this work will
be abbreviated *SHB*.

Although none of Bronte's biographers suggest that her ambivalent feelings about
Branwell may have contributed to her characterization of Bertha, there are a number
of similarities—drunkenness, violence, and what Charlotte believed was excessive
passion.

⁶Most critics dismiss Bertha as an irrelevant Gothic element, a remnant of Bronte's
Angrian fantasies, or simply as a lapse of artistic good taste. Of those who discuss
her, most see her as a part of Rochester:

Mark Kinkead-Weekes says, "...the mad woman does not simply represent an
external impediment, but also something within Rochester himself which he tries
to deny, to escape, to imprison." "The Place of Love in *Jane Eyre* and *Wuthering
Heights*," *The Brontes: A Collection of Critical Essays*, ed. Ian Gregor (Englewood
Cliffs, N.J.: Prentice-Hall, 1970). p. 83.

M.H. Scargill analyses Bertha's function: But behind Mr. Rochester...is Bertha
Mason, the mad wife. Rochester symbolizes uncontrolled physical passion, and with
uncontrolled passion there is always the menacing figure of complete degeneracy
and madness." "All Passion Spent: A Revaluation of *Jane Eyre*," *University of Toronto
Quarterly*, 19 (1950), pp. 122-23.

Richard Chase argues, "May not Bertha, Jane seems to ask herself, be a living
example of what happens to a woman who gives herself to the Romantic Hero,
who in her insane suffragettism tries herself to play the Hero, to be the fleshly vessel
of the *elan*?" "The Brontes: A Centennial Observance," *The Brontes: A Collection
of Critical Essays*, p. 24.

John Hagan says, "The double imprisonment of Rochester is imaged in the
mysterious third-story room which confines Bertha, who is both the wife who enslaves
him and, in her raging madness, his grotesque *alter ego*—a hideous mirror of his

own licentiousness," "Enemies of Freedom in *Jane Eyre*," *Criticism*, 13 (1971), p. 357.

One of the few essays to explore the important similarities between Bertha and Jane is Karen B. Mann, "Bertha Mason and Jane Eyre: The True Mrs. Rochester," *Ball State University Forum*, 19 (1978), 31-34. Mann argues that Bertha had "her future mapped out for her according to the pretensions of her family. In that sense, her rage is in some ways as justifiable as Jane's had been against the Reeds." (pp. 32-33)

[7]Cynthia Griffin Wolff observes Bronte's preoccupation with the condition of women:

> Now Bronte did not accept the drastic reductions that had been dictated by the Gothic tradition—her novel offers neither a never-never land of fantasy nor a puppet heroine—but neither does it reject the validity of the Gothic tradition altogether. Bronte addressed herself to the underlying problem of Gothic fiction, the dilemma of feminine sexuality, and carried it into the penetrating light of realistic limitations and real world constraints. (p. 217)

[8]Both Mrs. Gaskell and Winifred Gerin refer to autobiographical elements in *Jane Eyre*. While Gerin analyses Bronte's childhood suffering at Cowan Bridge, her ordeals as a governess, and her unrequited love for Monsieur Heger, Gaskell refers to an episode which, although not autobiographical, forms the core of the novel:

> A young lady, who held the situation of governess in a very respectable family, had been wooed and married by a gentleman, holding some subordinate position in the commercial firm to which the young lady's employer belonged. A year after her marriage, during which time she had given birth to a child, it was discovered that he whom she called husband had another wife. Report now says, that his first wife was deranged, and that he had made this an excuse to himself for his subsequent marriage. But at any rate, the condition of the wife who was no wife—of the innocent mother of the illegitimate child—excited the deepest commiseration....

> *The Life of Charlotte Bronte*, ed. Alan Shelston (Baltimore: Penguin Books, 1975), pp. 159-60.

[9]Rosemarie Bodenheimer's analysis of *Jane Eyre* ("Jane Eyre in Search of Her Story," *Papers on Language and Literature* 16 [1980], 387-402) focuses on Jane as a new kind of heroine, her story a new kind of story:

> ...her narrative is persistently set in relation to other, more conventional kinds of stories—not only the fairy tales, Gothics, and "governess tales" which have received critical attention, but also the internal, interpolated narratives like Rochester's story about his affair with Celine Varens, St. John Rivers' version of Jane's inheritance story, or the innkeeper's tale about the burning of Thornfield. Jane's insistence on the originality of her character and voice must therefore be seen as taking shape in a world of fictions, which often prove to be in curiously instable relations with her own. (387)

[10]In a footnote, Edgar F. Shannon Jr. provides the etymology of 'eyre.' It means "journey in a circuit" and derives from "OF *eire, erre*, journey, way, from Latin *iter, iteris*, way, from the root of *ire* to go." "The Present Tense in *Jane Eyre*," *NCF*, 10 (1956), p. 145.

The Oxford English Dictionary provides two more clues. In Medieval England, 'eyre' referred to a kind of circuit court and the proceedings of that court. It is also an obsolete form of "air."

In keeping with the notion of movement, Jane Millgate notes how many of the books to which Jane alludes are books that deal with real or fictional travels: Bewick, *Gulliver's Travels, Rasselas, The Arabian Nights* the two ballads, *The Pilgrim's Progress.* "Jane Eyre's Progress," *English Studies,* 50 (1969), xxi-xxix.

Tracy's study of the Gothic points to the metaphoric significance of wandering in Gothic novels:

> In short, the one place the protagonist almost never finds himself is at home. (Like mankind, according to some religious views, he is just a stranger; his home is always somewhere else.) (p. 6)

Bronte, however, takes this characteristic and translates it to Jane's search for a place "within her society."

Finally, although the suggestions of travel and movement are an important part of Jane's character, the reader should not forget the one play on Jane's name that Bronte includes in the novel. Adele misunderstands Jane's name and thinks it is the French word *aire,* which means area, space, threshing floor, and the nest for a bird of prey.

[11] This passage is analysed by R.E. Hughes, "*Jane Eyre*: The Unbaptized Dionysos," *NCF,* 18 (1964), p. 358:

> ...now the fiend in the attic (symbolically Jane's own irrationality) appears to her in a mirror. As she gazes through to the nether world...she sees herself as she is capable of becoming... And the next morning [sic] Jane surveys herself in the same mirror, and for a moment sees a stranger.

One should also remember Emily Bronte's use of the same image in *Wuthering Heights,* when the desperately ill Catherine Earnshaw stares in the mirror and is unable to recognize herself. Both Brontes use the mirror (a symbol of women's supposed narcissism) to point to the fact that nineteenth-century women must create a new sense of self, far different from the concept of self that was so often forced upon them.

[12] The possibilities of literal death are discussed by Nancy Pell, "Resistance, Rebellion and Marriage: The Economics of *Jane Eyre*," *NCF,* 31 (March 1977), pp. 397-420. Pell argues that "it is against the background of the very real possibility of death, emphasized by both the novel's plot and its imagery, that we see Jane's strategies for life being worked out."

Tracy provides a reminder that such references to death are common in Gothic novels:

> Death is perhaps the most striking difference between the Edenic and the blighted worlds, and Gothic fiction has always at hand some *memento mori* to remind us which world we are in. (p. 5.)

[13] Hagan makes a similar point when he discusses Jane's quest for freedom. He argues that Jane escapes from a "series of prisons or conditions of servitude which...would have imposed an alien role on her...." (p. 353).

[14] Bronte suggests this conclusion in a letter to her friend Ellen Nussey, May 15, 1840, *SHB,* I, p. 206:

> ...as to intense *passion,* I am convinced that it is no desirable feeling. In the first place, it seldom or never meets with a requital; and, in the second place, if it did, the feeling would be only temporary; it would last the honeymoon, and, then, perhaps, give place to disgust. Certainly this would be the case on the man's part; and on the woman's—God help her, if she is left to love passionately and alone.

[15]Hagan develops this point, explaining that Bronte develops the characters of Georgiana and Eliza Reed because "their characters present a striking contrast between the puritan and the voluptuary" which is the "counterpart of that to be developed between the fanatically messianic St. John and the unregenerate Rochester themselves" (p. 363).

[16]In his discussion of image patterns in the novel, David Lodge notices this need to strike a balance and argues that Jane must mediate between external forces which are—in T.S. Eliot's terms—objective correlatives for her emotions. "Fire and Eyre: Charlotte Bronte's War of Earthly Elements," *The Brontes: A Collection of Critical Essays*, pp. 110-36.

[17]Virginia Woolf, *A Room of One's Own* (1929; rpt. New York: Harcourt, Brace and World, Inc., 1957), p. 72.

[18]Pell refers to this act—rightly, I believe—as Bertha's revenge, "the revenge of the marriage object, the woman who was traded fifteen years before." Sadly ironic is the fact that Bertha lives in a world, where her only choice is death, not life.

[19]Kathleen Tillotson, *Novels of the Eighteen-Forties* (London: Oxford University Press, 1954), p. 300.

Susan Siefert (*The Dilemma of the Talented Heroine: A Study in Nineteenth Century Fiction* [Montreal: Eden Press, 1977]) also focuses on Jane's rebellions:

> It is appropriate that the novel begins with the scene of Jane's first rebellion...because Jane's story is essentially one of resistance to those who attempt to debase her, depersonalize her, or thwart her aspirations to self-fulfillment. Jane's first childhood act of rebellion and self-assertion is followed by a series of like incidents and each punishment prompts a bolder external response from Jane and a greater internal sense of outrage at injustice. (p. 40)

[20]For a study of many of these allusions, see Paula Sulivan, "Fairy Tale Elements in *Jane Eyre*," *Journal of Popular Culture*, 12 (1978), 61-74.

Similarly Bodenheimer notes that Bronte works with other narrative conventions to create a new kind of fiction:

> Yet this quiet but constant undertow of concern to claim originality for Jane's character and narrative actually takes the form of using, then apparently disengaging from, literary models, as though the only possibility of originality in a world full of other stories were the ability to draw back and recognize them as conventions. The stance is really a dependent position of independence; but it is certainly a self-conscious one, containing and making a subject of the stresses Bronte must have felt as she worked out the narrative of *Jane Eyre* in full awareness of the conventional fictions she scorned. (p. 396)

[21]Martin S. Day, "Central Concepts in *Jane Eyre*," *The Personalist*, 61 (1960), p. 498.

[22]John Reed's social background is rather sketchy though Jane mentions the important facts that Mr. Reed was a magistrate (and, therefore, responsible for enforcing the law) and that Mrs. Reed sneers at John Eyre for being in trade. She is more precise about Rochester's background. Jane refers to Thornfield as "a gentleman's manor house" (Ch. XI) and provides him with an ancestor who fought in the English Civil War and a father who is unwilling to divide his property between his two sons. In fact, one very important reason Rochester marries Bertha is to acquire her property and to obtain the wealth to which, as a younger son, he was not entitled. It is only his brother's death that makes him a landed gentleman.

[23]Scargill says that the burning of Thornfield is artistically appropriate, that "Bertha Mason has destroyed herself, the madness that can accompany unrestrained passion has burned itself out, though it has left Rochester, who gave way to it, disfigured and blinded" (p. 124).

Day refers to Rochester at the conclusion as a "dependent child" (p. 502).

Chase observes that the catastrophe is Bronte's attempt to chasten the universe that had conspired against her: "And so she sends Rochester's house up in flames and makes him lose his eyesight and his left hand in a vain attempt to save Bertha. Rochester's injuries are, I should think, a symbolic castration" (p. 25).

Elaine Showalter, who describes Rochester's injuries as "symbolic immersions of the hero in feminine experience" (*A Literature of Their Own: British Women Novelists from Bronte to Lessing* [Princeton: Princeton U. Press, 1977], p. 152) is, I believe, closer to the truth of Bronte's novel, for it is a way of making Jane and Rochester physically equal as they are economically and intellectually equal. One should also remember their first meeting, when Rochester briefly allows Jane to assist him and, therefore, begins their relationship on an equal footing.

[24]Ruth Bernard Yeazell, "More True than Real: Jane Eyre's 'Mysterious Summons'," *NCF*, 29 (1974), p. 128.

[25]Yeazell, p. 143. However, Cynthia Griffin Wolff is, I think, closer to the truth of Bronte's novel though she sees the final sections as awkward for a slightly different reason: They "suggest just how violently the conventions and assumptions of this work contend with the limitations of realistic fiction" (p. 220).

[26]Gallagher observes that "metaphors are a hallmark of Dickens's style." She notes, however, that *Hard Times*, the novel right after *Bleak House* is a "book *about* metaphors" (pp. 159-60). Gallagher warns readers about certain dangers in reading or misreading Dickens's metaphors in *Hard Times*:

> It is also...a book in which metaphors often break down or reveal themselves to be pure illusions, mere shows that conceal (and often ill-conceal) seamy actualities. In *Hard Times* even metaphoric connections are ambivalently presented. Indeed, as we will see, if the novel can be said to endorse unequivocally any connections at all, it endorses the connections made not by the fanciful narrator but by...the single character incapable of seeing anything in terms of anything else—Sissy Jupe. The novel, therefore, actually exhibits a distrust of its own metaphors at the same time that it explicitly recommends them. (p. 160)

In *Bleak House*, the comparisons are made by characters in the story, and the reader is expected to recognize certain similarities in the vampire and the human character.

[27]John Kucich is correct to argue that the "role of Chancery has been exaggerated, since only a few of the characters actually struggle against or within it." *Excess and Restraint in the Novels of Charles Dickens* (Athens: The University of Georgia Press, 1981), p. 94. Nonetheless, the Court of Chancery is a graphic image of the way that institutions can destroy the lives of individuals.

[28]See Douglas Hammer, "Dickens, The Old Court of Chancery," *Notes and Queries* (September 1970), p. 342; George Ford and Sylvere Monod, "Introductory Note on Law Courts and Colleges," *Bleak House* (New York: Norton, 1977), xvi-xx.

[29]Dickens's attitude to his own parents—especially after his tenure in the blacking factory—is well known. However, in *Corrupt Relations: Dickens, Thackeray, Collins, and the Victorian Sexual System* (New York: Columbia University Press, 1982), Richard Barickman, Susan MacDonald, and Myra Stark link the family and institutional corruption:

The workhouse, the debtors prison, Chancery, the government bureau, the aristocratic social system, the stock exchange, the school, and the factory are always presided over by a mock-patriarch: Bumble; William Dorrit—the "father of the Marshalsea"; the Lord High Chancellor.... The claims for any real personal authority are fatuous. But the symbolic accuracy of the patriarchal parody is deadly. All the massive institutions satirized by the novels have been modeled on a bloated version of the father's role in the family. (p. 63)

[30]Gallagher offers a brilliant discussion of some reasons for Victorian interest in the family and for the family-society metaphor in the late 1840s, 1850s, and 1860s, one that suggests that Dickens's interest in families may have stemmed from beyond his own personal situation:

Important as the rhetorical strategy of the Tory reformers was in popularizing the family-society metaphor, that metaphor was by no means their exclusive property.... According to some historians, nearly all of the parties to the ideological combat over industrialism used the family-society metaphor.... Classical political economy was undergoing a theoretical crisis; the threat of Chartism required an emotionally effective ideological alternative to Utilitarian individualism; change in industrial equipment and organization required that workers identify strongly with their employers' enterprises; the repeal of the Corn Laws made the manufacturing middle classes more secure, and other economic conditions gave them a sense of greater prosperity.... In short, the manufacturing middle class was itself beginning to assume a father's perspective. It was resolving...its Oedipal struggle with the landed classes and was simultaneously threatened by its own rebellious male offspring in the form of the Chartists. Thus, some historians have claimed, new, modified justifications of fatherly authority were both possible and necessary. (p. 125)

[31]Aside from the image of their living in a kind of tomb, Dickens does not explicitly use the vampire image to characterize the Smallweeds; he does, however, use another predatory image:

The father of this pleasant grandfather...was a horny-skinned, two-legged, money-getting species of spider, who spun webs to catch unwary flies, and retired into holes until they were entrapped. (Ch. XXI)

[32]Kucich comments on Tulkinghorn's lack of humanity:

Like Jaggers, Carker, and Rigaud, Tulkinghorn thrives on the contrast between the guilt of others and his own indifference; he pursues just such a contrast through Lady Dedlock.... The reader knows that Tulkinghorn deliberately tries to empty himself of all human content for the sake of his appearance to others. (85)

[33]Esther is a problem—so much so that many recent studies focus on her self deception and neurosis. See, for example: Joan D. Winslow, "Esther Summerson: The Betrayal of the Imagination," *Journal of Narrative Technique*, 6 (1976), 3; Valerie Kennedy, "*Bleak House*: More Trouble With Esther," *Journal of Women's Studies in Literature*, 1 (1979), 330-47; William Axton, "The Trouble With Esther," *Modern Language Quarterly*, 26 (1965), 545-57; Alex Zwerdling, "Esther Summerson Rehabilitated," *PMLA*, 88 (1973), 429-39; and Judith Wilt, "Confusion and Consciousness in Dickens's Esther," *Nineteenth-Century Fiction*, 32 (1977), 285-309. Moreover, Kucich points to "ominous parallels between her world and the world of the third-person narrator":

> What is the difference...between the chaos of Chancery and the "pleasant irregularity" of Esther's Bleak House? Certainly, too, Esther's mind is a labyrinth.... Esther's egotism has bothered many readers, but still more disturbing is the way Esther's control over others echoes Tulkinghorn's. Both are in everyone's confidence yet tell nothing about their own deeper intentions; both have a collection of keys and locks; both harp on their all-justifying sense of duty...there is never any doubt whose side Dickens is on. Nevertheless, these strange, insistent resonances, by making Esther herself ambiguous, make it difficult to specify what kind of change—or what kind or repetition—is involved in the most prominent action of the ending, Esther's movement from one Bleak House to another. (p. 146)

While most recent studies focus on Esther's neurosis, Dickens's contemporaries were inclined to see her favorably. W.L. Williams, for example, makes the following comment during the discussion period after a lecture on Dickens's women characters:

> Mr. Rideal had mentioned his favourites amongst the heroines of Dickens, and he (the speaker) would not dispute the high place given to them; he had his own likings, and they lay with Agnes in 'David Copperfield' and Esther in 'Bleak House.'

Charles F. Rideal, *Charles Dickens' Heroines and Women-Folk* (1896; rpt. New York: Haskell House Publishers, 1974), p. 62.

In addition, Ford and Monod explain that Georgina Hogarth, supposedly the original for Esther, remarked late in her life that "although she strongly disliked to be identified with the character Agnes in *David Copperfield*, she did not object to being likened to Esther in *Bleak House*." (p. 895)

One of the few modern critics who agrees that Esther is a positive force is Marilyn Georgas:

> Recognizing Tulkinghorn as the personification of the evil that dominates in the omnisciently-narrated part of the novel provides a counterpart character to Esther as the personification of compassion, selflessness, and devotion to duty who dominates the parts of the book which she narrates.

"Dickens, Defoe, the Devil and the Dedlocks: The "Faust Motif" in *Bleak House*," *Dickens Studies Annual*, 10 (1982), 41.

[34]The writers of *Corrupt Relations* also notice this power:

> This wholesale dereliction of patriarchal values helps account for the alliance between the benevolent patriarchs like Jarndyce and the virtuous sons like Woodcourt to "feminize" the family. When Jarndyce imports Esther Summerson to manage all his self-created family's affairs, he consciously tries to substitute "feminine" values for the rapacious and fraudulent patriarchal values of Chancery. (p. 65)

[35]Michael Ragussis, "The Ghostly Signs of *Bleak House*," *Nineteenth-Century Fiction*, 34 (1979), 258.

[36]Kennedy, pp. 336-37.

[37]Sissy Jupe in *Hard Times*, one of Dickens's most feminine characters, is also concerned for the individual as her discussion with Louisa Gradgrind reveals:

> I thought I couldn't know whether it was a prosperous nation or not, and whether I was in a thriving state or not, unless I knew who had got the money, and whether any of it was mine.... And my remark was—for I couldn't think of a better one—that I thought it must be just as hard upon those who were starved, whether the others were a million, or a million million.

Hard Times, ed. George Ford and Sylvere Monod (New York: Norton, 1966), p. 44.

³⁸Leonard W. Deen, "Style and Unity in *Bleak House*," *Twentieth Century Interpretations of Bleak House: A Collection of Critical Essays* (Englewood Cliffs, NJ: Prentice-Hall, 1968), p. 46.

³⁹John Kucich, "Action in the Dickens Ending: *Bleak House* and *Great Expectations*," *Nineteenth-Century Fiction*, 33 (1978), 102. Thorell Tsomondo concurs, arguing that "Esther ventures a 'beginning,' a youthful and continuous one that counterpoints the eternal decline of the world that the third person narrator delineates." " 'A Habitable Doll's House': *Beginning* in *Bleak House*," *The Victorian Newsletter*, 62 (1982), 7.

⁴⁰Included in *Charles Dickens: A Critical Anthology*, ed. Stephen Wall (Baltimore: Penguin Books, 1970), pp. 434-35.

⁴¹A number of studies, including Harry F. Stone's *Dickens and the Invisible World: Fairy Tales, Fantasy, and Novel-Making* ([Bloomington: Indiana University Press, 1979]) point to Dickens's use of unrealistic elements. However, one study is especially relevant to Dickens's use of the vampire motif: James E. Marlow, "English Cannibalism: Dickens After 1859," *Studies in English Literature*, 59 (1983), 647-666. Although Marlow's essay is primarily concerned with cannibalism in *A Tale of Two Cities*, he observes that the "regular recurrence of ogre-figures in his novels indicates Dickens's permanent fascination with the theme of eater and eaten" (p. 648).

⁴²Stone, xi. Boris Suchkov makes a similar observation in *A History of Realism* (Moscow: Progress Publishers, 1973). Suchkov goes on to explain, however, that including romantic elements is a characteristic of nineteenth-century realism:

> Realism was reborn in the same historical sod as romanticism and faced the same ideological task—that of presenting the real substance and direction of historical progress. Hence the similarities between realism and romanticism, the presence of romantic elements in the works of Pushkin, Balzac, Dickens, Gogol, and Stendhal, not to mention the realists of lesser stature. (p. 80)

⁴³Dickens's continued interest in the vampire motif is revealed by the fact that he includes a long essay on "Vampyres and Ghouls" (probably not written by Dickens himself) in the May 20, 1871 issue of *Household Words*—almost twenty years after the publication of *Bleak House*.

⁴⁴Kucich first drew my attention to the fact that Dickens continued to be interested in this paradigm:

> In "A Preliminary Word" to *Household Words*, Dickens claims...that he wants to "show to all, that in all familiar things, even those which are repellant on the surface, there is Romance enough." (p. 193)

⁴⁵John Romano, *Dickens and Reality* (New York: Columbia University Press, 1978), p. 2.

⁴⁶Romano, p. 24. Henry James makes a similar observation in "The Art of Fiction" (included in *Myth and Method: Modern Theories of Fiction*, ed, James E. Miller, Jr. [Lincoln: University of Nebraska Press, 1960]):

> The characters, the situation, which strike one as real will be those that touch and interest one most, but the measure of reality is very difficult to fix. The reality of Don Quixote or of Mr. Micawber is a very delicate shade; it is a reality so coloured by the author's vision that, vivid as it may be, one would hesitate to propose it as a model.... It goes without saying that you will not write a good novel unless you possess the sense of reality; but it will be difficult to give you a recipe for calling that sense into being. Humanity is immense, and reality has a myriad forms. (p. 12)

[47]Edgar Johnson, *Charles Dickens: His Tragedy and Triumph*, revised and abridged (New York: Viking, 1977), p. 391.

[48]Romano, pp. 75-76.

[49]George Levine, *The Realistic Imagination: English Fiction from Frankenstein to Lady Chatterley* (Chicago: University of Chicago Press, 1981), p. 11.

[50]Romano, p. 113.

[51]Levine, pp. 147-48.

[52]D.A. Williams, "The Practice of Realism" in *The Monster in the Mirror: Studies in Nineteenth-Century Realism*, ed. D.A. Williams (Oxford: Oxford U.P., 1978), p. 265.

[53]D.A. Williams, p. 275.

[54]Patsy Stoneman, "G. Eliot: *Middlemarch* (1871-2)," in *The Monster in the Mirror*, p. 103.

[55]Stoneman, p. 111.

[56]John P. McGowan, "The Turn of George Eliot's Realism," *Nineteenth-Century Fiction*, 35 (1980), 171.

[57]McGowan, p. 172.

[58]Stoneman, p. 127.

[59]Williams, p. 262.

[60]Stoneman, pp. 104-105.

[61]Gordon S. Haight, ed. *The George Eliot Letters* (New Haven: Yale University Press, 1955), V. 168.

[62]David Carroll makes a similar observation in "*Middlemarch* and the externality of fact," in *This Particular Web: Essays on Middlemarch*, ed. Ian Adam (Toronto: University of Toronto Press, 1975):

> Now all this, especially the glimpse of vampires feeding off each other, may seem a long way from the exact functioning of a scientific hypothesis. But I suggest that one leads to the other, that George Eliot's scientific conceits...lead logically to these monsters, vampires, and assorted succubi...who live a subterranean metaphoric life beneath the provincial surface of the novel. The mind in its pride seeks to redeem by fiat the fallen world in which it lives, but instead turns it into an inferno where it is hunted down by monsters of its own creating. Although the relation between Raffles and Bulstrode is the most violent in the novel,...it can be seen as a paradigm, a clear means of understanding what is happening in several other important relations—those between Casaubon and Dorothea, and Lydgate and Rosamond, for example. The same pattern of tampering with the evidence of reality, of bribery and blackmail, the rapid escalation of demands on each side, plotting and counter-plotting, and finally open hostility. In each case, the monsters creep out of their holes at the end. (p. 84)

[63]Levine, p. 293.

[64]J. Hillis Miller, *The Disappearance of God in Victorian Fiction* (Cambridge, Mass: Belknap Press of Harvard University Press, 1963), p. 12.

[65]Northrop Frye, *Anatomy of Criticism* (1957; rpt. New York: Atheneum, 1965), pp. 139-40.

[66]While all of Eliot's novels are concerned with the lives of women, *Middlemarch* is particularly interesting because of the larger social context in which it was written. As Eliot worked on *Middlemarch*, Mill delivered his plea for women's suffrage before the House of Commons; and Eliot was asked by feminist friends like Barbara Smith Bodichon, Emily Davies, and Sophia Hennell to lend support to their endeavors.

Thus her desires to see women gain equality with men, her respect for the traditional elements of the feminine character, and her fears of the feminist movement get incorporated into *Middlemarch*. There is also some evidence of a changing perspective between the first and second edition. The second edition, as Haight notes on page 612 of the Houghton Mifflin edition of *Middlemarch*, tones down several passages that deal specifically with the oppression of women.

[67]Asa Briggs (*The Making of Modern England: 1783-1867* [New York: Harper and Row, 1959]) explains how bankers gained power in the late eighteenth and early nineteenth century—precisely the period that Bulstrode came to Middlemarch:

> Improvements in banking facilities were as urgently necessary in the late eighteenth century.... Businessmen might obtain fixed capital by borrowing from relatives or merchants or by ploughing back profits, but they needed circulating capital to buy raw materials, to pay wages and to keep their factories and workshops in running order. They needed both small cash, which was in short supply particularly in the industrial districts, and short-term capital. To meet their needs, however imperfectly and unsystematically, country bankers began operating in various parts of the country.... By 1784 there were more than a hundred country banks in England alone; during the next ten years their number trebled.... Together they made up a hidden national credit network operating with London as a centre (page 31).

[68]Stoneman, p. 119.

[69]Dickens uses the traditional power of the vampire over its victims to illustrate Jasper's power over Rosa in the following passage from *The Mystery of Edwin Drood* (1870; rpt. New York: New American Library, 1961), p. 70:

> "He has made a slave of me with his looks. He has forced me to understand him, without his saying a word; and he has forced me to keep silence, without his uttering a threat. When I play, he never moves his eyes from my hands. When I sing, he never moves his eyes from my lips.... I avoid his eyes, but he forces me to see them without looking at them."

[70]Barbara Hardy comments on the flower imagery in *The Novels of George Eliot* (New York: Oxford University Press 1967):

> The image [i.e. of the basil plant] is the last ironical comment on the images of flowers first associated with their love, and perhaps even with the names of Laure and Rosamond, in a novel where women's names are not without significance. (p. 124)

In addition, the flower imagery distinguishes Rosamond from the other vampires; unlike more aggressive vampires, Rosamond's destructiveness is her passivity.

[71]H. Lawrenny, review of *Middlemarch*, *The Academy*, Jan. 1, 1873. Included in John Holmstrom and Laurence Lerner, ed. *George Eliot and Her Readers: A Selection of Contemporary Reviews* (New York: Barnes and Noble, 1966), p. 96.

[72]T.S. Eliot, "The Three Voices of Poetry," *Atlantic Monthly*, 193 (April 1954), p. 40.

[73]Stoneman, p. 108.

[74]Like most of Thackeray's mythic allusions, the following passage, which compares Becky to the ancient Greek sirens has a certain tongue-in-cheek quality. Instead of emphasizing monstrous qualities, the comparison merely shows her to be a manipulative, but very human, woman:

> In describing this siren, singing and smiling, coaxing and cajoling, the author, with modest pride, asks his readers all round, has he once forgotten the laws of politeness, and showed the monster's hideous tail above water?

No! Those who like may peep down under waves that are pretty transparent, and see it writhing and twirling, diabolically hideous and slimy, flapping amongst bones, or curling round corpses: but above the water line, I ask, has not everything been proper, agreeable, and decorous, and has any the most squeamish immoralist in Vanity Fair a right to cry fie? When, however, the siren disappears and dives below, down among the dead men, the water of course grows turbid over her, and it is labour lost to look into it ever so curiously. They look pretty enough when they sit upon a rock, twanging their harps and combing their hair, and sing, and beckon to you to come and hold the looking-glass; but when they sink into their native element, depend on it those mermaids are about no good, and we had best not examine the fiendish marine cannibals, revelling and feasting on their wretched pickled victims. And so, when Becky is out of the way, be sure that she is not particularly well employed, and that the less that is said about her doings is in fact the better..

Vanity Fair, ed. Joseph Warren Beach (New York: Vintage Books, 1950), pp. 671-72.

[75]George R. Creeger describes egoism in a way that provides an analogy to the vampire in "Introduction," *George Eliot: A Collection of Critical Essays* (Englewood Cliffs, NJ: Prentice-Hall, 1970). p. 6;

The self, in its attempt to achieve fulfillment through the gratification of private desires, causes the destruction or wounding of the other self (or selves) upon which it has been battening. In so doing, it is brought to a dead standstill and forced to survey both the wreckage it has caused and the barrenness in which it lives. Sometimes the wreckage involves a literal death; and where it does not, death is nevertheless present in the form of privation and suffering— the necessary pre-conditions in George Eliot's scheme of things, for any radical reorientation of personality.

[76]In *The Condition of the Working Class in England*, Engels refers to "the capitalist vampires" and to the "vampire middle classes," using the vampire motif in much the same way that Eliot does.

[77]E.P. Thompson (*The Making of the English Working Class* [1963; rpt. New York: Vintage, 1966]) comments on the decline in the ribbon industry in the early years of the nineteenth century, brought about by "a passing change of fashion (lace for ribbon)," p. 205.

[78]Briggs, p. 301.

[79]Thompson, p. 296.

[80]Thompson, p. 277; the quotation is taken from the weavers' petition in favor of a minimum wage bill, 1807.

[81]Patsy Stoneman uses Rosamond's education as a means of demonstrating the way that the past influences the present:

Formal codes of behavior and dress limit...those members of the middle class who do not put themselves in 'attitudes of receptivity' to new ideas. Thus Rosamond's education consists almost entirely of learning rules of etiquette...and Mr. Casaubon is dominated by cut-and-dried rules. (p. 124)

On the other side are characters who are receptive to new ideas:

Will displays more marked unconventionality by giving picnics to groups of ragged children, and by lying full-length on the rug in houses where he becomes familiar. (pp. 124-25)

One should not forget that the vampire in both folklore and literature is, like so many of Eliot's egoists, a creature that is trapped by his/her past.

[82]Eliot, "Margaret Fuller and Mary Wollstoncraft," *Essays of George Eliot*, ed. Thomas Pinney (New York: Columbia University Press, 1963), pp. 204-205.

[83]The contrast between helpless women and women who are capable and useful is quite common in nineteenth-century fiction and is particularly striking when one looks at the contrast between Dora and Agnes in *David Copperfield*, Rosamond and Dorothea in *Middlemarch* and Gwendolyn and Mirah in *Daniel Deronda*. In each novel, a vampiric character is supplanted by a woman of emotional strength and maturity; and in each novel, this shift is given the author's tacit approval.

[84]In *The Novels of George Eliot*, Barbara Hardy refers to the marriages in *Middlemarch* as "different versions of the same story":

> There are four pairs, linked by love and marriage: the Casaubons, the Lydgates, the Bulstrodes, and Fred and Mary. The correspondence is one of moral implication but George Eliot often uses a relatively trivial coincidence to draw our attention to the greater coincidence, or to put us into her habit of seeing the similarities of 'human lots'. She uses the trivial fact that Casaubon is courting Dorothea at the same time that Lydgate is getting to know Rosamond in order to point to other similarities and other differences. (p. 98)

[85]George Eliot, *Daniel Deronda*, ed. Barbara Hardy (Baltimore: Penguin Books, 1967), p. 367.

[86]A number of recent articles address the question of Eliot's treatment of history. Among them are the following: Joy W. Hooton, "*Middlemarch* and Time," *Southern Review*, 13 (1980), 188-202; Sara Moore Putzell, "George Eliot's Location of Value in History," *Renascence*, 33 (1980), 167-76; Brian Rosenberg, "George Eliot and the Victorian 'Historic Imagination'," *Victorian Newsletter*, 61 (Spring 1982), 1-5.

[87]Bonnie S. Zimmerman, " 'Appetite for Submission': The Female Role in the Novels of George Eliot," Diss. SUNY Buffalo 1974, p. 195.

[88]Fifty years later, another woman writer was to despair that "history is too much about wars; biography too much about great men." Virginia Woolf, *A Room of One's Own* (1929; rpt. New York: Harcourt, Brace, 1957), p. 112. The gap that both Eliot and Woolf attempted to fill is now an accepted aspect of social history.

[89]Ellen Moers states succinctly—if ironically—that there were lots of people who never thought of Saint Theresa:

> Carlyle, for example, in his lectures on heroism did not dwell at all on that strong-minded, adventurous, efficient, saintly heroine...though he might well have done so had it occurred to him to refer to *any* woman as a type of heroism.

Literary Women: The Great Writers (New York: Doubleday and Company, Inc., 1976), p. 124.

[90]Gallagher traces the serious treatment of the working class in nineteenth-century literature to the "influence of the political economists, who raised the category of labor to new heights in their theories, making it the very source of all value":

> The theories of political economy made it possible to conceive of workers in tragic heroic terms, not just because it made them seem destined to suffer, but also because it made them seem important. (p. 56)

[91]Erich Auerbach, *Mimesis: The Representation of Reality in Western Literature*, trans. Willard R. Trask (Princeton: Princeton U.P., 1953), 491; Auerbach also makes an interesting comment on the historical consciousness:

> For it is precisely in the intellectual and economic conditions of everyday life that those forces are revealed which underlie historical movements; these, whether military, diplomatic, or related to the inner constitution of the state,

are only the product, the final result, of variations in the depth of everyday life. (p. 33)

[92]There are a number of good feminist readings of *Middlemarch*. A brief overview of these readings is found in Ellin Ringler, "*Middlemarch*: A Feminist Perspective," *Studies in the Novel*, 15 (1983), 55-61.

[93]Letter of October 12, 1867; cited in *The George Eliot Letters*, IV, p. 390.

[94]Edith Simcox, *Autobiography*; cited in Haight, *George Eliot: A Biography*, p. 535.

[95]Letter to Emily Davies, August 8, 1868; cited in *The George Eliot Letters*, IV, p. 468.

[96]Letter of October 4, 1869; cited in *The George Eliot Letters*, V, p. 58.

[97]Karl Marx, *Capital*, Vol. I, trans. from the 3rd German ed. by Samuel Moore and Edward Aveling (1887; rpt. New York: International Publishers 1967), Ch. 10, p. 233.

[98]Marx, Ch. 10, p. 256.

[99]Friedrich Engels, *The Condition of the Working Class in England*, trans. W.O. Henderson and W.H. Chaloner (Stanford: Stanford U. Press, 1958), Ch. 9, p. 270.

[100]Engels, Ch. 12, p. 313.

[101]Frayling, p. 40.

[102]Levine, p. 7.

Chapter Six

[1]The following historical works were among those consulted to prepare this chapter: Asa Briggs, *A Social History of England* (New York: Viking, 1983); Peter Gay, *The Bourgeois Experience, Victoria to Freud*, Vol. I: Education of the Senses (New York: Oxford University Press, 1984); Gay, *The Bourgeois Experience*, Vol. II: The Tender Passion (NY: Oxford, 1986); Jane Lewis, *Women in England 1870-1950: Sexual Divisions and Social Change* (Bloomington: Indiana University Press, 1984); Paul Robinson, *The Modernization of Sex: Havelock Ellis, Alfred Kinsey, William Masters and Virginia Johnson* (New York: Harper & Row, 1976); Sheila M. Rothman, *Woman's Proper Place: A History of Changing Ideals and Practices, 1870 to the Present* (New York: Basic Books, 1978); Lawrence Stone, *The Family, Sex and Marriage In England 1500-1800*, Abridged Edition (New York: Harper & Row, 1979).

[2]Claire Kahane, "Gothic Mirrors and Feminine Identity," *The Centennial Review*, 24 (1980), 43-64.

[3]Stone, p. 50.

[4]Stone, p. 22.

[5]For a more thorough discussion of the Victorian romance with death, see John Kucich, *Excess and Restraint in the Novels of Charles Dickens* (Athens: The University of Georgia Press, 1981); James Stevens Curl, *The Victorian Celebration of Death* (London: David & Charles, 1972); and John Morley, *Death, Heaven, and the Victorians* (Pittsburg: University of Pittsburg Press, 1971).

[6]Curl, p. 185.

[7]Morley, p. 14.

[8]Curl, p. 185.

[9]Curl, p. xiii.

[10]Nancy K. Hill, *A Reformer's Art: Dickens' Picturesque and Grotesque Imagery* (Athens: Ohio University Press, 1981), p. 81.

[11]Ronald Chetwynd-Hayes, *The Monster Club*, pp. 189-90.

[12]Briggs, pp. 250-51.

[13]Briggs observes that "commercial broadcasting began in 1955 and between 1956 and 1960, the number of television licences doubled. As 'instant pictures' came into the home they speeded up reactions and gave a new significance to the day and its events" (p. 302).

[14]Briggs, p. 258.

[15]Briggs, p. 295.

[16]Gay, p. 60.

[17]Briggs, p. 308.

[18]Pirie comments on the religious connotations of the vampire:

It would be hard to imagine a supernatural and religious concept more appropriate to the second half of the twentieth century than the vampire. In the context of waning spiritual convictions, vampirism remains the most physical, the least spiritual of all supernatural manifestations. It records the triumph of sex over death, of flesh over spirit, of the corporeal over the invisible. It denies almost everything other than the gratification of the senses by physical means. It is the most materialistic of all possible cosmologies. (p. 6)

[19]Briggs, p. 302.

[20]Gay, p. 49.

[21]For an interesting, though sometimes oversimplified, discussion of the differences in nineteenth-and twentieth-century attitudes to sexuality, see Paul Robinson, *The Modernization of Sex: Havelock Ellis, Alfred Kinsey, William Masters and Virginia Johnson* (New York: Harper and Row, 1976):

...sexual modernism represented a reaction against Victorianism—a term I use here as shorthand for the dominant sexual tradition of the nineteenth century....Against the Victorians, the modernists held that sexual experience was neither a threat to moral character nor a drain on vital energies. On the contrary, they considered it an entirely worthwhile, though often precarious, human activity, whose proper management was essential to individual and social well being. (p. 2)

[22]Frayling, p. 66. Margaret L. Carter makes virtually the same point: "In the Decadent period, the Fatal Woman...dominated literature, as opposed to the Fatal Man...of the Romantic period" (p. 36).

[23]Praz observes:

For, once a fashion is launched, the majority imitate its external aspects without understanding the spirit which originated it.

The same can be said of Vampirism, and for this fashion also Byron was largely responsible.

Mario Praz, *The Romantic Agony*, 2nd ed., p. 78.

[24]Newton, p. 3.

[25]Gay, p. 207.

[26]Gay, p. 201.

[27]Rothman, p. 177.

[28]Rothman, p. 6.

[29]See Stone, for example, on eighteenth-century sexuality.

[30]Lewis, x.

[31]Stone, for example, cites some of the more explicit advertisements for prostitutes and brothels:

> In 1773...*The Covent Garden Magazine or Amorous Repository*...contained
> sexually provocative stories, and advertisements.... Some years earlier, there
> had begun publication of *Harris' List of Covent Garden Ladies*, an annual
> directory of call-girls, with prices, specialties, and descriptions which combined
> lyrical enthusiasm with extreme anatomical precision.... So popular was the
> demand that in the very late eighteenth and early nineteenth centuries....
> England's most famous caricaturist, Thomas Rowlandson, was turning out
> pornographic prints, some of them for special customers like the Prince Regent.
> (pp. 336-37)

Stone adds, however, that such advertisements were not restricted to specialized
publications:

> ...it was in the late eighteenth century—in 1782 to be precise—that respectable
> London newspapers like *The Herald* were publishing advertisements by men
> openly 'soliciting female friendships', a phenomenon which has only reappeared
> in England and America in the last few years. (p. 330)

Roy Porter makes a similar observation in "Mixed feelings: the Enlightenment and
sexuality" (in *Sexuality in eighteenth-century Britain*, ed. Paul-Gabriel Bouce
[Manchester: Manchester University Press, 1982]) though he argues that a more open
attitude to sexuality pervaded all aspects of life during the Enlightenment, when
thinkers "reconceptualised sexuality as being an essential part of Nature." Because
sexuality was an "important component of happiness," it was a subject for study;
and Porter mentions manuals discussing "sexual techniques, compatibility, venereal
diseases, fertility, birth limitation, and reproduction." He adds also that the "most
marked feature about Georgian sexuality was its public nature, its openness and
visibility":

> ...sex was a prominent part of the written and printed culture. There was
> both high class and popular pornography. Pornographical journals began
> appearing from the 1770s, starting with *The Covent Garden Magazine or
> Amorous Repository*, which contained sexy stories and advertisements for
> prostitutes and brothels (including prices). (pp. 7-8)

[32]Carl Degler, "What Ought To Be and What Was: Women's Sexuality in the
Nineteenth Century," *American Historical Review*, 79 (1974), p. 1469.

[33]Gay, p. 244. Gay adds that technological advances made contraceptives available:

> In 1839, Charles Goodyear had vulcanized rubber, and in 1844 he obtained
> his first patent on an invention that had eluded earlier, less fortunate tinkerers.
> These are cardinal dates in the calendar of modern sexuality. By 1850, Goodyear
> and rival inventors had improved on the original procedures, and fairly reliable
> condoms and diaphragms were for sale across the Western world. (p. 256)

Richard Allen Soloway (*Birth Control and the Population Question in England,
1877-1930* [Chapel Hill: The University of North Carolina Press, 1982]) disagrees
and argues that, "despite the introduction of new appliances and devices, including
the modern diaphragm and the latex rubber condom, the most prevalent restrictive
practices, coitus interruptus, abstention, douching, or some type occlusive pessary
had been known for centuries." (xiii)

Taking a slightly different approach, Lewis questions whether changes in birth
control technology affected the lives of women, for she says that most middle class
women would have been unable to procure birth control literature, since "all aspects
of sexuality were taboo topics for the late nineteenth-and early twentieth-century
middle class woman":

(Not even feminists made access to birth control information an issue before World War I.) The situation began to change during the inter-war years, when Marie Stropes' flowery prose and emphasis on 'married love' made the idea of sexual pleasure as well as birth control more acceptable. (p. 117)

Angus McLaren (*Birth Control in Nineteenth-Century England* [New York: Holmes and Meier, 1978]) insists that all people—women included—would have had access to birth control information much earlier because a major shift occurred during the 1890s:

> In the previous decade new vulcanization processes permitted the production of thinner, more comfortable sheaths and diaphragms. Cheap postal rates and advertising in the penny press gave entrepreneurs access to a national market. Surgical shops blatantly advertised their wares in window displays and their managers had leaflets distributed. By the turn of the century the channels of birth control information ranged from the local barbershop to the advertising columns of mass circulation dailies. (p. 222)

The discussion over the availability of birth control information will undoubtedly continue. What is important for us to recognize here is that the shift to a greater acceptance of sexuality did occur!

[34]Lewis, p. 81.

[35]Lewis, p. 82.

[36]Lewis, pp. 133-134. McLaren argues that such sexual equality occurred much earlier:

> Feminism and family planning were intimately related. Every writer who dealt with the issue of birth control expressed the belief that it would directly improve the physical and psychological life of the woman. Women by 1870 had at their disposal an articulated doctrine which held that they had a right and an obligation to limit their pregnancies. Thus when the decision was posed in the middle-class home whether or not to limit family size the question would not be resolved simply according to economic considerations; the health and happiness of the wife had now been raised in the eyes of many to a place of equal importance. (p. 101)

[37]Rothman, p. 231.

[38]Rothman, p. 240. For a more extensive discussion of this change in ideology, see *The Modernization of Sex*.

[39]Pirie observes:

> Surprising as it may seem, neither *Vampires of the Coast* (1909), *The Vampire* (1911), *The Vampire's Tower* (Italian, 1913), *The Vampire's Clutch* (1914), *Vampires of the Night* (1914), *Tracked by a Vampire* (1914), nor *A Village Vampire* (1916) have any supernatural content at all. Many of these movies use the word vampire simply as an innocuous alternative for *femme fatale* or vamp. There is, however, one British short, *The Vampire* (1913) in which a vampire woman in India kills two men, but the metamorphosis is into a snake rather than a bat. (p. 34)

[40]McNally, *Dracula Was A Woman*, p. 177.

[41]Cited by John Brosnan, *The Horror People* (New York: St. Martin's Press, 1976), p. 106.

[42]For a more complete discussion of lesbian vampire films, see McNally and Bonnie Zimmerman, "Daughters of Darkness: Lesbian Vampires," *Jump-Cut*, 24-25 (1981), 23-24.

[43]Carter, p. 126.

Bibliography

Alexander, Karl. *The Curse of the Vampire*. New York: Pinnacle, 1982.

Alley, Henry. "Allusion as a Technique of Characterization in *Middlemarch* and *Daniel Deronda*." *Greyfriar: Siena Studies in Literature* 19 (1978): 29-39.

———— "Literature and the Miscast Marriages of *Middlemarch* and *Daniel Deronda*." *Cithara* 19 (1979): 21-25.

The Annotated Dracula. Ed. Leonard Wolf. New York: Clarkson N. Potter, 1975.

Armstrong, F.W. *The Devouring*. New York: Tom Doherty Associates, 1987.

Astle, Richard. "Dracula as Totemic Monster: Lacan, Freud, Oedipus and History." *Sub-stance* 25 (1980): 98-105.

Atkins, Dorothy. "The Philosophical Basis for George Eliot's Feminist Stance in *Middlemarch*."*Publications of the Arkansas Philological Association* 5 (1979): 23-29.

Auerbach, Erich. *Mimesis: The Representation of Reality in Western Literature*. Trans. Willard R. Trask. Princeton: Princeton UP, 1953.

Auerbach, Nina. "The Power of Hunger: Demonism and Maggie Tulliver." *NCF* 30 (1975): 150-71.

———— *Woman and the Demon: The Life of a Victorian Myth*. Cambridge: Harvard, 1982.

Axton, William. "The Trouble With Esther." *MLQ* 26 (1965): 545-57.

Banks, J.A. *Victorian Values: Secularism and the size of Families*. Boston: Routledge and Kegan Paul, 1981.

Barickman, Richard, Susan MacDonald, and Myra Stark. *Corrupt Relations: Dickens, Thackeray, Trollope, Collins, and the Victorian Sexual System*. New York: Columbia, 1982.

Bayer-Bernbaum, Linda. *The Gothic Imagination: Expansion in Gothic Literature and Art*. Toronto: Associated University Presses, 1982.

Beaumont, Charles. "Blood Brother." *The Rivals of Dracula: A Century of Vampire Fiction*. 163-68.

Begnal, Michael H. *Joseph Sheridan LeFanu*. Lewisburg: Bucknell University Press, 1971.

Bentley, C.F. "The Monster in the Bedroom." *Literature and Psychology* 22 (1972): 27-34.

Bierman, Joseph S. "*Dracula*: Prolonged Childhood Illness and the Oral Triad." *American Imago* 29 (1972), 186-98.

———— "The Genesis and Dating of 'Dracula' from Bram Stoker's Working Notes." *Notes and Queries* 222 (1977): 39-41.

Birkhead, Edith. *The Tale of Terror: A Study of the Gothic Romance*. London: Constable, 1921.

Bleiler, E.F. "Introduction." *Varney the Vampyre*. New York: Dover, 1972. v-xv.

Blinderman Charles S. "Vampurella: Darwin and Count Dracula." *Massachusetts Review* 21 (1980): 411-28.

Bloch, Robert. "The Bat is My Brother." *The Rivals of Dracula*. 144-62.

Bodenheimer, Rosemarie. "Jane Eyre in Search of Her Story." *Papers on Language and Literature* 16 (1980): 387-402.

Bouce, Paul-Gabriel, ed. *Sexuality in Eighteenth-Century Britain*. Manchester: Manchester University Press, 1982.

Briggs, Asa. *The Making of Modern England: 1783-1867*. New York: Harper and Row. 1959.

——— *A Social History of England*. New York: Viking, 1983.

Briggs, Julia. *Night Visitors: The Rise and Fall of the English Ghost Story*. London: Faber, 1977.

Britton, Andrew, Richard Lippe, Tony Williams, and Robin Wood. *American Nightmare: Essays on the Horror Film*. Toronto: Festival of Festivals, 1979.

Bronte, Anne. *The Tenant of Wildfell Hall*. New York: Penguin, 1980.

Bronte, Charlotte. *Jane Eyre*. Ed. Richard J. Dunn. New York: Norton, 1971.

——— *Shirley*. Ed. Andrew and Judith Hook. Baltimore: Penguin, 1974.

——— *Villette*. New York: Everyman, 1972.

Bronte, Emily. *Wuthering Heights*. Ed. William M. Sale, Jr. New York: Norton, 1963.

The Brontes: A Collection of Critical Essays. Ed. Ian Gregor. Englewood Cliffs, NJ: Prentice-Hall, 1970.

Brosnan, John. *The Horror People*. New York: St. Martins, 1976.

Browne, Nelson. *Sheridan LeFanu*. London: Arthur Barker, 1951.

Brownstein, Rachael M. *Becoming A Heroine: Reading About Women in Novels*. New York: Viking, 1982.

Carlson, M.M. "What Stoker Saw: An Introduction to the Literary Vampire." *Folklore Forum* 10 (1977): 26-32.

Carroll, Bernice A., ed. *Liberating Women's History: Theoretical and Critical Essays*. Urbana: University of Illinois, 1976.

Carroll, David. "*Middlemarch* and the externality of fact." *This Particular Web: Essays on Middlemarch*. Ed. Ian Adam. Toronto: University of Toronto, 1975. 73-90.

Carter, Margaret L. *Shadow of a Shade: A Survey of Vampirism in Literature*. New York: Gordon, 1975.

Chandrasekhar, S. "*A Dirty, Filthy Book*": The Writings of Charles Knowlton and Annie Besant on Reproductive Physiology and Birth Control and an Account of the Bradlaugh-Besant Trial*. Berkeley: University of California Press, 1981.

Charles Dickens: A Critical Anthology. Ed. Stephen Wall. Baltimore: Penguin, 1970.

Charnas, Suzy McKee. *The Vampire Tapestry*. New York: Simon and Schuster, 1980.

Chase, Richard. "The Brontes: A Centennial Observance." *The Brontes: A Collection of Critical Essays*. 19-33.

Chetwynd-Hayes, Ronald. *The Monster Club*. London: New English Library, 1975.

Christ, Carol T. "Imaginative Constraint, Feminine Duty, and the Form of Charlotte Bronte's Fiction. *Women's Studies* 6 (1979): 287-96.

"Concerning Vampires." *Chamber's Journal* 73 (1896): 730-34.

Conger, Syndy McMillen. "The Reconstruction of the Gothic Feminine Ideal in Emily Bronte's *Wuthering Heights*." *The Female Gothic*. Ed. Juliann E. Fleenor, Montreal: Eden, 1983, 91-106.

Cooper, Basil. *The Vampire in Legend, Fact, and Art*. Secaucus, NJ: The Citadel Press, 1974.

Craft, Christopher. " 'Kiss Me with Those Red Lips': Gender and Inversion in Bram Stoker's *Dracula.*" *Representations* 8 (1984): 107-33.

Creegor, George R. "Introduction." *George Eliot: A Collection of Critical Essays.* 1-10.

Cunningham, A.R. "The 'New Woman Fiction' of the 1890's." *Victorian Studies* 17 (1973): 177-86.

Cunningham, Gail. *The New Woman and the Victorian Novel.* New York: Barnes and Noble, 1978.

Curl, James Stevens. *The Victorian Celebration of Death.* London: David and Charles, 1972.

The Curse of the Undead: Classic Tales of Vampires and Their Victims. Ed. Margaret L. Carter. Greenwich, CT: Fawcett. 1970.

Daleski, H.M. *The Divided Heroine: A Recurrent Pattern in Six English Novels.* New York: Holmes and Meier, 1984.

Daniels, Les. *The Black Castle.* New York: Ace Fantasy, 1978.

———. *Citizen Vampire.* New York: Ace Fantasy, 1981.

———. *The Silver Skull.* New York: Ace Fantasy, 1979.

Davidson, Donald. "What Metaphors Mean." *On Metaphor.* Ed. Sheldon Sacks. Chicago: U of Chicago, 1978. 29-45.

Davis, G.A. Wittig. "Ruskin's *Modern Painters* and George Eliot's Concept of Realism." *English Language Notes* 18 (1981): 194-201.

Day, Martin S. "Central Concepts in *Jane Eyre.*" *The Personalist* 61 (1960): 495-505.

Deen, Leonard W. "Style and Unity in *Bleak House.*" *Twentieth Century Interpretations of Bleak House.* 45-57.

Degler, Carl. "What Ought To Be and What Was: Women's Sexuality in the Nineteenth Century." *American Historical Review* 79 (1974): 1467-90.

Demetrakopoulos, Stephanie. "Feminism, Sex Role Exchanges, and Other Subliminal Fantasies in Bram Stoker's *Dracula.*" *Frontiers: a journal of women studies* 2 (1977): 104-13.

Dickens, Charles. *Bleak House.* Ed. George Ford and Sylvere Monod. New York: Norton, 1977.

Documents of Modern Realism. Ed. George J. Becker. Princeton: Princeton UP, 1963.

Dowling, Linda. "The Decadent and the New Woman in the 1890's." *NCF* 33 (1979): 434-53.

Drake, David. "Something Had To Be Done." *The Rivals of Dracula.* 168-73.

Dubois, Ellen et al. "Poetics and Culture in Women's History: A Symposium." *Feminist Studies* 6 (1980).

Eagleton, Terry. *The Rape of Clarissa: Writing, Sexuality and Class Struggle in Samuel Richardson.* Minneapolis: U of Minnesota. 1982.

Eliot, George. *Adam Bede.* Boston: Houghton Mifflin, 1968.

———. *Daniel Deronda.* Ed. Barbara Hardy. Baltimore: Penguin, 1967.

———. *Essays of George Eliot.* Ed. Thomas Pinney. New York: Columbia UP, 1963.

———. *Middlemarch.* Ed. Gordon S. Haight. Boston: Riverside, 1956.

Eliot, T.S. "The Three Voices of Poetry." *Atlantic Monthly* 193 (1954): 38-44.

Engels, Friedrich. *The Condition of the Working Class in England.* Trans. W.O. Henderson and W.H. Chaloner. Stanford: Stanford UP, 1958.

Estleman, Loren D. *Sherlock Holmes vs. Dracula or The Adventure of the Sanquinary Count.* New York: Penguin, 1979.

Farson, Daniel. *The Man Who Wrote Dracula: A biography of Bram Stoker*. London: Michel Joseph, 1975.

Fernando, Lloyd. *"New Women" in the Late Victorian Novel*. University Park: Pennsylvania State UP, 1971.

Fleenor, Juliann E., ed. *The Female Gothic*. Montreal: Eden, 1983.

Fry, Carrol L. "Fictional Conventions and Sexuality in *Dracula*." *Victorian Newsletter* 42 (1972): 20-22.

Frye, Northrop. *Anatomy of Criticism: Four Essays*. New York: Atheneum, 1970.

_____ *The Secular Scripture: A Study of the Structure of Romance*. Cambridge: Harvard UP, 1976.

Gallagher, Catherine. *The Industrial Reformation of English Fiction: Social Discourse and Narrative Form 1832-1867*. Chicago: U of Chicago, 1985.

Gardner, Craig Shaw. *The Lost Boys*. New York: Berkley, 1987.

Garton, Ray. *Live Girls*. New York: Pocket Books, 1987.

Gaskell, Elizabeth. *The Life of Charlotte Bronte*. Ed. Alan Shelston. Baltimore: Penguin, 1975.

Gates, Barbara. "Suicide and *Wuthering Heights*." *The Victorian Newsletter* 50 (1976): 15-19.

Gay, Peter. *The Bourgeois Experience, Victoria to Freud*. Vol. I. Education of the Senses. New York: Oxford UP, 1984.

Georgas, Marilyn. "Dickens, Defoe, the Devil and the Dedlocks: The 'Faust Motif' in *Bleak House*." *Dickens Studies Annual* 10 (1982), 23-44.

George Eliot: A Collection of Critical Essays. Ed. George R. Creeger. Englewood Cliffs, NJ: Prentice-Hall, 1970.

George Eliot and Her Readers: A Selection of Contemporary Reviews. Ed. John Holmstrom and Lawrence Lerner. New York: Barnes and Noble, 1966.

The George Eliot Letters. Ed. Gordon S. Haight. New Haven: Yale UP, 1955.

Gerin, Winifred. *Charlotte Bronte: The Evolution of Genius*. New York: Oxford UP. 1967.

_____ *Emily Bronte: A Biography*. Oxford: Clarendon, 1971.

Gezari, Janet K. "Marriage or Career: Goals for Women in Charlotte Bronte's Novels." *Bucknell Review* 24 (1978): 83-94.

Gilbert, Sandra M. and Susan Gubar. *The Madwoman in the Attic: The Woman Writer and the Nineteenth-Century Literary Imagination*. New Haven: Yale UP, 1979.

Glut, Donald F. *The Dracula Book*. Metuchen, NJ: The Scarecrow Press, 1975.

_____ *The Frankenstein Legend: A Tribute to Mary Shelley and Boris Karloff*. Metuchen, NJ: The Scarecrow Press, 1973.

The Gothic Imagination: Essays in Dark Romanticism. Ed. G.R. Thompson. Pullman Wash: Washington State UP, 1974.

Grand, Sarah. *The Heavenly Twins*. London: William Heinemann, 1893.

Griffin, Gail B. " 'Your Girls That You All Love Are Mine' ": *Dracula* and the Victorian Male Sexual Imagination." *International Journal of Women's Studies* 3 (1980): 454-65.

Hagan, John. "Enemies of Freedom in *Jane Eyre*." *Criticism* 13 (1971): 351-76.

Haight, Gordon S. "The Heroine of *Middlemarch*." *Victorian Newsletter* 54 (1978), 4-8.

Hamer, Douglas. "Dickens, The Old Court of Chancery." *Notes and Queries* 17 (1970): 341-47.

Hardy, Barbara. *The Novels of George Eliot*. New York: Oxford UP, 1967.

Hatlen, Burton. "The Return of the Repressed/Oppressed in Bram Stoker's *Dracula*." *Minnesota Review* 15 (1980): 80-97.

Hill, Nancy K. *A Reformer's Art: Dickens' Picturesque and Grotesque Imagery*. Athens: Ohio UP, 1981.

Homans, Margaret, "Dreaming of Children: Literalization in *Jane Eyre* and *Wuthering Heights*." *The Female Gothic*. Ed. Juliann E. Fleenor, 257-79.

Hooton, Joy W. "*Middlemarch* and Time." *Southern Review* 13 (1980): 188-202.

Horne, Margot. "From the Window-Seat to the Red Room; Innocence to Experience in *Jane Eyre*." *Dutch Quarterly Review* 10 (1980): 199-213.

The Hour of One: Six Gothic Melodramas. Ed. Stephen Wischhusen. London: Gordon Fraser, 1975.

Hughes, R.E. "*Jane Eyre*: The Unbaptised Dionysos." *NCF* 18 (1964): 347-64.

James, Henry. "The Art of Fiction." *Myth and Method: Modern Theories of Fiction*. Ed. James E. Miller, Jr. Lincoln: U of Nebraska Press, 1960. 3-27.

James, Louis. *Fiction for the Working Man. 1830-1850: A Study of Literature Produced for the Working Classes in Early Victorian England*. New York: Oxford UP, 1963.

Jennings, Jan. *Vampyr*. New York: Tom Doherty Associates, 1981.

Johnson, Edgar. *Charles Dickens: His Tragedy and Triumph*. New York: Viking, 1977.

Johnson, Ken. *Hounds of Dracula*. New York: Signet, 1977.

Jones, Ernest. *On the Nightmare*. New York: Liveright, 1971.

Kahane, Claire. "Gothic Mirrors and Feminine Identity." *The Centennial Review* 24 (1980): 43-64.

Kaminsky, Stuart. *Never Cross A Vampire*. New York: The Mysterious Press, 1984.

Kennedy, Valerie. "*Bleak House*: More Trouble With Esther." *Journal of Women's Studies in Literature* 1 (1979): 330-47.

Kiessling, Nicholas K. "Demonic Dread: The Incubus Figure in British Literature." *The Gothic Imagination*. 22-41.

Killough, Lee. *Blood Hunt*. New York: Tom Doherty Associates, 1987.

King, Stephen. *'Salem's Lot*. New York: NAL, 1976.

Kinkead-Weekes, Mark. "The Place of Love in *Jane Eyre* and *Wuthering Heights*." *The Brontes: A Collection of Critical Essays*. 76-95.

Kucich, John. "Action in the Dickens Ending: *Bleak House* and *Great Expectations*." *NCF* 33 (1978): 88-109.

———. *Excess and Restraint in the Novels of Charles Dickens*. Athens: U of Georgia, 1981.

Lamb, Lady Caroline. *Glenarvon*. Delmar, NJ: Scholars' Facsimiles and Reprints, 1972.

Leatherdale, Clive. *Dracula: The Novel and the Legend*. Wellingborough: The Aquarian Press, 1985.

Lee, Tanith. *Sabella or The Blood Stone*. New York: Donald A. Wollheim, 1980.

LeFanu, Joseph Sheridan. "Carmilla." *A Clutch of Vampires*. Ed. Raymond T. McNally. Greenwich, CT: New York Graphic Society, 1974. 69-154.

———. *Uncle Silas: A Tale of Bartram-Haugh*. New York: Dover, 1966.

Leiber, Fritz. "The Girl with the Hungry Eyes." *The Midnight People*. 191-205.

Lerner, Gerda. "New Approaches to the Study of Women in American History." *Liberating Women's History*. 349-56.

"Letters on the Truths Contained in Popular Superstitions." *Blackwoods* 61 (1847): 432-40.

Levine, George. *The Realistic Imagination: English Fiction from Frankenstein to Lady Chatterley*. Chicago: U of Chicago, 1981.

Lewis, Jane. *Women in England 1870-1950: Sexual Divisions and Social Change*. Bloomington: Indiana UP, 1984.

Liberating Women's History. Ed. Bernice A. Carroll. Urbana: University of Illinois, 1976.

Lidston, Robert. *"Dracula* and *'Salem's Lot:* Why the Monsters Won't Die." *West Virginia University Philological Papers* 28 (1982): 70-78.

Linton, E. Lynn. *Witch Stories*. London: Chapman and Hall, 1861.

Lodge, David. "Fire and Eyre: Charlotte Bronte's War of Earthly Elements." *The Brontes: A Collection of Critical Essays*. 110-36.

Lozes, Jean. "Joseph Sheridan LeFanu: The Prince of the Invisible." *The Irish Short Story*. Ed. Patrick Rafroidi and Terence Brown. Atlantic Highlands, NJ: Humanities, 1979. 91-101.

Ludlam, Harry. *A Biography of Dracula: The Life Story of Bram Stoker*. New York: W. Foulsham and Co., 1962.

MacAndrew. Elizabeth. *The Gothic Tradition in Fiction*. New York: Columbia UP, 1979.

McCormack, W.J. *Sheridan LeFanu and Victorian Ireland*. Oxford: Clarendon, 1980.

MacDonagh, Oliver. *The Nineteenth Century Novel and Irish Social History: Some Aspects*. Cork: University College, 1970.

MacGillivray, Royce. *"Dracula:* Bram Stoker's Spoiled Masterpiece." *Queen's Quarterly* 79 (1972): 518-27.

McGowan, John P. "The Turn of George Eliot's Realism." *NCF* 35 (1980): 171-92.

MacKay, Charles. *Extraordinary Popular Delusions and the Madness of Crowds*. New York: Farrar, Straus and Giroux. 1974.

McLaren, Angus. *Birth Control in Nineteenth-Century England*. New York: Holmes and Meier, 1978.

McLemore, Joy Ellis. "Edgar Linton: Master of Thrushcross Grange." *RE: Artes Liberales* 8 (1981): 13-26.

McNally, Raymond T. *Dracula Was A Woman: In Search of the Blood Countess of Transylvania*. New York: McGraw-Hill, 1983.

Mann, Karen B. "Bertha Mason and Jane Eyre: The True Mrs. Rochester." *Ball State University Forum* 19 (1978): 31-34.

————. *The Language That Makes George Eliot's Fiction*. Baltimore: Johns Hopkins UP, 1983.

Marlow, James E. "English Cannibalism: Dickens After 1859." *Studies in English Literature* 59 (1983): 647-666.

Martin, George R.R. *Fevre Dream*. New York: Pocket Books, 1982.

Marx, Karl. *Capital*, Vol. I. Trans. Samuel Moore and Edward Aveling. New York: International Publishers, 1967.

Masters, Anthony. *The Natural History of the Vampire*. New York: G.P. Putnam's Sons, 1972.

Matheson, Richard. *I Am Legend*. New York: Berkley, 1971.

Michelet, Jules. *Satanism and Witchcraft: A Study in Medieval Superstition*. Trans. A.R. Allinson. New York: The Citadel Press, 1939.

The Midnight People. Ed. Peter Haining. New York: Popular Library, 1968.

Miller, J. Hillis. *The Disappearance of God in Victorian Fiction*. Cambridge, Mass: Belknap Press of Harvard UP, 1963.

Millgate, Jane. "Jane Eyre's Progress." *English Studies* 50 (1969): xxi-xxix.

Moers, Ellen. *Literary Women: The Great Writers*. New York: Doubleday, 1976.

The Monster in the Mirror: Studies in Nineteenth-Century Realism. Ed. D.A. Williams. Oxford: Oxford UP, 1978.

Morley, John. *Death, Heaven, and the Victorians*. Pittsburg: U of Pittsburg, 1971.

Mrs. Lynn Linton: Her Life, Letters, and Opinions. Ed. G.S. Layard. London: Methuen, 1901.

Myth and Method: Modern Theories of Fiction. Ed. James E. Miller, Jr. Lincoln: U of Nebraska, 1960.

Nandris, Grigore. "The Historical Dracula: The Theme of His Legend in the Western and in the Eastern Literature of Europe." *Comparative Literature Studies* 3 (1966): 367-96.

Nethercot, Arthur H. "Coleridge's 'Christabel' and LeFanu's 'Carmilla'." *Modern Philology* 47 (1949): 32-38.

———. *The Road to Tryermaine*. New York: Russell and Russell, 1962.

James E. Miller, Jr. Lincoln: U of Nebraska, 1960.

Newton, Judith Lowder. *Women, Power, and Subversion: Social Strategies in British Fiction, 1778-1860*. Athens: U of Georgia, 1981.

Nichols, Nina da Vinci. "Place and Eros in Radcliffe, Lewis, and Bronte." *The Female Gothic*. 187-206.

On Metaphor. Ed. Sheldon Sacks. Chicago: U of Chicago, 1978.

Paris, Bernard. " 'Hush, hush! He's a human being': A Psychological Approach to Heathcliff." *Women and Literature* 2 (1982), 101-117.

Parsons, Coleman O. *Witchcraft and Demonology in Scott's Fiction*. Edinburgh: Oliver and Boyd, 1964.

Pell, Nancy. "Resistance, Rebellion and Marriage: The Economics of *Jane Eyre*." *NCF* 31 (1977): 397-420.

Penzoldt, Peter. *The Supernatural in Fiction*. London: Peter Nevill, 1952.

Pinchbeck, Ivy. *Women Workers and the Industrial Revolution: 1750-1850*. New York: Augustus M. Kelley, 1969.

Pirie, David. *The Vampire Cinema*. New York: Cresent Books, 1977.

Planche, James Robinson. *Recollections and Reflections: A Professional Autobiography*. London: Sampson Low, Marston and Co., 1901.

Popular Attitudes toward Birth Control in Pre-Industrial France and England. Ed. Orest and Patricia Ranum. New York: Harper and Row. 1972.

Porter, Roy. "Mixed feelings: the Enlightenment and sexuality in eighteenth-century Britain." *Sexuality in eighteenth-century Britain*. 1-27.

Praz, Mario. *The Romantic Agony*. Trans. Angus Davidson. New York: Oxford UP, 1970.

Ptacek, Kathryn. *Blood Autumn*. New York: Tom Doherty Associates, 1985.

Putzell, Sara Moore. "George Eliot's Location of Value in History." *Renasence* 33 (1980): 167-76.

Ragussis, Michael. "The Ghostly Signs of *Bleak House*." *NCF* 34 (1979): 253-80.

Railo, Eino, *The Haunted Castle: A Study of the Elements of English Romanticism*. London: Routledge and Kegan Paul, 1927.

Rapaport, Herman. "*Jane Eyre* and the *Mot Tabou*." *MLN* 94 (1979): 1093-1104.

"A review of two translations of Burger's *Lenore*." *The Monthly Review* 20 (1796): 322.

Rice, Anne. *Interview With the Vampire*. New York: Knopf, 1976.

———. *The Vampire Lestat*. New York: Knopf, 1985.

Richardson, Maurice. "The Psychoanalysis of Ghost Stories." *The Twentieth Century* 166 (1959): 419-31.

Ricoeur, Paul. "The Metaphorical Process as Cognition, Imagination, and Feeling." *On Metaphor.* 141-57.

Rideal, Charles F. *Charles Dickens' Heroines and Women-Folk.* New York: Haskell House Publishers, 1974.

Rieger, James. "Dr. Polidori and the Genesis of *Frankenstein*." *Studies in English Literature* 3 (1963): 461-72.

Ringler, Ellin. "*Middlemarch*: A Feminist Perspective." *Studies in the Novel* 15 (1983): 55-61.

The Rivals of Dracula: A Century of Vampire Fiction. Ed. Michel Parry. London: Corgi, 1977.

Robinson, Paul. *The Modernization of Sex: Havelock Ellis, Alfred Kinsey, William Masters and Virginia Johnson.* New York: Harper and Row, 1976.

Romano, John. *Dickens and Reality.* New York: Columbia UP, 1978.

Ronay, Gabriel. *The Truth About Dracula.* New York: Stein and Day, 1972.

Ronson, Mark. *Blood Thirst.* New York: Critic's Choice, 1979.

Rosenberg, Brian. "George Eliot and the Victorian 'Historic Imagination'." *Victorian Newsletter* 61 (1982): 1-5.

Rossetti, William Michael, ed. *The Diary of Dr. John William Polidori.* London: Elkin Mathews, 1911.

Roth, Phyllis A. *Bram Stoker.* Boston: Twayne, 1982.

―――― "Suddenly Sexual Women in Bram Stoker's *Dracula*." *Literature and Psychology* 27 (1977): 113-21.

Rothman, Sheila M. *Women's Proper Place: A History of Changing Ideals and Practices, 1870 to the Present.* New York: Basic Books, 1978.

Rudorff, Raymond. *The Dracula Archives.* New York: Pocket Books, 1972.

Russell, Jeffrey B. *A History of Witchcraft: Sorcerers, Heretics, and Pagans.* New York: Thames and Hudson, 1980.

Saberhagen, Fred. *The Dracula Tape.* New York: Warner, 1975.

―――― *The Holmes-Dracula File.* New York: Ace, 1978.

―――― *An Old Friend of the Family.* New York: Ace, 1979.

―――― *Thorn.* New York: Ace. 1980.

Saralegui, Jorge. *Last Rites.* New York: Charter, 1985.

Scargill, M.H. "All Passion Spent: A Revaluation of *Jane Eyre*." *University of Toronto Quarterly* 19 (1950): 120-25.

Schorer, Mark. "Technique as Discovery." *Myth and Method.* 86-110.

Scott, Jody. *I, Vampire.* New York: Ace Science Fiction Books, 1984.

The Shakespeare Head Bronte: The Life and Letters. Ed. Thomas J. Wise and J. Alexander Symington. Oxford: The Shakespeare Head Press, 1932.

Shirley, John. *Dracula in Love.* New York: Kensington, 1979.

Showalter, Elaine. *A Literature of Their Own: British Women Novelists from Bronte to Lessing.* Princeton: Princeton UP, 1977.

Siefert, Susan. *The Dilemma of the Talented Heroine: A Study in Nineteenth Century Fiction.* Montreal: Eden, 1977.

Skipp, John and Craig Spector. *Fright Night.* New York: Tom Doherty, 1985.

Smith, Evelyn E. "Softly While You're Sleeping." *The Curse of the Undead.* 175-94.

Soloway, Richard Allen. *Birth Control and the Population Question in England, 1877-1930.* Chapel Hill: U of North Carolina, 1982.

Somotow, S.P. *Vampire Junction*. New York: Berkley, 1985.

Southey, Robert. *Poetical Works*. IV. London: Longman, Brown, Green, and Longmans, 1846.

Stein, Karen F. "Monsters and Madwomen: Changing Female Gothic." *The Female Gothic*. 123-37.

Stoker, Bram. "Dracula's Guest." *The Bram Stoker Bedside Companion*. Ed. Charles Osborne. New York: Taplinger, 1973.

———— *Famous Imposters*. New York: Sturgis and Walton, 1910.

———— *The Jewel of Seven Stars*. New York: Kensington, 1978.

———— *The Lady of the Shroud*. London: Arrow, 1962.

———— *The Man*. London: William Heinemann, 1905.

Stone, Harry. *Dickens and the Invisible World: Fairy Tales, Fantasy, and Novel-Making*. Bloomington: Indiana UP, 1979.

Stone, Lawrence, *The Family, Sex, and Marriage in England 1500-1800*. New York: Harper and Row, 1979.

Stoneman, Patsy. "G. Eliot: *Middlemarch* (1871-2)." *The Monster in the Mirror: Studies in Nineteenth-Century Realism*. Ed. D.A. Williams. Oxford: Oxford UP, 1978. 102-30.

Strieber, Whitley. *The Hunger*. New York: Pocket Books, 1981.

Suchkov, Boris. *A History of Realism*. Moscow: Progress Publishers, 1973.

Sulivan, Paula. "Fairy Tale Elements in *Jane Eyre*." *Journal of Popular Culture* 12 (1978): 61-74.

Sullivan, Jack. *Elegant Nightmares: The English Ghost Story From LeFanu to Blackwood*. Athens: Ohio UP, 1978.

Summers, Montague. *The Vampire: His Kith and Kin*. New Hyde Park, NY: University Books, 1960.

———— *The Vampire in Europe*. New Hyde Park, NY: University Books, 1968.

Swanson, Don R. "Toward a Psychology of Metaphor." *On Metaphor*. 161-64.

Thackeray, William Makepeace. *Vanity Fair*. Ed. Joseph Warren Beach. New York: Vintage, 1950.

Thompson, E.P. *The Making of the English Working Class*. New York: Vintage, 1966.

Thompson, G.R. "Introduction: Romanticism and the Gothic Tradition." *The Gothic Imagination*. 1-10.

Tillotson, Kathleen. *Novels of the Eighteen-Forties*. London: Oxford UP, 1954

Todorov, Tzvetan. *The Fantastic: A Structural Approach to a Literary Genre*. Trans. Richard Howard. Ithaca, NY: Cornell UP, 1975.

Tompkins, J.M.S. *The Popular Novel in England 1770-1800*. Lincoln: U of Nebraska, 1961.

Tracy, Ann B. *The Gothic Novel 1790-1830: Plot Summaries and Index to Motifs*. Lexington: The University Press of Kentucky, 1981.

Tremayne, Peter. *Bloodright*. New York: Walker and Company, 1977.

Tsomondo, Thorell. " 'A Habitable Doll's House': Beginning in *Bleak House*." *The Victorian Newsletter* 62 (1982): 3-7.

Twentieth Century Interpretations of Bleak House: A Collection of Critical Essays. Ed. Jacob Korg. Englewood Cliffs, NJ: Prentice-Hall, 1968.

Twitchell, James B. *Dreadful Pleasures: An Anatomy of Modern Horror*. New York: Oxford UP, 1985.

———— *The Living Dead: A Study of the Vampire in Romantic Literature*. Durham, NC: Duke UP, 1981.

The Undead. Ed. James Dickie. New York: Pocket Books, 1976.

Ursini, James and Alain Silver. *The Vampire Film*. New York: A.S. Barnes and Company, 1975.

Utley, Steven. "Night Life." *The Rivals of Dracula*. 174-77.

The Vampire: Lord Ruthven to Count Dracula. Ed. Christopher Frayling. London: Victor Gollancz, 1978.

Vampires: Two Centuries of Great Vampire Stories. Ed. Alan Ryan. Garden City, NY: Doubleday, 1987.

"Vampires." *Household Words* 11 (1855): 42-44.

The Vampyre: A Tale. London: Sherwood, Neely, and Jones, 1819.

"Vampyres and Ghouls." *All the Year Round* 25 (1871): 597-600.

Vance, L.J. "Vampire Lore." *The Open Court* 13 (1893): 3607-8.

Varma, Devendra P. *The Gothic Flame*. London: Arthur Barker, 1957.

Varney the Vampyre. New York: Dover, 1972.

Veeder, William. "*Carmilla*: The Arts of Repression." *Texas Studies in Literature and Language* 22 (1980): 197-223.

Waller, Gregory A. *The Living and the Undead: From Stoker's Dracula to Romero's Dawn of the Dead*. Urbana: U of Illinois, 1986.

Wasson, Richard. "The Politics of Dracula." *English Literature in Transition* 9 (1966): 24-27.

Weissman, Judith. "Women and Vampires: *Dracula* as a Victorian Novel." *Midwest Quarterly* 18 (1977): 392-405.

Wiesenfarth, Joseph. "*Middlemarch*: The Language of Art." *PMLA 97 (1982): 363-377*.

Williams, D.A. "The Practice of Realism." *The Monster in the Mirror*. 257-79.

Wilson, Colin. *The Space Vampires*. New York: Pocket Books, 1976.

Winslow, Joan D. "Esther Summerson: The Betrayal of the Imagination." *Journal of Narrative Technique* 6 (1976): 1-13.

Wilt, Judith. "Confusion and Consciousness in Dickens's Esther." *NCF* 32 (1977): 285-309.

———— *Ghosts of the Gothic: Austen, Eliot, and Lawrence*. Princeton: Princeton UP, 1980.

Winter, Douglas E. *Stephen King: The Art of Darkness*. New York: NAL, 1984.

Wolf, Leonard. *A Dream of Dracula: In Search of the Living Dead*. Boston: Little, Brown and Co., 1972.

Wolff, Cynthia Griffin. "The Radcliffean Gothic Model: A Form for Feminine Sexuality." *The Female Gothic*. 207-23.

Wolff, Robert Lee. *Strange Stories and Other Explorations in Victorian Fiction*. Boston: Gambit, 1971.

Woolf, Virginia. *A Room of One's Own*. New York: Harcourt, Brace and World, 1957.

Woolrich, Cornell. *Vampire's Honeymoon*. New York: Carroll and Graf, 1985.

Worrell, Everil, "The Canal." *The Undead*. 192-208.

Yarbro, Chelsea Quinn. *Blood Games*. New York: Signet, 1979.

———— *Hotel Transylvania*. New York: Signet, 1978.

———— *The Palace*. New York: Signet, 1979.

———— *Path of the Eclipse*. New York: NAL, 1981.

———— *The Saint-Germain Chronicles*. New York: Timescape, 1983.

Yeazell, Ruth Bernard. "More True than Real: Jane Eyre's 'Mysterious Summons'." *NCF* 29 (1974): 127-43.

Zimmerman, Bonnie. " 'Appetite for Submission': The Female Role in the Novels of George Eliot." Diss. SUNY Buffalo, 1974.

———. "Daughters of Darkness: Lesbian Vampires." *Jump-Cut.* 24-25 (1981): 23-24.

———. "Gwendolen Harleth and 'The Girl of the Period'." *George Eliot: Centenary Essays and an Unpublished Fragment.* Ed. Anne Smith. Totowa, NJ: Barnes and Noble, 1980. 196-217.

Zwerdling, Alex. "Esther Summerson Rehabilitated." *PMLA* 88 (1973): 429-39.